M000007133

"A 73 year-old who climbs mountains, runs marathons, skis black diamonds and bikes across Cuba makes you wonder what he was doing 20 years ago. Now we know… he wrote the book."
Charlie Sturgis, past director Mountain Trails Foundation

"If you want to learn about traveling in remote places, listen to a guy who's been there.
If you want to know about beating prostate cancer, listen to a guy who did it.
Or you can just pick up this amazing journal. It's all in here."
Steve Dering, founder of Elite Alliance

"There was a time only a handful of guys in the world had climbed up an active volcano---and skied down it. One of those guys did that kind of stuff all the time---the guy who wrote these stories."
Max Doilney, author's son and travel sidekick

"Jim came to me as a prostate cancer survivor, but he wanted more. He is pioneering with us in cutting-edge regenerative treatments using his own stem cells. He's hoping one of these could be the game-changer."
Dr. Elliot Lander, Urologist and author of The Stem Cell Revolution

"Men with a prostate cancer diagnosis need to know that what Jim did 20 years ago with hormones, testosterone and other novel treatments---and what I wrote about 10 years ago--- is today supported by mainstream medical knowledge. The shame is that most of these men aren't told about it."
Dr. Ed Friedman, University of Chicago theoretical biologist

"I've been with him over the years as he beat a biopsy-verified Gleason 9 cancer. To me , that is more amazing than any mountain he climbed or any desert he crossed."
Dr. Kim Scott, personal physician

INTRODUCTION

This is the story of an implausible twenty-year saga which wanders across faraway deserts, mountains, and jungles—with astounding detours through the halls of academia and the American medical establishment.

Like the off-path explorer he is, Jim Doilney throws away the guidebooks and maps " . . . to see places where nobody goes, to meet people nobody knows." But in the midst of his decades long odyssey, he is diagnosed with life-threatening prostate cancer.

The state-of-the-art medical solutions he is offered— which he characterized as "butcher me, bake me, burn me, or break me"—he refused. And began his quest to find his own answers and ultimate cure.

All the years Jim battled his demoralizing cancer , he defiantly continued to travel to distant places. These are his detailed one-of-a-kind experiences. Along with his unique explorations of the foibles in American medicine.

The discoveries Jim makes and the lessons he learns were not in the medical journals and best practices. But the result may be one of the most important and life-changing guidebooks for tens of thousands of aging men who even now face the same grim diagnoses and brutal choices.

If you are an armchair adventurer, a weekend hiker, someone who just loves an authentic tale, or simply a past middle-age man wondering if prostate cancer has its sights on you—Doilney's journal is for you.

If you are a medical professional, you will be nodding your head as you read along. Because you know the book's title is cruel but true.

Copyright © 2021 Jim Doilney

All rights reserved. This book or any portion thereof
may not be reproduced or used in any manner whatsoever
without the express written permission of the author
except for the use of brief quotations in a book review.

Published in the United States by
Orrery Publishing
Park City, Utah

ISBN: 978-1-7376345-0-8

DISCLAIMER

The ideas, opinions, and suggestions In *Riding the Scalpel* are intended to
be used only to share the authors' opinions for educational purposes. This
book is sold with the understanding that the authors and the publisher are
not rendering medical advice of any kind nor is this book intended to replace
medical advice or to diagnose and prescribe or treat any disease, condition,
illness, or injury.

It is important, before beginning any medical treatment, that you receive full
medical clearance from a licensed physician.

The authors and the publisher claim no responsibility for any person or
entity because of any liability, loss, or damage caused directly or indirectly
as a result of use, application, or interpretation of the material in this book.

authors' photos by jon paul casella & patricia barrow
cover design by rick barrow

RIDING THE SCALPEL

Jim Doilney

Rick Barrow

FOREWORD

These are the stories my old friend, Jim, has been telling to strangers in bars and friends around the table for thirty-five years. There are a lot of laughs and a lot of hard truths here.

A lot of what- in -hell -made- you- try- that adventure. A lot of heart-pounding success and heart-breaking failure. A lot of things to make you think and reflect.

If it was only a journal of adventure travel, you'd enjoy a hell of a good read. Because there are a bunch of trip stories here you can pick it up and put it down at your own pace.

But it's also a journal of real life and death. And if you're a guy past fifty, or even forty, you need to read this. And pay attention.

Prostate cancer is a cold fact for hundreds of thousands of us. It's scary but you can deal with it. What you can't do is be ignorant about it. Because the price of too-little knowledge is years of agony and regrets.

Jim wrote this book to share with you what it takes. Because it really is up to you and no one else. You have to know what you are facing, what you are being offered. It's not pretty.

Luckily, there are a lot of new and better answers out there.

When I first sat down with Jim to help him record all these amazing adventures, he brought out boxes with thirty-five years of hand-written journals, old photos, scraps of notes, torn tickets, and trip leftovers in a dozen languages.

We spent months on Google Earth reconstructing and charting all of his trips. The technology in some cases let us virtually stand on mountaintops where he had climbed and see the same panoramas.(You can do the same).

I have never been lost in a fjord in Patagonia or freezing on a mountain pass in Nepal. I've never skied down a volcano or carried my bike across a crocodile-infested river. But now I have—in these pages.

I have never had my own experience with prostate cancer. I've known friends who died from it and friends who suffered such humiliating after-effects from prostate surgery they still regret it.

But now, after working with Jim on this book, I get the rage and I know the sadness that 200,000 American men will be feeling this year when they hear the prostate diagnosis. I can feel their fear.

Jim has done all the work—and we did this book—so they can also feel hope.

Rick Barrow
Wilmington, North Carolina
July 30, 2021

"If it is to be, it is up to me."

Jim's favorite quote.

Why I Wrote This Book

It took me almost thirty years to figure out what I should do with my life. It was actually simple. Get off the fuckin' highway. And then it took me another few years to find my off-ramp.

But I finally did.

This is how I did it.

Like most of you, I grew up following that double-white-line highway we all seem to get stuck on . . .

- Raised in a large, loving family
- Altar boy and future priest, a faithful Catholic
- Good student, did homework on time, followed the rules, Eagle Scout
- Solid scholar at a good university
- Grad student heading to a PhD, learned critical thinking
- Missed Vietnam and Woodstock, one intentionally
- Visiting Associate Professor of economics
- Loving husband to a beautiful blond wife.

Then I kicked it all away . . . my way is not the highway.

There I was at twenty-six, leaving my good life on the East Coast behind.

Moving my reluctant wife to the mountains of Utah.

Little bumfuck town nobody heard of called Park City.

Even convinced my big brother to uproot his family and join us.

Opened a sandwich shop and deli at the bottom of the town ski lift.

Now what do I do?

It took me a few more years but I decided building homes was better work for better money. Eventually it was great money.

That finally got me to my off-ramp.

I called it adventure travel.

Once or twice a year, sometimes more, I would take off to somewhere far away with nothing more than a backpack and a bedroll—sometimes a bike. And I would just go. No plan. No route. No goal.

Just a test of what I could do on my own with as little help as possible.

Going off-path. Finding my own way. My own destination.
I deliberately tried not to be among travelers and tourists like me. I wanted to go to places nobody goes, to meet people nobody knows.

It worked great for the next twenty years. And then some random cells in my body got crazy in a very bad place. I found out I had prostate cancer (PCa).*

And then I found I only had four choices—all bad.

I could undergo radical prostatectomy surgery, where they cut out your prostate and all around it, hoping to make sure they get all the cancer.

I could undergo intense radiation,* as precise as they could make it, but still like carpet-bombing your prostate area.

I could opt for chemotherapy,* which to me was like setting a fire to stop a fire.

Or I could do nothing—they call that watchful waiting*—and hope the slow-moving cancer didn't get me before I checked out.

I rejected all four.

I wanted a better way, or at least a different way.

I chose to go where I usually went—off path.

For the next twenty years, that's what I did.

I never stopped my adventure travels even when my health sometimes said I should.

I never stopped searching for off-path medical solutions. And prostate cancer has no guideposts.

I learned an enormous amount about cancer and how little we—even those expert doctors—really know about protecting prostates.

I learned an enormous amount about our medical establishment and how little real freedom and curiosity our doctors are able to safely deploy in how they treat patients.

I was an oddity. An off-path patient with a lot of notes and a lot of questions. Most doctors stay right down the double-white-line highway.

In all these years, I have traveled and explored some of the most remote places on our planet. I have hiked and biked thousands of miles.

But no path was less traveled or more challenging than the one I followed to my eventual cure.**

So no surprise ending to this book. Twenty-two years after diagnosis, I'm still alive.

I didn't get everything I wanted. I didn't get most of what I was promised.

I'm still traveling. Still off-path. And I can still do most—but not all—of what we need our prostates for.

And that's only because I found the fifth choice.

I wrote this book to show you the way.

Jim Doilney
Park City, Utah
July 30 ,2021

Follow Jim's travels on Google Earth

We think you'll enjoy how much you can see and learn
by using this amazing application.

Download it for free and enter the places we describe in every chapter.

TABLE OF CONTENTS

Pay attention to these* and these**

Asterisks (*) next to key words in the text to call your attention to further clarifications of medical terms. Double asterisks (**) alert the reader to additional reference sources or explanatory notes in the appendices. These asterisks delineate notes, sources, and explanations that are important to understanding the insights and experiences described. For example, we use the words "cancer free" and "cure" here as most people understand them, but a doctor will tell you those are really popularized shorthand for the correct term of "remission.*" We have strived to avoid assertions without supporting logic or sources. Conversely, appendices are provided which consolidate and/or restate author's PCa assertions that are spread throughout the book and often without specific support. You'll quickly find the asterisk definitions listed in the back of the book in the WebMD Glossary*.

For

Robert L. Leibowitz, MD (Dr. Bob)

and

Michelle Skally Doilney

CHAPTER 1
December 8, 1997—The Patagonia Coast

"The drip, drip, drip you can't ignore."

It all started with that middle-of-the-night desperation to pee. I was flat out on the bottom of a three-bunk tier in the darkness of a seven by seven cabin on a freighter sailing the Chilean Patagonian fiords. There was no denying the urge that woke me up.

Stepping blindly but carefully to avoid fellow sleepers and scattered backpacks, I made it down the hall guided by the ammonia stink of the head.

Gotta stop blaming the beer.

Just a few hours earlier, I had been serenaded by my drunken shipmates to celebrate my fiftieth birthday. That, too, was interrupted by an unrelenting need to piss.

Gotta see my doctor when I get home, I promise myself. I'm too young to have an old man's disease.

The wind outside is screaming. It hasn't let up for three days. The fog is so thick we get only glimpses of the glacier-covered mountains and an occasional whale.

So why am I on a stinking freighter in plunging seas off the coast of Patagonia? Because it is an adventure. And that all started some fifteen years ago when I committed myself to regular off-road, off-chart vacations. Treks to places nobody goes, for experiences and people nobody knows.

My version of adventure travel method is simple. I pick a place on the globe, decide whether I'm biking, climbing, or hiking, then I pack up and go. I do as little prep as possible. I don't consult guidebooks. I don't make anything but the most basic plans, i.e., if it's cold, bring a jacket. If it's hot, bring shorts.

So far, I have eaten dust and worse across much of Australia, both the north and south islands of New Zealand, the deserts and mountains of Mexico, the highest volcano in Ecuador, through Glacier National Park and western Canada, along the frozen coast of Chile, and now here—skipping over the ocean and leaving Patagonia.

Life is great as long as you've got your health, right?

So why Patagonia? I'll get back to that. But first I've got to pee.

And that became what felt like my main concern for the next nine months. Until I finally kept my promise.

CHAPTER 2
September 30, 1998—Park City, Utah

"Oh, yeah, that promise . . . "

I'm standing in the Park City Family Health Clinic with my friend and neighbor, Tek Kilgore, a nurse practitioner. My nighttime peeing has reached what seems like hourly levels—often stretching into the day. I've had enough.

Tek had just drawn some blood, taken a urine sample and introduced me to the unexpected sensation of DRE* — the dreaded greased-finger-up-your-ass prostate exam that scares men off in droves.

Tek is a fellow marathoner and he knows I plan to run the nearby St. George, Utah marathon the next day. So he tells me not to worry and he'll call me later that day.

Good news. Tek calls and says my urine is normal but something called my prostate specific antigen (PSA*) is 4.0 at the upper limit of normal. That sounds like a definition of me. I shrug it off and head to St. George.

CHAPTER 3
October 3, 1998—St. George, Utah

"If only I hadn't stopped . . . "

This is the first year I'm eligible for the over-fifty marathon age group and I had sacrificed and trained hard all summer. Bad luck the day of the race—strong headwinds negate all my extra effort. I ignore the pain and give it everything I have.

I finish third!

This is astounding. The two guys who beat me are from—naturally—California.

But I'm the fastest man from Utah over fifty.

At 3 hours, 1 minute, and 11 seconds, I am even within 15 percent of the fastest fifty- plus marathoners in the world!

But I can't help wishing I'd had the guts to just pee my pants instead of stopping a mile from the end for my usual can't fight it.

This is really starting to impact my life

CHAPTER 4
October 4, 1998—Salt Lake City, Utah

"My next doctor puts his finger on it."

S till high from my marathon finish, I'm packing to leave in two days for a twenty-day bike trip through Mexico but I want to make sure the 4.0 PSA really is nothing to worry about. I've convinced my regular doctor of fifteen years, Dr. Robert Wynn, to see me on a Sunday.

He walks me through the now familiar tests and then gives me my second invasion of the finger test.

Wynnie looks me in the eye and says what he felt seemed irregular. He tells me I'm fine to go on my trip but wants me to see a urologist colleague at the University of Utah sooner rather than later.

I am not messing around. In what will become a regular pattern of persistence, I start calling Wynnie's colleague, Dr. Snell, at the University immediately. He doesn't have any openings for weeks but I beg a nurse to take my name and number in case of a rare cancellation. She doesn't offer much hope.

I call Snell's office the next day just to check and the nurse laughs. She was about to call me—there is a cancellation available that afternoon.

Three hours later I am in the hands, literally, of the very attractive young nurse Linda as she takes my blood and urine samples and my clothes, then turns me over to the doctor.

Dr. Snell and I hit it off right away, laughing and exchanging stories. That's good because within minutes he's giving me my most intense DRE yet, probing and palpating my prostate as I wriggle and writhe. This time my urine sample reveals something that leads him to prescribe an expensive and exotic antibiotic. He wants me to start right away. No need to skip the bike trip, he advises, but schedules me to see him the day after I get back.

CHAPTER 5
October 6, 1998—Monticello to Manzanillo

"Burn the boats"

My meeting with Dr. Snell left me little doubt about the prostate cancer. But one of the best things to get you through the frequent hell of adventure travel is the art of denial. I am a master.

Two days later I've put PSA out of my mind and my camping gear and bike are ready to go. I'm hitching a ride with my friend Mark Oliver, who is driving south past Moab and will drop me off in Monticello. Why Monticello? Because I went to college at Virginia, Mr. Jefferson's university. And it sounded good next to my destination, Manzanillo

As Mark drives away, I'm standing there next to my bike, ready to start the 1,100 mile trek I had told Dr. Snell I was determined to do. Like Alexander and Cortes, I have burned my boats. There is no going back. Probably an easier decision to make when you're still left with a thousand soldiers—but all I've got is my shadow right there on the desert sand next to me.

Forty miles later I've biked a long stretch of desert highway with a lot of mountains keeping an eye on me. I'm heading to a campground in Bluff but first I've got an important stop.

I like to end a day's trip with a couple of cold beers, so, I try to find a store or gas station before I get to the campsite. Tonight's stop is Bluff, twenty-six miles away. So I stop at a lonely gas station a few miles south of Blanding. The Mormon proprietor regrets he can't sell me my beers and explains why.

A few years ago his Mormon neighbors got jealous of his booming beer sales and voted to extend the town boundary south to—you guessed it—fifty feet beyond his station. Beer sales are not allowed within town limits.

I pushed on, thinking about the limits of brotherly love and hoped I'd find some—along with a shower and a beer—in the Bluff campground.

6

Gratefully, I did.

Next morning, I'm heading west when I spot a famous landmark. Think of a four-story, red sandstone wedding cake with a stone cherry on top. Now put a sixty-foot wide stone sombrero flopped on top of the cherry. For hundreds of years, travelers have called this unworldly formation the Mexican Hat.

This area gets in the news from time to time because they keep screwing up at the nearby nuclear waste dump. You might also recognize it in the scene from the movie, *Forrest Gump*, where he finally stops running. Honestly, I didn't.

I passed on from Mexican Hat and rolled over the San Juan River bridge which will take me into the sprawling, 17-million-acre Navajo Reservation which runs through three states.

A little further south I'm suddenly in a John Wayne movie. All around me is red desert and on the horizon are the spectacular rock formations of Monument Valley. Even if you've seen these icons on TV and in the movies, you can't appreciate how magnificent they are in person.

I keep stopping and taking pictures. Before I get close enough for the real wow photos, I've used up all my film. There is nobody in sight but me. It's amazing and an experience everyone should try.

I take my time, for once reluctant to leave. As night falls, I pull into Goulding's Lodge and the kind desk folks offer me the vacant staff trailer because all the camp sites are full. The next day as I pull out, I see huge tourist buses loading up the crowds who will soon be looking out windows at the rocks I just biked under. I feel lucky to do it my way.

I'm thirty miles into Arizona that afternoon when I stop at the Gap Trading Post—hot, dirty, and hoping they sell ice cream. These trading posts still fill their historic purpose where far-flung Navajo can cross miles of dirt roads to pick up groceries, gas, and other necessities as well as a little gossip.

Today, that's me. To most Navajo, who are used to tourists, I look weirdly out of place. A pony-tailed old white guy covered in dirt and sweat, wearing baggy shorts and a faded tee shirt, sitting against the wall next to a battered bike with saddlebags. One guy decides to get the lowdown.

He squats next to me and wonders where I'm headed. When I say Tuba City, eighty miles away, he gives me a look and says he just drove from there to pick up his kids from boarding school. We chat for awhile and I find out he lives twenty miles north up a dirt road, has no electricity, gets his water from a windmill pump, and couldn't be happier. By now another guy has squatted down and he says he lives fifteen miles south toward Tuba City. They both invite me to camp on their land.

I ask them if they have any idea why a place in the Arizona desert is named Tuba City. They both smile and say, "Of course." Their ancestor who befriended the first Mormon settlers in 1847 was named Tuuvi. As usual, the white guys bungled the pronunciation.

I accept the invitation to the south and spend a beautifully restful night camped in a sagebrush thicket. My host sends me on my way with a warm breakfast beer for the road.

I'm a long way from my ultimate destination of Manzanillo with maybe eight hundred miles to go. But first I have to get out of America.

I finally hit Tuba City around dinnertime. Figuring my grubby state won't do in most eating places, I stop at a roadside burger shack with picnic tables. Two minutes after I sit down, a half-dozen Navajo cops are sitting with me. Turns out this is the best burger joint in town.

A little conversation brings up the guys I talked with back at the Gap Trading Post and one of the cops says, "That's my cousin." Before they leave, he answers my question about camping sites by directing me to an abandoned old hogan, a traditional Navajo dwelling, a mile west off Highway 89. It sounded perfect and it was.

I'm becoming addicted to nights in the desert—the smell of sagebrush, the incredible stars and all the rest of the song lyrics. I wake up this morning with the rising sun squarely in my eyes. By tradition, hogans are always built with a single door facing east. Some people think its religious. I think it's just an alarm clock.

8

By mid-morning, I pass the turnoff for Grand Canyon. I'm tempted but I've seen it before and my solitary travel has me feeling anti-tourist. I think I'm about an hour out of Flagstaff—my overnight destination—when I meet Carl.

Carl is standing by his camper pickup next to a sign that reads Sunset Crater. I stop in answer to his friendly wave. "A guy like you has gotta see it," he says. By it he means the crater formed when a volcano erupted nearby about thousand years ago. It left behind a distinct cone top formed by a wall of red, oxidized cinders that give it a fiery glow every sunset.

I ride along beside Carl's truck, thinking I really don't have time for a thirty-mile detour but Carl is a likeable guy. Turns out he works for the public works department of some town in California and gets ten weeks vacation a year which he spends tooling around the southwest. He likes to stop and look at everything. A kindred spirit.

Sure enough, we haven't gone four miles when Carl is pointing to what resembles a tumbledown stone wall. I'm wondering who built a wall in the middle of nowhere when he says, "Meteor strike." It seems many millennia ago a wayward meteor decided to commit suicide right here in the desert and the colossal impact threw up an outer ring twenty miles in diameter. And here it is.

Another five miles and Carl slows to a stop at a barely visible turnoff. "You gotta see these," he says. And sure enough, we round a curve and there is an entire cliffside of Anasazi ruins. Sometime back when London was just a smokey village, the local natives were building these elaborate multi-story ancient condos. Carl says they think this one was a trading center for people from hundreds of miles around. Turns out his daughter is an archeologist and told him how to find the place.

At that point, I'm already ten miles out of my way and I'm thinking the crater can't beat this, so, I thank Carl and head back to the highway. But I make sure to tell him that sidetracks like this are what I travel for.

I make Flagstaff in time to get a cheap room, a shower, and a good Mexican dinner. Other than that, my impression boils down to the trains that run right through the middle of town and what looked like several thousand college

9

girls—all with the same blonde hair, cut-off jeans, and tank tops—and no curiosity at all about a gray-haired, pony-tailed biker.

Leaving Flagstaff, I follow Route 89A as it drops down into Oak Creek Canyon which some folks call the Little Grand Canyon. It's a river gorge that runs about twelve miles from here to Sedona and it's gorgeous.

Following a series of hairpin turns that reveal one eye-popping view after another, I descend about a thousand feet to where Oak Creek, what else, winds along the bottom. The walls and banks are heavily wooded, there are hundreds of small gushing streams, and there is wildlife everywhere. Along with a lot of dedicated fly fishermen looking for trout.

Once again, I stop to smell the roses. Reluctantly, I pedal back up to the top where the road dumps into the picturesque town of Sedona. This is the area famous for the red rock color and cliffs but, after the canyon, I was jaded and hungry. I treated myself to a nice room in a famous resort, a great meal, and a restless sleep because I was no longer used to air-conditioning.

Next morning I'm off at sunrise to miss the traffic as I head east to get back on Interstate 17. It's a long highway slog from there down to Phoenix, about a hundred miles.

By the time I get to Phoenix, I've already forgotten the numbing and uneventful highway miles, truck stops, and desert campsites. My travel, like big mountaineering, is not glamourous in the moment but, rather, filled with masochistic endurance which yields unique memories.

The city of Phoenix is huge, sprawling for miles over what used to be Paradise Valley but now looks like Endless-Affluent-Suburbs-Valley. Not a great place for a desperate-looking old biker. Mothers are grabbing their children and men are reaching for their concealed-carry as I pass by—or at least it feels like they are.

I go halfway around the city to get to the home of my friends, John and Katy. I had told them I might stop by on my trip. Unfortunately, John is away on his own trip but a forewarned Katy recognizes me after a startled hello. We enjoy a great restaurant dinner followed by my nine-hour collapse in the guest room.

After a quick coffee with Katy in the morning, I'm heading south. But I've had enough of interstates. I follow the more sedate Highway 79. It seems to take me the better part of a day to escape the sprawl of Greater Phoenix which I realize when I bike past Florence's prison farms.

The desert really surrounds me now and I am surprised at the amazing diversity and beauty. The ever-changing light creates spectacular effects, long shadows, and amusing mirages.

I'm rolling without a plan or itinerary, so, if I see a place I want to sleep, I rent a room. If not, I camp out under the stars. The total flexibility frees me. All options are open.

Which is how I got to Biosphere 2.

You might remember when it opened in 1991. It was the biggest thing since moon travel. They built this gigantic glass dome to be a fully-enclosed, independent environment. The four acres under the dome were supposed to be a separate environment with everything controlled for air, water, and plant life. And then they picked four women and four men to live in it and see what happened. I think the idea was to test if humans could live in a self-contained environment—like a spaceship—for long flights out into the Solar System.

Things apparently went okay for a few years but by 1994 the systems weren't always working right, the scientist-residents weren't getting along, and they were running out of money. So the head financier brought in a money guy from Beverly Hills to tighten the operation. His name was Steve Bannon—yeah, the same guy. And he didn't last a year before he was fighting with everyone. Calling the chief lady scientist a frustrated bimbo didn't help.

So, yeah, I took the detour down to Oracle to see it for myself. It was now being run by Columbia University. Well, those guys had dumped all the human residents and were now running some pretty important experiments on something they were calling global warming. Al Gore, are you listening? But it no longer had the morbid fascination of the early days. It was just a big glass dome. So, I pedaled on.

11

After a couple of nights camping in RV parks, I'm rolling into Tucson to stay with a running buddy.

Beth and I had competed together in Marin County's famous Double Dipsea race from the hills to the sea, run every year since 1905. The next day her husband, John, has volunteered to drive down to meet us in Nogales where I will cross the border. Meanwhile, Beth and I will bike the sixty miles down a mountain valley along rural Route 82 through Sonoita and Patagonia.

As the eternal macho man, I assume I will be leading Beth the entire route even with her twenty-year age advantage. As we cross the rolling hills and long curves, I begin to notice that she is slowly pulling away. I respond with reckless downhill acceleration and furious pumping but she is soon out of sight. Until I round a curve and she is waiting for me! Now I remember it was the same in the Double Dipsea. Humbly, I follow her into Nogales and our rendezvous with John. Dinner that night was a lot of laughs. Mostly hers.

Afterward, they drive off into the sunset heading home, while I stand in my motel parking lot. I can almost smell those ships burning again.

I'm now two weeks into my trip. The next segment I had decided was a long stretch of nothing so I planned on taking the bus down to Mazatlán on the coast, about five hundred miles. I had, after all, biked these same latitudes in Baja a few years earlier.

Long distance bus travel is routine in Mexico and often first class. I leave my motel early in the morning and cross over the border without a hassle. My Spanish, based on hazy memories from high school and movies, gets me the right directions to the bus station. I find out the overnight bus to Mazatlán leaves in eight hours. I'm happy for the break.

I never mind long waits when I'm biking because I always carry good books with me. Today I find a good nearby shady spot and settle back.

After the sun sets, I get a cheap and tasty Mexican dinner. An hour later, I'm settled in to a big comfortable bus seat in first class and the bus attendant brings me a cold Coke. Surprise! The movie tonight is Air Force One in English with Spanish subtitles, starring Harrison Ford. That's good karma because his Indiana Jones is one of my role models for my travel mode. Stay cool, don't worry, it always works out.

Ten hours later I wake up in Mazatlán, refreshed and ready to hit the road.

I haven't thought about cancer for almost a whole day.

A ten-peso breakfast gets me on my way. Manzanillo is another five hundred mile trip down the coast and for the first half I'll be following a road that skips along the beach, squeezed between a bunch of wetlands and lakes.

This is farm country. I see nothing but planted fields to my left and zero resorts along the beach. Which means places to buy meals and sleep are rare. I usually rent a bed but I am always prepared to camp, a lot of times I prefer it. The trick is to get well off the road in some bush when no one is looking, and keep my reading light concealed.

Eventually the beach road detours inland and I get a long stretch of country highway. Late in the day, I spot the turn off toward San Blas and look forward to reaching Puerto Vallarta further down the coast. It's beach time again. Long interludes here of surf, wind, and very hot sun. I'm happy when I round a point and see one of Mexico's biggest resort cities.

Puerto Vallarta was pretty much unknown until almost forty years ago when Hollywood arrived to shoot a movie called *Night of the Iguana*. It starred Ava Gardner and Richard Burton, but he was embroiled in a scandalous affair with Elizabeth Taylor. When she showed up on the set, it was an affair heard around the world and the Puerto Vallarta tourist boom was on.

Today as I ride through the city all I see are wealthy Mexican families and visiting tourists. I pass a hotel where I once happily vacationed with my family. Sheryl Crow's voice blares from a bar about just wanting to have fun.

I pedal beyond that world to the part of the city devoted to less prosperous visitors and rent a cheap room. Another ten-peso breakfast gets me rolling in the morning for the last half of this leg and the finish line in Manzanillo.

Leaving the beaches behind, I'm crossing alternating jungle and farmland and climbing toward the mountains. When I top out a mountain, I pass a

13

coffee plantation. I throw down my bike in the shade by a half dozen dangerous looking guys sitting under the trees. I'm damn thirsty. I decide to plead, "Agua fria por favor?"

They look at each other, then at this sweaty old gringo, and then one of them grins and says, "Cerveza?" Two cold beers later, we are speaking like old friends. I think that's what they are saying. As I mount up to leave, it sounds like they are warning me to be careful about some place up ahead. But everyone always tells old guys on a bike to be careful.

Reaching the flatlands, I'm rolling pretty good past what looks like a banana plantation when I see both sides of the road occupied by groups of scruffy guys chopping with machetes. A guard with a shotgun is watching them and me. Suddenly, one of the guys yells, "Toro," and another repeats it. I roll on.

A hundred yards later the machete guys are everywhere along both sides of the road and there are dozens of shotgun guards. As a I ride between them, they start the Toro chant again. I have an inspiration. I pedal faster and faster and lift my hands above my head like I'm crossing a Tour de France finish line. Now two hundred guys are waving their machetes above their heads, screaming, "Toro, Toro," and I keep pedaling with no hands, hearing the music from *Chariots of Fire* in my head and grinning like an idiot.

It was exhilarating. And a great finale to my ride.

An hour later, I am nearing Manzanillo as I pull off at a roadside stand for my last meal. An old lady takes my order for a Coke and I think she offers a chicken special. A minute later, I see her chasing chickens around the yard and, just as she is about to wring the head of one she caught, I beg her to cancel my order.

I hear the now familiar, "Gringo loco," but the chicken is saved. My final good deed before I reach the airport.

My bike is packed and loaded with my gear and I'm sitting in the airport lounge with my latest book. An older American nearby notices the cover and says, "I knew the guy who wrote that." And that's how I met Jay who I discover was once Marlon Brando's manager. In between Hollywood tales, he tells me he is flying home after a two-month bus trip around Mexico,

14

something he does every year somewhere in the world. He tells some great stories about Brando and Tahitian girls . . .

I'll save those for another time.

CHAPTER 6
October 25, 1998—Park City, Utah

"Family comes first."

Three weeks and 1,700 Mexican kilometers later, I'm back from my trip but my mother-in-law is gravely ill and I have to fly to the east coast. I call to postpone Dr. Snell and nurse Linda tells me there are no openings for two months.

I'll have to wait.

CHAPTER 7
January 8, 1999—Salt Lake City, Utah

"It takes a worried man to sing a worried song."

For two months I've been getting up at night to pee more and more often. And I've done way too much reading about prostate cancer. Detected at my age, it is likely a fast-growing form. Even worse, nobody really seems to know if any of the radical treatments routinely prescribed are actually effective.

One school of thought even argues it's better to watch and wait, although that's mainly for much older guys. There's not much certainty. I am here to see Dr. Snell and get his opinion.

The lovely nurse Linda is still on duty. Once again she puts me through my paces and leaves me in my stupid half-gown to hear the oracle.

Dr. Snell doesn't waste any time. "How was the bike trip? Did the antibiotics help with the urination?"

Before I can answer, he asks me to turn around and bend over, his finger is up my ass and he is probing with conviction. He wipes up and walks away saying, "Come into my office." As I sit down, he leans forward and drills me with his eyes. "I think you may have prostate cancer. Call me on Monday so we can schedule a biopsy* and discuss a treatment program."

I croak back, "But I've heard there's nothing that really works without some pretty awful side effects—and even then you're not cured."

"Don't believe everything you read," Snell says, "modern science offers many options."

I leave his office in a daze. I had half-suspected what his answer would be but I also half-hoped I could dodge the obvious.

I call my wife, Diane, who is helping to cater an event where the noise is so loud we can barely hear each other. I shout into the phone, "I have prostate cancer!" Stunned, she says she is heading for home and will meet me there.

I hang up and crawl into the back of my SUV where I lie shaking and weeping for an hour before I can attempt to drive home. I am stunned, angry, crushed, despondent, and belligerent—all at the same time.

By the time I pull into my driveway, I have decided that this cancer cannot beat me.

CHAPTER 8
January 9, 1999—Park City, Utah

"Let's ask Google."

L ast night I remembered I am a PhD in Economics, once sponsored by the National Science Foundation. The path to answers is research and analysis.

So, the first thing I will do is learn everything I can about prostate cancer. I will not limit myself to the opinions of one or two doctors. I will not limit my options to the prejudices of one or two specialists.

My beautiful and devoted wife Diane throws herself into it immediately, immersing herself with our home computer to become my research partner in whatever Google can teach us about prostate cancer. We quickly discover it will take weeks. But we learn some basic facts:

Your prostate* is a walnut-sized gland between your bladder and your penis. It wraps around your urethra which is the tube through which urine flows.

Your prostate secretes the fluid which mixes with sperm and is ejaculated as semen.

Cancer growth in your prostate interferes with your ability to urinate and ejaculate.

Primary treatment for an enlarged, cancerous prostate initially presents you with three basic choices:

1. Radical prostatectomy, which is surgery to remove all of the prostate gland plus some margins while trying to preserve the urethra and erectile nerves.

2. Radiation, in the form of external beam radiation (EBR*), where the oncologist targets the cancerous prostate gland and attempts to spare surrounding tissue. An alternative to that is brachytherapy,* where

radioactive seeds are inserted or implanted into the prostate via long steel needles.

3. Chemotherapy,* which is another attempt to balance between destroying the cancer cells without killing off the tissue you need.

The side effects of any of these treatments often lead to the unfortunate and unpleasant results we labeled D.U.P.E. which stands for the precious bodily functions you may never perform normally again: Defecate. Urinate. Penetrate. Ejaculate. And almost all men whose entire prostate is treated— 190,000 or more each year**—never again ejaculate.

A fourth treatment, known as hormone therapy,* is often represented as a treatment of last resort ,applicable only after all else has failed.

Little wonder that the choice of treatment for many affected men was something called "watchful waiting." Unfortunately, that often only works if your PSA level is at a midrange around 4.0 and moves up slowly. For many men, the choice eventually cannot be avoided. The gallows humor expression for your three choices is, "Butcher me, burn me, or bake me."

CHAPTER 9
January 11, 1999—Park City, Utah

"If it is to be, it is up to me."

Those ten two-letter words have always made a lot of sense to me. After a sleepless weekend researching the internet, Diane and I agree I will take charge of my health. It will now be my full-time job.

So, first I need to share my condition with my workmates and my investor partners. At that time, I was building my BlackHawk community in Park City and my team needed to be brought up to speed.

My twelve employees step up immediately with, "We've got you covered . . . take the time you need." My investor partners offer unwavering support, condolences, and suggestions. One of them, Paula Swaner-Sargetakis, tells me about her friend David who just completed his own nationwide search for answers to his prostate cancer. Five minutes later I am on the phone with David who quickly volunteers the important things he has learned:

- "You've got to take your time. Don't let someone railroad you into a particular treatment until you've looked at everything."
- "You've got to take charge and do your own research."
- "I chose nerve-sparing surgery . . . and then I went and got the best, a guy at Johns Hopkins. Recent follow-up tests show he got it all."
- "I am about 80 percent capable of what I was, but I can still enjoy my life without most of the side effects."
- "You might want to talk to my urologist, Chris Jensen, in Salt Lake City . . . "

Salt Lake City is less than an hour from my home in Park City. I call Jensen's office. They can fit me in if I get there within the hour. I risk a speeding ticket.

CHAPTER 10
January 11, 1999—Salt Lake City, Utah

"Go find your own solutions."

My mind is whirling as I drive to Salt Lake City. I am a driven multitasker. In my phone notes, I have the numbers for two brachytherapy clinics that were noted in a Newsweek article about Intel founder, Andy Grove. He preceded his brachytherapy by obtaining for his surgeon a set of images from a unique MRI* machine that used spectroscopy to provide a visual guide to the cancerous areas of his prostate.

Grove reasoned that the more precise and accurate his surgeon could be, the smaller the chance of collateral damage would be.

I arrive at Dr. Jensen's office. I am younger than all of the men in the waiting room by what looks like twenty years. Dr. Jensen is pleasant and runs me through the usual routines and offerings of my body parts and fluids. In short order, he confirms what Dr. Snell has already led me to believe, that there is an 80–95 percent probability I have prostate cancer. Time to face facts, old man.

I ask Dr. Jensen if he can book me for a biopsy. I don't want to wait for Snell.

I drive back to Park City thinking about Andy Grove's lesson. If you don't like what you're being offered, go find your own alternative solutions. It seems pretty clear that no one yet has the best answer.

CHAPTER 11
January 11, 1999—Park City, Utah

"Time to face facts."

O ver the weekend, I had shared the whole prostate story with my older brother, Mike. I decide I need to call my kids, Max and Molly, who are away at college. For a change, I will be calm and confident. I tell them what we have learned and quickly add that prostate cancer is not usually fatal, that very few men who get it cannot find a cure, that they know I am a guy who always beats the odds and doesn't take no for an answer. I will see them soon, they will be okay. I could have told them more of what I had learned:

- Every year about 250,000** more or less American men are diagnosed with PC. About 30,000 of them will die from it.
- If you get PC in your fifties, chances are you've got the fast-growing form. If you get it after your mid-sixties, chances are you have the slow-growth form and you may be one of the lucky ones who can watch and wait*.
- If the first doctor you are referred to is a urologist and/or a surgeon, you're going to be steered toward surgery. If it's a radiation oncologist, it's those little seeds. And so on.

And that was the next fact that stood out. The medical community has so much invested in different approaches and specialties, it's hard to escape bias or even self-interest.

I'm starting to suspect doctors are often unable to provide unbiased referrals, due to loyalty to their team or institutions. I'll come back to that point later.

I decide it is not yet time to tell my elderly parents about my cancer.. They had a very rough time with the death of my sister Mary Ellen from ovarian cancer five years before, with many false hopes and starts. I would wait until I could be definitive. In the meantime, I will keep learning.

CHAPTER 12
January 12, 1999—Park City, Utah

"Don't spit in the wind."

In bed that night, wide awake and staring out the window , the howling wind reminded me of one of my first solo trips. I was biking 1,500 miles down the coast of eastern Australia, fighting unrelenting ocean-born headwinds the whole way . . . compounded by my own failing spirit and stamina. I felt over my head and beaten down, alone, and exhausted . . . in short, defeated. But somehow, my lifelong determination to never quit on anything pulled me through.

I figured it out. I kept going. I even escaped a near-death event. I beat the sun, the heat, the nasty wildlife and, yes, the headwinds. I made myself proud . . . in the way only overcoming something on your own can do.

I was remembering all of that as I fell asleep. And I thought back to the wind and the rain fifteen years ago . . .

CHAPTER 13
November 2, 1985—Cairns, Australia

"You're headed where?"

Rain. And more rain. Sheets of it. Cold and opaque, drowning the airport parking lot outside the glass doors. At four in the morning, it's only me and the airport cop there to curse it.

I had just flown in from Utah, via Hawaii, and here I was, twenty-two hours later in the underwhelming airport lounge of Cairns, Australia. Make that eastern Australia. Which I always thought was mainly hot, dry desert.

Why Cairns? I picked it out on a map for my first of many Blind Adventure Tours. The idea is that I just pick a spot in some remote part of the world. No Plan. No Research. Just go and let the chips fall.

And get this. I do it all on my bike. Just me, a sleeping bag, a wrench, and a spoon. Living off the land. Going native. And soaking in all the unimagined experiences the tourists never taste.

First regret of No Plan: Of course I didn't bring a rain jacket . . . it's supposed to be desert! And I was going to be biking 1,500 miles along the coast down to Sydney.

First surprise of No Research: It rains a lot this time of year in eastern Australia. And I am on the tropical coast—not the desert which is fifty miles inland, just over the mountains. But here I am.

So, with a few hours until dawn, I haul out the box my bike was packed in and set up for the trip.

As the weather cleared with a glorious sunrise, my spirits lifted and I was smiling with anticipation as I pedaled up to the just opening doors of Cairns' only bike shop . . . courtesy of some research by the friendly airport cop. My packing had omitted a few things experienced long-distance bikers tend to cherish . . . like spare tire tubes, patches, spokes, and the always handy water bottle. But the lads approved of my minimalist packing style.

25

Everything fit in my two custom-made bike panniers borrowed from Park City champion, Tom Noaker, plus my bivvy sack rolled and strapped on top.

Turns out Aussie bike shop owners, like their airport cops, all subscribe to the God loves a fool philosophy, and couldn't have been more helpful, cheerful, and friendly. I was feeling good the way things were working out until . . .

Second surprise of No Research: My new mates kept chuckling every time I talked about my projected travel speed over the 1,500 mile route down the coast to Sydney. They mercifully explained, "Surprised you didn't hear, mate, but nobody rides a bike from Cairns to Sydney because the stiff ocean wind blows in your face the whole way. Everyone knows you only ride the opposite way."

Second surprise of No Plan: At home in Utah, I can ride my bike all day at 10–15 miles per hour. A hundred miles a day is no problem. My new friends thought I'd be lucky to do half that, day after day, against the wind. So my two week journey just became a grueling month. But hey, they tell you to stop and smell the roses, right?

Cairns itself was pleasantly low-key. There's a lovely esplanade through the middle of town lined with bars and restaurants around a swimming lagoon. But the long ride out of town is typical suburbs following the A1 highway and then nothing but miles of blue skies, relentless sun, and turgid humidity. I hardly see anyone. The roads are empty. Which is weird, considering the number of roadkill kangaroos I've counted.

I'm feeling jet-lagged and uninspired, so, I decide to take the rest of the day off and try a snorkel boat tour my bike shop mates suggested. Out to the Great Barrier Reef to spot some Great White Sharks! The water was teeming with them. Closer to shore, the ocean is full of very poisonous jellyfish. Don't ask me why they called it a snorkel tour.

Caught up on my sleep that night, the next day I biked the first sixty-mile leg down to a river town called Innisfail. A curious sign brought me to a halt. "Caution! Cassowary Crossing!" And below that was an intimidating black image of an ostrich-looking bird. It turns out your cassowary is a very large and nasty wingless bird, indeed, up to six feet tall with a nine-inch claw that can rip out your guts if you park your bike on its private crossing.

I'm starting to think the reason Australian people seem so friendly is because their wildlife is definitely not.

That curious contrast was confirmed a few days later outside a little town called Tully. I had decided to get off the highway and hug the coastline. Hammered by the heat and desperate to escape the humidity of the surrounding rainforest, I finally stopped my bike on a grassy slope above a sparkling creek, tumbled off, and headed down for a cooling plunge.

Just up the creek, a young Aboriginal boy was energetically waving, so, I waved back as I started to pull off my shirt and boots.

I now know the Aboriginal word for crocodile.

The boy rushed up to me just in time to remember his English and warn me that the creek was infested with reptiles who lunch. See what I mean about good people and bad animals?

Sometimes there are exceptions, from a seafood lover's perspective. For example, I grew to love the bugs. That's because along this coast of Australia you can feast very inexpensively on small, clawless lobsters everyone calls bugs. One memorable night at Nick's Hideaway, I enjoyed their all -you- can eat special for only $13. The same price as my room.

But you noticed I said exceptions? Because the next day I was enjoying a flat stretch just outside of Townsville when I spotted another one of those uniquely Australian road signs. There was an image of what looked like a dive bomber and just two words, "Magpie Zone."

Magpies, like apparently all Australian animals, deeply resent our trespassing. So it turns out the local magpies build nests atop poles along the road and then ruthlessly defend their territory for about six hundred feet in every direction.

And their very effective defense is to madly dive at any intruder with an arsenal of beaks and claws until the unwary offender is dead or has fled.

I can go pretty fast on my bike when I really hit it and I have a good helmet. So I got through the half-mile danger zone with a lot of shrieking and the odd scratch . . . and a nostalgic memory of Park City building inspection days back in my general contracting days.

Townsville is an oddly-named beach town, well-known for its offshore Magnetic Island. With about 250 miles already under my belt, I decided to loaf for a day and I left my hostel bed early to watch the famous lifeguard competition. It looked to me more like training to be a Navy SEAL. But it was a great intro for me to the beloved Aussie friendliness.

By that night, the lifeguards were my best mates and I think they had bought me as many beers as I bought them. Best of all, my new friend, Mick, traded for my old East Canyon Triathlon t-shirt and I was now the proud wearer of a genuine Magnetic Beach Lifeguard shirt. Admiring glances the rest of my trip guaranteed. The only setback was when a local policeman stopped me as I was weaving home on my bike. "Where is your light?" he demanded. But then, hearing my accent, he read at my shirt and snorted, "Not likely," and sent me on my way.

I then left behind rolling farmland and colorfully-named villages like Mooroobool, Bambaroo, Helen's Knobs, and Rollingstone and was tooling down the rain forest-lined coast through more conventional sounding beach towns like Mission Bay, Palm Grove, and Queen's Beach. It was there, in a delightful little seaside rooming house, that I was just finishing my sundowner with a new friend as I floated in the pool, when suddenly he jumped up and cannonballed on top of me. Sputtering to the surface, drink obliterated, I yelled, "What the fuck!" as he pointed to a large sodden spider.

"That's a funnel-web, mate, and one bite from her puts you in a coffin in a few hours unless you get the antidote shot. How about a fresh drink?"

Remember what I said about Aussies and their wildlife?

The next few days took me past Dingo Beach, Pindi Pindi, and Wedgie Island—by now a seamless blend of hot, lonely, biking by day and cheery drinking with a cast of friendly characters by night.

My typical hotel was a caravan park surrounded by beat-up old camper trucks and gleaming SUV behemoths. They dwarfed my little bivvy tent.

28

Aussies must be the least class-conscious folks on earth. I never knew who I was drinking with or whether they had money or not. Many nights I would finish dinner by the fire and crawl into my bivvy, slipping into my sleeping silk. I would no sooner open my book and turn on my headlamp than I would hear, "Can't have that, mate. Come join us for a beer. Tell us your story." And off the night would go. Everyone I met was happy and seemingly carefree.

Apparently you didn't need to be rich to live by the ocean. Food was fresh and cheap, the beer was cold, and did I mention that many of the women on the beaches didn't bother with tops? I compared it all to southern California and it crossed my mind I could be very happy here.

I was now well into my second week on the road and settled in to the routine. Nearing the small coastal city of Mackay, I encountered the first biker I had seen in days—naturally he was wisely riding north with the wind at his back. I asked about my prospects to the south and he answered, "If you liked the last sixty miles you just did, you'll love the next three hundred." He then described the lack of services like camping spots and even fresh water. I knew, I had often been reduced to begging for water from local farmers' cisterns.

When I got to Mackay, I stopped in a local bike shop for advice. They described the next 250 mile stretch south as the horror highway . . . at least that's what the people driving cars called it. Spotting a pamphlet in a next-door pub for train service to Rockhampton, about 280 miles to the south, I opted for a day of air-conditioned butt sitting and loaded my bike on.

Below Rockhampton, the coastal road opened up to endless panoramas of beach and ocean and those topless Aussie surfer girls. Eventually I developed a crick in my neck from constantly looking to seaward. I was nearly halfway through my trip and really into my rhythm. The only problem was the never-ending ocean breeze always right in my face. It was also what I called cooling but fooling . . . hours of riding into wind deceived me about the broiling heat and blistering sun.

It was only when I stopped that I realized I was sitting on a two-wheeled frying pan.

As I got further south, I started to hit the southern California stretches around Brisbane and Surfer's Paradise . . . still beautiful but getting too developed for my solo biker sensibilities. I remembered a Joni Mitchell song about parking lots.

On my twenty-seventh night, I had an epiphany. Lulled into half-sleep by the usual cold beer and hum of friendly conversation, I was suddenly startled by a premonition that I was going to die on this trip. Not because of heat, or wildlife, or an enraged boyfriend, but because of a truck. The ominous image of the deadly on-rushing truck stayed with me all night. The next morning, tired and stupidly nervous about a dream, I left the town of Newcastle for my final leg.

After what I hoped might be one of my last lunches on the side of the road, I was under a hundred miles north of Sydney and the finish line. The wind had finally let up and I was easily keeping pace with the steadily increasing traffic. That's when a roar like a locomotive horn blasted my helmet and a huge double-tractor trailer swept by with a gust of sidewash that pushed me and my bike right off the road into a ditch.

A few minutes later, I put myself and my gear back together and was just lifting my bike back onto the shoulder when another monster—this time a garbage behemoth—rumbled by so close that his projecting rearview mirror almost beheaded me.

I looked up at the sky and mumbled, "Okay, I get it," and, as soon as the traffic died down and my legs stopped shaking, I rode meekly back to Newcastle.

From Newcastle, I am not ashamed to say, I rented a car with a bike rack and drove the last hundred miles into Sydney . . . passing trucks along the way and honking merrily all the way to the airport.

I've definitely got mixed feelings about Australia. I love the people, not so much the traffic, and definitely give the wildlife a wide berth. But there is a fascination I can't deny. I'll be back.

On the plane home, I proudly wore my Magnetic Beach tee and talked about my mates. Good on ya.

CHAPTER 14
January 13, 1999—Park City, Utah

"Putting the pieces together."

It's been less than three months since the big C entered my daily life but I've already attacked it like one of my off-road trips. I'm not going to stay on the typical path and accept the expected conclusion. This is my job now. I know how to go off-path for unexpected and usually better results.

Early this morning, I'm en route to see Scott Jobs, a Doctor of Oriental Medicine recommended by my D.O.M. friend, Laurel. On the way, I place several calls trying to unearth Andy Grove's elusive MRSI machine location. I finally connect it to University of California, San Francisco. Four calls later, I have a researcher there named Andrew on the line. He confirms the machine is theirs, he says the wait list is over a month long, and no one ever cancels. I doggedly persuade him to take my name and number just in case.

Dr. Jobs' examination doesn't really add anything, but he agrees I should pursue the MRSI machine, no matter the odds. As I say goodbye and walk out the door, my phone rings. Unbelievably, it's Andrew from UCSF. They have a rare cancellation. He felt he had to call me. I have to be in San Francisco later today by 5:30 p.m! Dr. Jobs volunteers to help me by faxing the required physician requests and medical records. I rush to catch a flight.

There's also a message on my phone from Dr. Snell. I call and his nurse confirms that my blood test from January 8 showed a now higher PSA of 5.1. He still cannot see me until the end of the month. She will meanwhile check on earliest dates for the biopsy. I take small solace in the knowledge that I already have one biopsy scheduled with Dr. Jensen in five days. First come, first served.

CHAPTER 15
January 13, 1999—San Francisco, California

"I want Andy's guys."

Hello, San Francisco! UCSF's MRSI machine is in a concrete bunker under a parking garage. I arrive just in time to sit down with Dr. Jim Krakauer, a medical physicist, who waxes eloquent on the magic of their MRSI.

"I am amazed you caught a cancellation."

"Our machine is 95 percent accurate and we have the only clinically operational one in the world."

" Good thing you haven't had a biopsy already because the resulting blood marks make it hard to read tumors."

"If I were you, I'd make sure to use a UCSF urologist/radiation oncologist* team."

"You'll probably get today's results in a week."

Once again, I run into the mainstream medical fraternity where patients are always loyally referred within the network of the doctor you are talking to. Many good reasons for this if you are on the team, but it tends to limit the options you are going to hear.

You are your own best resource —but you really have to work at it. If all goes according to plan here, I know I will need a biopsy. So I take the initiative and decide I want UCSF. I book myself for February 3 with the recommended Dr. Shinohara and then cancel the dates with Jansen and Snell.

Within an hour, I am strapped onto a platform inside a giant tube as the MRSI electronics and whatever is stuffed up my ass talk to each other and compare snapshots. After an hour of that, I'm sitting in the lobby checking for night flights home when the radiologist who will study my exam results,

32

Dr. Amos Cokeley, pages me. He's going to work tonight and volunteers to meet me first thing in the morning. Of course I'll stay over.

At 9:30 a.m. the next day, Dr. Cokeley looks up at me and smiles, "You may be lucky . . . I don't see anything outside the prostate area . . . I'll need some time to study this more . . . "

CHAPTER 16
January 14, 1999—San Francisco, California

"Unexpected news."

Not expecting to hear from my new best friend, Amos, for another day or so, I stop by the MRSI office that morning on my way to the airport. I've learned that a meaningful thank you is always worth it.

As I walk out down the hall, Dr. Krakauer calls out my name. Waving a handful of blueprint- size films, he smiles broadly and says, "Dr. Cokeley wanted me to catch you . . . he now says he is almost certain . . . you don't have cancer!"

I am stunned. A few minutes later, after tearful hugs and goodbyes, I am sitting on the grass by the road outside their office. Alternately laughing and crying, I keep trying to dial my phone and call Diane, my kids, my investors, my co-workers, my close friends, and I can't remember who else. But I remember to call Dr. Shinohara's office and ask nurse Jill to cancel my biopsy. She congratulates me on my good news.

I get to my car and, before I drive anywhere, I sit and mediate for close to an hour on what I will do with this gift of the rest of my life.

When I'm back at work, my duel with cancer is already becoming a bad memory. Within a few days, I'm already sitting down to pick my next trip. I stare out at the mountains and remember other mountains and a another trip that was just over a year ago. How my world has changed . . .

CHAPTER 17
November 23, 1997—Temuco, Chile

"Excuse me, how far to the end of the world?"

It was my fiftieth birthday. My son Max, twenty, was joining me on one of my wayward trips for the first time. Joined by my nephew Jake, twenty-six, who just traveled the west coast of Mexico with me a year earlier. We three thought it sounded great to do one together. I wonder what they're thinking now.

Our trip began with a simple plan. We'd use Temuco, Chile as our jumping off point. We'd highway bike 350 miles south through the lake district, then follow a 700 mile seldom used dirt road bordering Patagonia's mystical fjords, then catch a freighter 500 miles along the Atlantic to Puerto Natales, and a final 200 mile bike leg to our southernmost point, Punta Arenas. It's in what they call Antártica Chilena, exactly what it sounds like.

But simple plans never end up being simple.

Our first day was a long one. Thirty hours and 6,000 miles of flying got us from Park City to Santiago and then a last leg on to Temuco. It's mid-morning as we unpack, assemble our bikes, and sort out our gear. The airport is in the middle of nothing way south of the city but conveniently just a few miles off of Highway 5, the famed Pan American Highway, which is our route south.

Tailwinds push us fifteen miles down the smooth highway, then shift with us as we turn east at the town of Friere, following Highway 199 toward our night's stop at Villarica, another thirty-five miles or so.

Villarica is a tourism town where I can buy bike tube patches I'd forgotten to pack. And it's the gateway to the lush lake district and a wall of volcanos guarding the Andes. The biggest lake and the most active volcano are both named Villarica. The volcano last erupted twenty years ago. We'll be biking through the national park named for both of them.

Our ride was easy even after thirty hours of travel. We'd stopped for lunch and a beer at a roadside café. Max wonders why we warned him about the tough trip but Jake advises he's been on one of my no plan trips. "Just wait."

Our hotel, Hosteria de Colina, is actually a plush B&B. The ex-pat American owners are in awe of our plan to bike across the Andes into Argentina, much less ride down to Patagonia. With a fifty-mile day under our tires, we head off to sleep.

Dawn finds us already on our way in a misty fifteen-mile climb to a village called Licanray on the shore of the beautiful Lago Calafquen. In the distance, we can see snow-capped volcanic peaks. This is a luxury resort home area. Passing a local school, we draw titters from the kids with our cold-weather tights that are not often seen in this locale. We decide we look like Robin Hood's Merry Men---not the" ballerinas on bikes" the kids were describing.

Another easy fifteen-mile run to the end of the lake brings us to the village of Conaripe. We stop for drinks at a country store where Maria, the eighty-year-old owner, smiles and calls Max "Senor Nureyev" when he poses for a photo. Max is too young to remember the famous Russian ballet dancer.

From here, the road turns to rutted dirt, winding between a massive cliff to our left and the tree-covered shores of Lago Pellaifa on our right. We've seen the last of smooth asphalt and easy riding. We cross over the raging Llancahue River and I can see a steep switchback through the forest up ahead.

I tell the guys it's time to switch tires. We'll swap our smooth road tires for knobby tires, a little wider to gain traction. Who says I don't plan? I am commenting to Max and Jake that we are now where no bikers dare come when up rides a couple who stop to chat—Bruno, a German architect, and the lovely Nicole, a city manager. Bruno begins advising us on the correct way to change and mount tires. He can't resist showing us. It's not until the third tire that he overhears Jake telling Nicole about our thousands of miles on bike trips.

The five of us start the climb and within a few miles we get our first flat. Bruno shows us the proper way to patch it. A few miles later we have another. And then another. Bruno has now decided to retire from showing the ignorant Americans how to bike. He and Nicole pedal on ahead. I can't figure out why we keep getting flats with patches that don't hold.

An hour later we pull into the tiny village of Llonquen, just a dirt road crossroads really, but it boasts the only store and pension for miles.

Our room will be $8 a night, breakfast included. Bruno is loudly complaining about the lack of cleanliness. We ask him to cap it. If he pisses off the owner, we'll be out in the coming rainstorm.

Luckily, Sergio the pension owner, is a portly, balding charmer with a big smile. He looks at our bikes and tells us over a cerveza how he was once the Chilean national bike champion. Bruno's raised eyebrows again put hospitality at risk but Nicole wisely engages Sergio in some stories of past glories.

The next morning we leave at first light, allowing time for the now expected flat tires. We have a thirty-mile run we can't blow because we are racing to catch the only ferry that gets us across the next lake. It usually leaves around noon but we're on Latino time. Bruno and Nicole left an hour before us. They're on German time.

We're headed due south in steady rain, skirting a huge unbroken forest on the slope to our left. The edge of the dirt trail drops off on our right, plummeting down to some river bottom land. Whatever bulldozer graded this road has never been back. Edges are crumbling and there are frequent huge holes—many filled with logs where some unlucky trucks got stuck. There are frequent short bridges over gullies—many with waterfalls—but most of the bridges are missing decking with holes the size of our bikes. Concentration takes the place of conversation.

By now, I realize I made a huge mistake in my choice of which bikes to bring. Our hybrids were fine for highways and minor roads. We need mountain bikes for these mountains. Duh.

Eight flats and numerous slips later, Max and I limp into Puerto Fuy. It's past noon. Jake, who went ahead to delay the ferry if needed, strolls out of the only café. The ferry is still docked and Jake is chewing on a foot-long plant that looks like a flimsy cucumber—it's called "narco." He got it from some local kids. When he asked what they were chewing, they shared. Jake says it tastes like coconut but there is no effect like the name suggests. Bruno and Nicole are inside the café, enjoying the only lunch on the menu—cheese and instant coffee. The ferry leaves in an hour.

The ferry will take us and our bikes on a long, meandering twenty-mile cruise down Lake Pirihueico to the town at the end with the same name. The ferry is just a flat bed, about sixty feet by thirty feet, with an enclosed shed along one rail. The shed is maybe four feet wide and barely high enough to stand inside.

There is a single truck and a car on the deck. The truck belongs to some foresters, the car to a vacationing Chilean family. The rain forces us all into the shed—three ferrymen, four foresters, the family of four, and five bikers.

It's a long ride. Lots of Spanish we didn't understand. The never-pleasant odor of wet wool and muddy bikers mixed with other smells you pick up in a long confined period where you can barely move. There was probably some spectacular scenery of forests and volcanoes reflected in a still, misty lake. But the shed had no windows.

We finally arrive at the landing dock. The Chilean family offers smiles all around, hops in their car, and drives away. The ferrymen tie up and tell us the Argentine border station is maybe twenty miles east. They climb in the truck with the foresters, everyone waves, and they are soon out of sight.

There are only four buildings in view—a barn, a shed, a shack, and a dilapidated farm house. Nicole looks at Bruno. Max looks at me. Jake smiles—he's been here with me, the no-planner, before.

We walk our bikes down to the farmhouse in a drizzle. There is smoke from the chimney. An ancient farmer wrapped in wool steps out and, from his wrinkled face flashes the huge smile of perfect white teeth. He is Armando, and we are welcome to leave our bikes and gear in his barn once we relocate the pigs, goats, chickens, dogs, cats and the cow.

Armando invites us into his house to meet his equally ancient wife who promptly asks us to stay for dinner. But we notice there is nothing on the wood stove. We discover the shack next door is actually a restaurant, now closed for the season. Armando's wife knocks determinedly on the locked door and Señor Diaz, the owner, appears. No, he will not open but he will sell us the last of his supplies—some cheese, a wrinkled tomato, and a single hot dog complemented by nine warm beers. We conclude negotiations and retreat to the farmhouse where I borrow a rusted pot from the Señora, clean it with sand, and prepare my famous Doilney Camp Stew. The recipe matches the food we just bought plus some wild onions Nicole has picked. What a meal!

After dinner, the Señora has a bit more beer than she is used to and reveals that when she married eighty-six-year-old Armando seventy years ago she was only nineteen.

Armando jumps up and exclaims, "But you told me you were sixteen, the same as me!" He married an older woman and never knew it.

After that, we are ready to retire. Armando shows us the ladder that leads to his loft, a four-foot clearance shelf under the roof where we can stretch out our sleeping bags. In consideration of our dinner contribution, he is willing to let us have the entire loft for only $40 for the night. It's better than the muddy ground and at least out of the rain. Over Bruno's outraged protest, we accept. Armando is pleased to note that morning coffee is included.

Morning comes early with an unexpected adventure. One of us left a barn door unlocked and now we have to help Armando catch his cow. An exhausted hour later, the fastest cow in Chile is back in the barn and we are underway.

At last the rain has stopped. Our trail runs through a forest, following alongside the Huaham River. After fifteen miles of nothing but trees, wooden bridges, and the placid river, Max has renamed it the Ho Hum River.

The trail opens up on a clearing and we are at our first border station, about to enter Argentina. There will be three more. Station #1 is where we get a piece of paper that warns us we are leaving Chile. A mile further, Station #2 receives our paper and gives us another that tells us we have officially left Chile. A few yards away, Station #3 welcomes us to Argentina with a paper we will deliver to Station #4 where we will swap it for another paper that notes we are now officially within Argentina. Bruno is now mumbling loudly about bureaucrats and German efficiency. But he quiets when we pull up on the shore of Lago Nonthue.

Our trail begins a forty-mile trek along the north shore of this lake and then Lago Lácar which will eventually take us to the famous resort town of San Martin de los Andes. This will be a long, sometimes steep climb through the mountains that come all the way down to the lake shore. There won't be any easy parts.

It seems like every thirty minutes one of us has another flat tire. How could I have screwed up on this so badly! The steep mountain terrain seems endless. For Max, who has 8,000 miles of western US motorcycle camping rides under his belt, this is an eye-opener. Jake and I have been through the pain. Because of our flats, Bruno and Nicole are far ahead, out of sight. At the top of the last and longest climb of the day, Max throws down his bike and swears at the pointless stupidity of actually volunteering to do a ride like this. Jake reassures him that he'll remember the top, not the climb. The final long downhill restores his smile.

San Martin de los Andes is an Argentine Park City. We immediately feel right at home with the stylish mountain architecture, chic shops, and kids in logo outfits everywhere. Even the restaurants are familiarly expensive.

We're relaxing in a sidewalk café when Uwe, a Swiss ski racer at the next table, smiles at our bad Spanish and American wisecracks and leans over. He offers friendly tips about the better restaurants, the right hotels, and the best bar. We thank him as he smiles and gets up to leave in, naturally, a gleaming Mercedes station wagon stocked with a gorgeous wife and two beautiful kids. Almost makes us homesick.

We check into the hotel Uwe suggested, do some laundry, and track down some powerful painkillers for Max's knee tendonitis. Snug in our cocoon, we spend the next morning over a leisurely breakfast and then visit local stores to stock up on provisions. We can't find a bike shop but a hardware store has one last box of tire patches. We know we'll need them.

At noon we're back on the highway. Max is all smiles as we speed down smooth pavement for the next seventeen miles south. We spot the turn to enter the national park road. Back on the dirt, we're now following a river valley bordering a mammoth lake called Maliquina. Snow-capped mountain peaks are all around us. It's a beautiful sunny day and we haven't had a flat yet.

At the end of the lake, we come back to civilization with a broad flat area, lake beaches, vacation homes, and a lunch stop called Todas Cambia—"All Cash." We're quickly back on our bikes, enjoying the ride as we re-enter the solitude of our trail along the rushing Rio Maliquina surrounded by deep forests.

We stop at a bridge to pump some cold water to purify for drinking. We're sitting on the edge soaking our bare feet, dirty and sweaty but stupidly happy, when a four-wheel adventure tour bus pulls up and very slowly glides past. The tourists inside are glued to their windows looking at the strange barbarians, barefoot in the middle of wilderness. Jake quickly dubs them "the prisoners of the bus on a ride to nowhere."

That night, we pitch our tents by the river and sit around a big fire. Eating chocolate, drinking packed-in beers, we analyze the lyrics of Bob Dylan songs we can remember, especially "…how does it feel to be on your own, no direction home, a complete unknown, like a rolling stone … " We decide it feels pretty good.

Dawn comes and we are up and on our way with just a long drink of water.

The sunny weather can't be wasted. We've left the Rio Maliquina and now our dirt road has become gravel. We're following a wide whitewater river called Caleufu. We stop for breakfast—three mouths with three apples, three juices, and three chunks of bread.

We can feel our legs when we start a long uphill climb, switching back and forth as we head between peaks to the Paso Cordoba. Six miles later, we reach the top of the pass, immediately leaping off for a team pee in celebration. The only observers are a pair of Huemul, the rare Patagonian deer. They'll report back on the unique habits of the human male species.

We're astounded by our panorama of the seemingly endless Andes, rolling off in every direction.

Now we get an equally long and winding downhill run broken by the excitement of several high-speed flat tires. Exhilarated and tired, we stop where the gravel meets the paved road at the bottom and we enjoy a gourmet gas station lunch.

This is where we turn south toward the famous ski resort area of Bariloche. It's about forty-five miles and, as usual, we will follow a narrow road bordering a fast-flowing mountain river. This one is called Rio Negro because its black rock bottom makes the water look dark.

The riding is fairly easy, we're the only ones on the road, and we're making good time when the bike gods step in and say not so fast. Max loses a spoke on his rear wheel. Ordinarily, that's an adjustment I can work around but this one is on his rear gear side and cannot be touched without a special tool I never thought to bring. For three hours we use up the file on my Swiss Army knife, and then some rough river rocks, wearing down the point of the broken spoke to finally pull it off, then resetting the other spokes to compensate.

Back on our bikes at last, we pedal like mad, chasing the setting sun. Fifteen miles out from Bariloche, the sun is gone, the rain has begun, and we pull in to a small village on a big lake. Dina Huapi is not much more than a crossroads but we spot a small restaurant with three tables out front. There's a lady putting up chairs and about to close. We beg sixty-year-old Marta, who says I look like her late husband, for anything she has left. That turns out to be a delicious soup, grilled steaks, salads, and cold beer. Full as ticks and too tired to set up tents, I wonder to Marta if we can just lay out our bedrolls on her floor for the night. She says that would be scandalous but there is an empty storage shed next door we can use. She even promises hot breakfasts in the morning. We call it quits on a great day.

Morning brings the promised breakfast, a nostalgic hug from Marta, and a rainy seventeen kilometer ride into Bariloche. This is the end of our first week on the road and the ferry we have to catch doesn't leave until tomorrow. Our first stop is a bike shop. Where all of us get much-needed care for our battered bikes. After a relaxing lunch, we walk over to the ferry office to launch our Week Two Plan.

Having already crossed the Andes on bikes, we had no need to turn around and do it again. Our plan was to split up the rides between a series of long ferry rides on the lakes that ran like links in a chain between Argentina and Chile. The first was leaving the next morning from the dock at Llao Llao. Twenty-five kilometers west of where we were now. We decide to bike there now and grab a ferry-side room.

It's now snowing heavily and walking our bikes out of the town we admire that Bavarian feel of Bariloche. We make quiet jokes about Nazis fleeing here after the war and building a place like home. Pedaling along the lake in the snow, Jake remembers reading that President Clinton had stayed at the Llao Llao Hotel on a recent diplomatic trip here. We choose a more modest place, the six-room Hotel Katy. The owner and guests speak only German to us, leading to more sniggering among us about fake identities. Who knows?

The next morning we breakfast quickly and sprint-pedal the half-mile to the 8:00 a.m. ferry departure. We make it by one minute. As we park our bikes and drop our packs, I approach a trio of lovely Latina young women and ask in my best Spanish if one will take a picture of us on the snowy lake with my camera. "Step over here, guys," says Rosa, a University of Chicago MBA grad. She and her two friends, Melissa and Zan, are third-generation Latina Americans on a tour. They think our Spanish is pretty lame. Jake and Max perk up.

The snow and clouds drive us inside the ferry's warm lounge but we still get views of glacier waterfalls and giant peaks. Twelve miles cruising later, we're at Puerto Blest where we disembark to go overland to the next ferry boarding at Puerto Alegre and Lago Fria. Everyone else climbs into four-wheel drive vans but we jump on our bikes and disappear into the snow. We make it with time to spare, disappointing fellow passengers who had confidently bet against us. Rosa and her friends collect their winnings.

Crossing Lago Fria, well-named for its icy winds and cobalt water, we land at Puerto Fria and clear Argentine customs. We do it here because the actual border is at the top of one of the peaks above us. We have to ride up to that peak and over it, then follow a slowly descending fish-hook trail that meets up on the Chilean side with the Rio Puella. That gushing mountain stream will lead us down to the Puerto Puella and our next ferry.

None of our passenger buddies seem to envy us as they board their warm buses for the seventeen mile ride.

It's a bitch. And we can't be late. The first mile or so feels straight up. Max and Jake pedal all the way, I pretty much walk my bike. By the time we reach the crest, the snow has stopped. Through mist below, we can get glimpses of the whitewater river plunging over huge boulders. The road down is bordered by trees with mattress-sized leaves. Hopefully we won't get so many flats.

We fly down the mountain, screaming at the top of our lungs. A dozen waterfalls go by in a blur of spray. The windchill from our speed is frigid but somehow exhilarating. At the bottom, we pull up, slapping high fives and tumbling off our bikes for a desperate piss. A wild boar ambles out of the bushes, looks at us curiously, then bolts as the tour bus catches up and we hurriedly put ourselves back together. Bussers and bikers have different etiquette.

We've made it back to Chile but now we have to bust ass to get in to Puella in time for the ferry. It's the last one of the day.

We meet up with the Chicago girls at a grand hotel lodge in town. We have just enough time for a couple of rounds and a toast, enjoying our first taste of Pisco Sours—apparently Chile's national drink.

The ferry ride is eighteen miles across another mammoth mountain lake, Lago Todos los Santos, buried in between more peaks and plunging valleys with glacier waterfalls everywhere. By the time we dock at Petrohue, we'd had enough Pisco Sours to qualify as Chileans. Everyone disembarks as we make vague plans to meet the girls the next day in Puerto Montt. Too tipsy to trust our biking skills at sunset, we decide to overnight in the luxurious Petrohue Lodge.

It's still off season, so, the staff is happy to have some guests. The head porter, noting our wobbly arrival, makes an amusing show of valet parking our bikes as we stumble into the lobby. An hour later we have donned our only dry clothes and are enjoying a gourmet dinner in front of the fireplace while the piano player does Sinatra.

Morning comes with headaches and cold but sunny skies. We are eager to get going but spend a futile hour trying to get the tire patches we bought to stick. Nothing works, it's a mystery. We have no choice but to squeeze back into yesterday's warm but still wet clothes. We'll dry off on the road.

Our route now is due southwest to Puerto Montt, following Route 225 along the Rio Petrohue. This is definitely a Class 5 with continuous white water, serious rapids, and a dozen waterfalls. High above our right shoulders is the

9,000 foot snow-covered peak of Volcan Osorno. We have to stop four times to walk around long stretches of highway that have been wiped out by recent mudslides caused by heavy rain on the volcano slopes. At one stop, we enviously eye a group of Chilean kayakers heading back up the road for another run down the river. We talk about coming back one day for a skiing-kayaking vacation—without bikes.

By mid-morning, we reach the town of Ensenada and begin a long cruise on a highway hugging the shore of another huge lake, Lago Llanquihue. It's an easy and welcome ride, admiring the reflection of the volcano on the placid lake surface. Twenty miles later, we ride in to Puerto Vera, a pretty resort town at the end of the lake. A quick stop for fruit and cheese at a roadside market serves for lunch and we turn south for the last leg of the day to Puerto Montt.

We're in flat land now and whitewater rivers, glacier waterfalls, and volcanos give way to the Pan American Highway, truck traffic, overpasses, and warehouses. Luckily, two lanes of the highway are closed off for construction, giving us a private route most of the way.

Puerto Montt is at the northern head of a huge bay that winds down to the Pacific Ocean. It's a busy major port and looks it, with a little suggestion of a Vancouver or Seattle. We ask for directions to the city's best bike shop and end up at a place called Keiffer's.

At Keiffer's, we are the day's entertainment. They laughingly explain the mystery behind our constant flat tires and patches that don't work.

It seems that bike tubes in South America are made of good old-fashioned rubber—not the synthetic material that comes on American and European bikes. And, as apparently everyone else knows, the perfectly good rubber patches we bought locally do not stick on synthetic tubes. After getting a few photos of us for their wall, they fix us up with what we need.

That night we rendezvous with our Chicago girls and they again drink us under the table. The next morning, I find out Jake had promised we'd join them for a bus ride and hike up the slopes of Volcano Osorno—the same volcano we rode by the day before. My mood wasn't improved after paying $50—times three—for a simple guided walk up a mountain.

It gets even better when we return to the hotel and management greets us with an eviction notice. Our behavior at the bar the night before qualified us to leave. After much protest and loud indignation from the girls, they relent and let us stay overnight as long as we are gone the next morning.

Considering the room rate was only $7 a night, we didn't know they had such high standards.

We head off to dinner in the Angelmo district of the port and their famous seafood market. Over seventy stalls are selling every sea creature I've ever heard of and twice as many I've never seen. Behind most stalls is a tiny enclosed room where you can squeeze onto a bench at a skinny table and enjoy a continuous feast of cooked and raw samples—one of the strangest and most delicious meals I can remember. We limit ourselves on the cerveza and make it back to our rooms with suitable decorum.

In the morning, we bid the girls farewell and leave Puerto Montt in a light rain. We luck out again with another lane closed to cars, but not bikes, and sail down the smooth asphalt for the next fifteen miles to catch the ferry at Pargua. We're heading out to Chiloe Island, more like a huge peninsula that juts down into the Pacific.

Our plan is to cross Chiloe Island along its Pacific coast, then catch another ferry to connect to the mainland further south. From there we'll be on the famous Carretera Austral, the primitive 1,200 kilometer southern highway that connects northern Chile to Patagonia. It's a mythical route to adventure travelers with spectacular scenery, untamed wilderness, and unknown perils. My kind of place.

But first, we have to cross Chiloe. We hop off the ferry in Pargua and roll into a steady downpour of cold rain. We decide it's the perfect time for lunch. At a small Chacao restaurant, we steam in our clothes in front of a roaring fire and devour seafood chowder, sea bass, and shrimp for the next two hours.

We finally admit the downpour isn't going to let up, so we force ourselves back out into the rain. Twenty miles down the coast, the rain finally relents as we pedal into a picturesque fishing village called Ancud with pastel cottages shining in the golden Pacific sunset. Dinner in front of another fire where we talk and read, then head off to our dry beds.

46

The next day begins dry and sunny with a bracing breeze off the ocean as we ride down island. I'm riding behind Max and noticing that his bike stroke is ragged as hell. The tendonitis he has been fighting the entire trip is winning the fight. His knee is giving out.

We come to a roadside café at another river bridge and I call a halt.

We sit in front of another fire, drinking coffee and holding a team conference. I vote we need to close down our ride and plan a way home. Max begs us to go on to the end without him. Jake won't leave his cousin. I explain that this trip was a kind of fiftieth birthday celebration for me and I won't consider any plan that doesn't keep us together. We drink more coffee and figure it out.

We've had two great weeks. We don't have to be anywhere for at least ten days. Our prepaid plane tickets home are expensive to change. Plan B is to fly 1,000 miles south right over the Carretera Austral down to our original destination and pick up our trip from there—including a cruise through the supposedly spectacular fjords of Chile. Agreed. So, first we have to catch a bus back to Puerto Montt. From there, we'll fly to the combo airport/air force base that serves a town called Punta Arenas.

We're in our rental car a few miles north of the airport when we can't resist stopping to chat with a couple of fellow bike tourers. The twenty-six-year-old couple are Swiss and they humble us with their trip description.

They started by biking from Lucerne to London and rode Great Britain top to bottom. Then they flew to America and biked New England to Florida. From Miami, they flew to Cancun and biked from Mexico up through the American Midwest, cut over to Utah, and rolled on to Anchorage. Then they decided to fly down to Santiago and were just finishing the Carretera Austral by adding a leg down to Ushuaia, the southernmost inhabited town in the Western Hemisphere, just below Tierra del Fuego.

We cheered them on their way and rode the next half hour in silence with our thoughts and imagination. Then we drive in to the valley leading to Torres de Paine and our minds are blown again.

I wish I could adequately describe one of the most visually stunning landscapes I have seen on earth—and I've been to the Himalayas. Try to

47

imagine something like the sculpted peaks of Monument Valley, only much taller, capped with snow and floating on a turquoise blue lake.

We checked in to the Refugio Paine Grande and spent the next two days walking for hours. We saw herds of guanacos—elk-sized cousins of llamas and nandus—five-foot-tall ostrich-like flightless birds, and airplane-sized condors floating overhead. We walked along immense glacier icefields and on rickety suspension bridges over raging rivers. We talked with a group of baquenos—Chilean cowboys—who rode by, and we petted a ranger's domesticated fox.

The most brilliantly blue water I've ever seen was in the Bahamas but the simply-named Lago Paine, high up in a glacier-fed valley, was a blue even Van Gogh would have marveled at. Years later, I found out the English-sounding Paine is pronounced pie-nay and is the local Indian's word for blue. Yes, it is.

Our next stop was the gray everyday dull world of Puerto Natales, a port city on the Golfo Montt where we would begin a long, winding sea cruise through the mountains until we reached the Pacific.

Our cruise ship was a freighter ferry named Eden for no apparent reason. The eighty passengers and sixty crewmen were crammed in with trucks, cattle, and horses. There was no place to go except the windswept deck, your seven by seven shared room, and a single community room where everyone ate, read, drank, and sang.

Our plan was to experience the famous fjords from the sea—all 900 miles of them—on an exotic three-day cruise. I would describe it to you in more detail but basically I already did in Chapter 1.

We gratefully left the Eden in Puerto Monte on the twentieth day of our trip—happy to begin our long connecting flight home, happy to have shared the whole experience, and happy to have the family home for Christmas.

CHAPTER 18
January 26, 1999—Park City, Utah

"Really Unexpected News."

I'm marking off dates on my calendar when I realize I somehow forgot to call Dr. Jobs with my happy news. Even though I only met him briefly and he never treated me, I got him involved that day he sent my files in to UCSF MRSI by acting as my doctor of record.

Dr. Jobs comes on the phone right away when I call and says, "I was wondering why I hadn't heard from you."

I assume Dr. Jobs has heard the good news and I apologize for not calling while I was celebrating.

"What were you celebrating?"

"The fact that my report says I am cancer free**."

"That's not what their report says."

Silence.

It turns out that Dr. Amos's boss and mentor later examined my reports and concluded that I do, in fact, have cancer in my prostate. Their official protocol is to notify the doctor of record, not the patient, so that is what they did.

I choke out my thanks to Dr. Jobs, ask him to send me a copy of their report, and put down the phone.

I don't know how or what to tell anybody. I can't really process this. But I am not the guy who does nothing.

I pick up the phone and call nurse Jill. "Can Dr. Shinohara still keep my biopsy exam on February 3?"

"Yes."

I am rebooked in San Francisco.

Before my reprieve, I had been leaning toward a form of radiation treatment called Brachytherapy. One of the best at that was Dr. Max Roach at UCSF which is where I would be in a week. I call his office. His earliest opening is March 16, six weeks away. I don't think I can wait that long. I need to do something now!

I talk with Diane and this time we decide I will be tight-lipped, at least until we have the biopsy results from next week. In the meantime, I start rereading all my notes and research. I have got to make a decision soon.

CHAPTER 19
February 3, 1999—San Francisco, California

"The fastest gun in the west."

Nurse Jill welcomes me back to the MRI center and ushers me into an exam room to slip into my ridiculous gown. I am convinced they make you wear these because, even if you chicken out, you can't run anywhere dressed like this.

Dr. Shinohara introduces himself and he is all business. Within minutes, I am laid out on the exam table on my side with my knees up to my chest. This time, instead of the greased-up finger, I get a metal instrument shaped like a pistol right up my ass.

He explains the procedure involves moving the gun barrel around following ultrasound images. When he stops, he triggers a loud pop followed by a dull pain and the gun extracts a small cylinder of my prostate. My jerk reaction almost takes me off the table.

I'm cold and shaking and he asks if I am okay. I blurt out that he should take as many as he wants today because I am not doing this again! I may have shrieked that last part. Fourteen pops later, he is finished and I am done.

At the airport later that day, I am walking like a man with a gun up his ass. Slowly and carefully. So slow I miss my car rental bus but I finally get on the plane. Have you ever noticed how uncomfortable those seats are?

Now we wait.

CHAPTER 20
February 8, 1999—Park City, Utah

"Math matters."

I am on the phone with nurse Jill to hear my biopsy report. She gently tells me that two of the six areas they checked, the lower left and mid left, show cancer in 5–10 percent volume. The other four areas are clean.

The two positive areas have Gleason* scores of 3 plus 4. I express my relief because Gleason scores under 6 are generally successfully treated.

Jill gently explains I don't have it quite right. You must add the two numbers together to get your Gleason score, putting me at 7. I remember the famous PC surgeon at Johns Hopkins who treated John Kerry and Paula's friend, Dave. He doesn't even accept patients with a Gleason of 7 or higher.

This is where the concept of staging becomes important. That is how the medical folks rate your cancer condition. You are staged according to various markers and symptoms: your age, cancer cell type, MRI and DRE results, Gleason, etc.

My current staging on something called a Parton Table indicates I have an 80 percent probability that my cancer has reached beyond my prostate. That diagnosis means I am facing a much tougher menu of treatments. I am shocked. Again.

I am desperately trying to escape the D.U.P.E. consequences of the conventional treatments and now I am being herded back into line.

I end the call with nurse Jill and start paging through my notes and files. There is something I am trying to remember about Loma Linda.

CHAPTER 21
February 9, 1999—Loma Linda, California

"Is this the future?"

I had read about a new kind of precise treatment for prostate cancer called a proton beam machine . . . or maybe I saw it on Star Trek?

In any case, I had tracked it down. The only clinical proton beam machine in the world! And it was in Loma Linda, California.

Yesterday I called and asked for an appointment. As usual, they had no openings for weeks. But as usual, I ordered roses delivered to the reception desk the next day while I caught a flight to Loma Linda .

Now, here I was, refreshed from my rush flight and six hours sleep in the only cheap motel, courteously asking if they can squeeze me in to see a doctor.

I couldn't help but smile at my roses and note on the reception desk. After filling out the usual forms and verifying my insurance coverage, an admin lady comes out and tells me if I come back Friday, they will fit me in.

CHAPTER 22
February 12, 1999—Loma Linda, California

"No D.U.P.E. for me."

The excitement about proton beam radiation is that it can pinpoint its destructive force on precise, small locations. In contrast, external beam radiation can often harm surrounding healthy tissue. It's sort of the rifle versus shotgun analogy we've all heard . . . particularly with women who now often choose a smaller lumpectomy over a mastectomy.

It's Friday and I'm back.

Dr. Christian Wright has my immediate trust when I hear he is a sub-three-hour marathoner. My theory is that doctors who take care of themselves will take better care of me.

Initially, I am also impressed by the Loma Linda published data until I realize it only addresses claimed D.U.P.E. side effects, not mortality. But then facts begin to emerge. They have pretty much the same incidence of impotence. And it turns out they only beam the entire prostate! So much for the pinpoint effect I was hoping could save my healthy tissue.

I tell Dr. Wright I appreciate his squeezing me in but I need to reflect. I am actually crushed and I think he can sense it. I don't want to be D.U.P.E.'d.

CHAPTER 23
February 16, 1999—Seattle, Washington

"Sharing with my son."

After getting my biopsy news a week earlier, I called my kids, Max and Molly, and told them I was back in the ring but I still had plenty of fight in me.

Tonight I am having dinner with my son, Max, who drove up from his campus in Olympia to meet me in Seattle. Why Seattle? Because it's where I will meet my preferred brachy therapist tomorrow. He is Dr. Hakon Ragde, Swedish born and today one of the world's most experienced in his field. As usual, I'd done my research. And I called his office the day I left Loma Linda.

Max is a bright, analytical guy and it helped my thinking to lay out my options with him.
I tell him I have ruled out the proton beam because it is not nearly as precise as I wanted.

A radical prostatectomy surgery is also a no go, mainly because my Gleason score of 7 makes me an undesirable candidate for top surgeons. I don't know what their reasoning is but it sure makes their batting average better. And, as I tell Max, the radiation solution pretty much guarantees you're going to have disappointing problems with impotence and incontinence. I assure Max us old guys worry about both.

As I lay it out and we talk, I realize that my first goal of getting the cancer out means that Dr. Ragde's style of brachytherapy is probably going to be best for me. And I'm thinking about foot-long needles.

CHAPTER 24
February 17, 1999—Seattle, Washington

"I'm feeling like shish kebab."

My usual roses are sitting on the reception desk as I arrive to meet with Dr. Hakon Ragde who turns out to be a fellow graduate of the University of Virginia.

We exchange Charlottesville memories as he bends me over for the now routine DRE. What a way to make friends. Though guys like the famous surgeon at Hopkins think my Gleason 7 prostate score eliminates me as a surgery candidate, Dr. Ragde decides it's worth a deeper look.

Off I go to Dr. Ragde's ultrasound lab where I am quickly settled into the stirrups on the cervix exam table followed by a sportscaster-like technician who stuffs his imaging equipment up my ass and begins reading off a play-by-play of what he is seeing in real time.

"You're going to live by the looks of things . . . "

" Oh, this is what he was feeling, I bet . . . "

"He's going to want to look at this . . . "

"Yeah, most guys can still get it up. Of course, you will never ejaculate again."

The instruments are gratefully removed but the nurse tells me to lie on the next table on my side with my knees against my chest.

I know what comes next. Dr. Ragde has his own gun and he can't wait to shove it up my ass and pop off a couple more biopsy samples. At this rate, I may not have any prostate left to operate on.

Turns out what Dr. Ragde felt in the DRE led him to question the readings from Dr. Shinohara's biopsy at UCSF. When I meet with his oncologist associate, Dr. Kon tells me their findings have convinced Dr. Ragde that I need both brachytherapy and the dreaded External Beam Radiation (EBR*) which is the very prostate treatment I was avoiding by not going back to Loma Linda. He shows me a sheaf of computer printouts that predict the odds of my cure* approach 90 percent, about the same level as guys who do nothing as far as I can tell. But hey, I just want to get the cancer out—seems the least I should do.

Then the doctors show me a foot-long, shiny steel needle they use to deliver the radiation pellets with such precision. I can't help but shift in my chair as they describe how the needle is inserted in my perineum. (In school, we jokingly called it your t'aint. If you're still not clear, try Google.) The needle deposits the seeds as it is pulled out and then you go your merry way with very little surgical effect. Just don't try any squats for a few days.

I am pretty much depressed by the best-of-a-bad-thing choices I have but this is state of the art for 1999. Dr. Kon helpfully signs me up for five weeks of pre-brachytherapy EBR at my nearby University of Utah and then I will return to Seattle for Dr. Ragde and his little needle.

CHAPTER 25
December 1996—Mexican Riviera

"Down Mexico Way."

Ten years ago, I promised myself I would stick to my travel plans no matter the timing. My goal was to travel from the top of North America to the tip of South America.

I didn't plan to do it all in one trip. And I didn't think I would cover every mile. I'd just do bites, covering most of the latitudes going one way or another.

So here it was, a few weeks before Christmas, with my forty-ninth birthday coming up. Recently, I'd been chiding my twenty-six-year-old nephew, Jake, about getting some excitement back in his life.. The guy was a Stanford grad, almost US Ski Team in skiing, and now all he was doing was dabbling at being a local real estate agent. But he could still my over-confident butt in some biking we'd been doing.

"I'm off to bike the Mexican Riviera," I challenged. "Think you're up to doing it with me?" Two days later he was packed and boarding the plane with me.

We landed in Acapulco at 2:00 p.m. in the middle of siesta time. In less than an hour, we'd assembled our bikes and were on the road—actually a freaking busy highway. We're headed up the coast to Mazatlán, 500 miles north.

Thirty minutes of barely-controlled highway traffic convinces us we need to get better fortified. We pull off and walked into the luxurious Princess Hotel for an ice-cold Coco Loco. Or four.

With our judgement improved, we hit it again, this time ignoring the trucks brushing past our elbows. Before long, the congestion of Acapulco city swallowed us with increasingly tall buildings. An hour of pedaling around a crescent bay lined with luxury condo towers and hotels has Jake throwing dark glances at me.

We finally escape the city and follow the highway along the coast. It's getting dark. Our campsite is some unknown distance ahead. And Jake is saying nothing.

Then I spot a group of men standing around a pickup truck, supervising a guy changing a tire. I use my best high school Spanish to beg a ride to our campsite "dos kilometers" (I am guessing) up the road. They confer and agree. We hop in the truck bed with our bikes and four of them join us, carrying rifles I hadn't noticed.

In a few minutes, the leader points to his nose and sniffs, "Quiera coca?"

My Spanish tells him, I hope, that we are too poor to buy coca. We can only afford bicycles. But we will trade our bicycles for women. I laugh so he will get my macho joke.

Dead silence. Then one of them quickly converts my butchered Spanish into the real words. They all laugh loudly. They like my humor. But that didn't stop them from depositing us and our bikes at the first intersection we came to—a dirt road to nowhere they smiled and pointed down.

We're standing in the dark with our bikes. Jake is waiting to hear my plan. And out of the darkness shuffles a large soldier with a machine gun in his hands. Again, my Spanish conveys our need to find the campground nearby. He laughs. Very happy guys here in Mexico. But there is no campground. Only a hotel down the road we are looking at. Gratefully, it is toward the beach. I ask how much. He replies, "Cinco mil dollars." Jake gleefully translates that as $5,000 a night, and laughs as the soldier hustles us on our way.

Were you waiting for a happy ending to our first day?

We got one. The real price was fifty pesos. And for the equivalent of $8, we enjoyed a fresh grilled fish dinner on the beach with numerous cervezas, clean sheets, soft beds and ocean breezes. I give Jake a smug smile as I turnout the l;ight.

Next morning we awoke in our Pie de la Cuesta resort feeling refreshed and optimistic. But then suddenly fiercely itching all over. Invisible biters decided to share our overnight and they were everywhere. We jump in the cold ocean for relief and decide we'll skip the resort breakfast. Jake shakes his head as mounts up before me and heads out.

Forty-two miles later, I catch up with him sitting at a roadside market, drinking something cold and grinning. I pull over , ready to give him his due. But when my foot hits the ground, I catch the mother-of-all charley horses. Which quickly spreads to both legs and my back. I collapse like a jelly man. Thirty very touchy minutes later, I can slowly climb back on my bike. It's time to head for our campsite.

I still don't know if Jake was impressed by the next ten miles' ride up a narrow strip of beach between Laguna Coyuca and the Pacific Ocean. I still don't know how he crossed the river at Playa Azul. Or how he followed the broken-line beach highway all the way to Boca Chica. But knew he had to wait up for me so we wouldn't miss the turnoff to the twisting highway north toward Tecpan.

Jake just smiled when I finally caught up. And smiled more at each of my questions. "Quien sabe?" was his enigmatic reply, sipping on his cold cerveza. Revenge comes in all forms. Especially between family.

We decide I will now ride ahead as Jake rides leisurely ski patrol behind me , just in case I cramp up again.. I decide to redeem my pride by speeding ahead, cramps be damned.

When I finally pull up at the turn for our campsite , fate steps in again. As Jake pedals into sight, I'm about to wave him over. Then I see a truck overhauling him to pass. I'm afraid to yell because he might turn in front of the speeding truck. The truck roars by, screening Jake from my view. I look up and down the road and then spot him, already out of shouting distance, pedaling furiously to catch up to the stupid uncle who was supposed to be waiting.

I have no choice but to painfully follow him. To wherever he finally stops. Eighteen miles later Jake is well beyond our campsite, all the way to Tecpan. Neither of us is happy with our explanations. But we find a cheap hotel in the town, lock up our bikes, and find a cab to take us back toward the beach where we are supposed to be camping. At least we'll get in a swim.

By this point, you'd think Jake would be questioning my leadership. You'd be right. Especially when my Spanish directions to the cab driver brings us to the end of the paved road, miles from anywhere. He hauls out a map and shows us the playa, another eight miles away. I agree to the extra pesos.

Soon we are on a dirt road passing through a huge banana plantation. And something more. Under most of the banana trees, concealed under the fronds, are leafy coca plants lovingly guarded by unsmiling men holding rifles. We roll on. And our dirt road ends at a river.

I'm getting those looks from Jake again. Now the driver explains that he whistles for the ferry that will then float us down to the beach. Our driver Manuel, now my trusted compadre, says he will come back for us in three hours. To cement our trust, I rip a 100 peso bill in halves and give him one. I will give him the other when he returns. He is not at all insulted and smiles thanks.

Twenty minutes later we are swinging in hammocks on the beach, the only visitors to a beautiful resort with outdoor dining, icy fruit drinks, terrific body surfing, and soft breezes meant for naps.

The twenty-five-year-old chef proprietor has recently come home from picking produce in Fresno. I can see he has no reason to go back. His ten-year-old brother is our waiter and is fascinated how we seem to appear from nowhere. As the sun sets, we head back on the ferry and find Manuel waiting. I think Jake has forgiven me.

Next morning, we are up early to start a long fifty-mile inland route that will take us through jungles and farmland and up and down mountains. We want to make it to Petatlán, about halfway to the big resort area of Ixtapa/Zihuatanejo.

Every ten miles or so, the highway dips down to the beach then climbs back up the hills. It's tough no-thrill biking with the only break from boredom the nerve-racking traffic. The highways here do not have shoulders and the curves often lack guard rails. The truck drivers have all they can handle just staying on the road, so, we do lots of steer-into-the-bushes and climb-out-alive.

Every time our slower pedaling on long ascents holds up all the truck drivers, I think about how they will get their revenge on the descent. Nothing like a blasting horn in your ear and a five-ton truck up your ass, wondering how often Mexican trucks have their brakes checked.

We make Petatlán alive, helped, I am sure, by grace of the city's Sanctuary de la Padre Jesus de Petatlán and its 400-year-old statue of Christ. The Catholic in me is always trying.

Dawn finds us at a roadside coffee stand, waiting for light safe enough for biking. Our plan is to kick it early and get forty miles up the beach to Zihuatanejo for breakfast, then cruise through next-door Ixtapa and find a highly-touted hideaway resort called Troncones. Outside magazine called it "a secret gem of bohemian American luxury" and it's right in our flight path. We are figuring on a day or two of just what they described.

Our fellow coffee drinkers that morning have heard our story and, as they repeat it among themselves, I heard the words, Tio and Sabrino. Jake asks and they point to me, "Tio," and him, "Sabrino." Uncle and nephew. We get it.

Jake is still interested in showing me who is the better-trained biker, so we take turns blowing by each other, many times pedaling out of sight. . I wasn't worried when I arrived in Zihuatanejo first, collapsing on a grassy patch with no Jake in view.

An hour later, I'm getting seriously worried. Either he's hurt or he was so far ahead of me now that I'll never catch up. We didn't even name a precise meeting spot. Americans on bikes on the Mexican highway tend to stick out.

Finally, I see him come limping into sight. He's pedaling with only one gear. His derailleur is broken and his bike speed is barely beyond walking. He tells me he stopped at one point and tried to do a repair in a small village square. He was soon surrounded by school children, excited to see the strange looking Yankee tourist dressed like a surf bum, trying to fix a weird looking bike. They laughed when he said his name was Sabrino.

We start asking around. There's got to be a bike mechanic in town. Luck has put one less than a mile away. We call and he has the parts. Twenty minutes and twenty pesos later, we are back on the road.

Zihuantanejo is basically a great big village sprawled around a wide, protected bay. It's historic, hilly, and packed with Mexican tourists. It has lots of beaches with gentle waves. Next door Ixtapa is crammed with the usual big hotels, condo towers, and North American tourists.

Leaving the city, we come to an overlook on the mountain road above Ixtapa. It looks to us like more of what we just left , but on steroids. We decide to pass and start winding through the mountains. Our forty-mile jaunt to the beach is starting to feel like forty up and forty down. Once again, Jake's twenty-year age advantage, and nothing else, lets him climb a little faster. An hour later, I catch up to the familiar scene of Sabrino drinking a cold one by the road as I gratefully roll to a stop.

We chat with the Mexican owners who lived for many years in San Diego playing a lot of golf. Somehow, they have decided the mountain air and ocean views they have here are a good trade-off.

We hear this almost every time we meet a Mexican who lived in the States and returned here. The slower pace, better environment, lower costs of living, and the overall enjoyment of life obliterate any comparison to their life north of the border. Can't say I disagree with them.

Finally, we spot a sign pointing down a dirt road off to our left toward Troncones. Three miles later, we pass through a modest village to a string of beachfront villas and retro motels. We're back in the bubble of flush toilets, safe water, air-conditioning, and ice-cold Cokes. The resort is pleasantly laid back and our B&B room is $80 a night—more than all our other accommodations combined. Good old America—even in Mexico.

We're soon hanging out at the Burro Boracho—Drunken Donkey—with owner-proprietor Mike, an escapee from San Francisco and a grad of the California Culinary Institute. The man paid attention in class. His food is mouthwatering, fresh, and perfect. But it's also priced like San Francisco. We eat and drink all we can afford, bodysurf and nap, then come back for more. Luckily, we can only stay one night.

The next day is going to be a long one. We have to climb back up to the highway, then get as far as we can—seventy miles, we hope—to our next planned stop.

We biked ten miles before sunrise. It's good to be back in our minimal comfort, on-our-own bubble. Fifteen miles later, we're crossing a river bridge when Jake gets a flat. I get a break. We both get breakfast—fresh oranges, cheese, crackers, cold filtered water.

We're sitting on the bridge rail, taking in the miles of empty wetlands and farm land all around us. Unknown birds and insects keep up a good buzz and the gentle breeze rustles the palm trees. The traffic has magically thinned out and it's pretty peaceful. Jake nudges me.

Walking along the highway, leading a shuffling donkey, is a guy who looks like Juan Valdez. I'm ready to ask him about Colombian coffee when he walks up to us and asks if we have any Gatorade. He says he's a little dehydrated. And he's speaking with a pure Southern California accent.

A few hours later, we can tell we are beginning a long stretch of foothills and mountains. We're forced to follow the highway as it turns more inland. Now we are leaving the Mexican state of Guerrero and entering Michoacán. They have a little problem hereabouts called the Zapatistas --- armed rebels who like to blow up government places.

Our detour inland takes us over the broad Rio Balsas and a huge dam. Truckloads of soldiers are everywhere. We see concrete guard houses with rifle ports and sand-bagged machine gun nests. A lot of grim faces and signs warning against photography. Apparently the dam is a major rebel target.

Once across the river, we head south as fast as we can, finally coming to an industrialized zone around the city of Lazaro Cardenas. There's an airport here and I want to try and find a more detailed map. For some reason, maps are hard to find in Mexico. Maybe they are just hiding them from the Zapatistas. We finally chat up a helicopter pilot who once trained near Provo. He remembers it never got over ten degrees and he's happy to be here. He gives us an old flight map, better than anything I have. Jake is very happy. He's been less than complimentary about my navigating.

To which I usually respond, "When the big water is on your left, you're going the right direction." Our pilot friend warns us that the mountain roads ahead are frequent ambush sites because the rebels can sit on the high ground and shoot down at the soldiers in the trucks below.

As we leave the city, I am checking the map for how long it will be before our turn toward the beach and our overnight. It's a place called Las Penas. I tell Jake it's going to be hard. He says I need to work on my sense of humor.

The only hotel in Las Penas is closed for remodeling—all five rooms—but the little old lady who runs it lets us have a room not too torn up for ten pesos. We're the only guests. Our balcony is seventy feet above the surf and the beer in the open-air restaurant on the beach is ice cold. Dinner is grilled fish caught about a hundred yards away and the fishermen who caught them are soon at the table next to us holding a spirited town meeting. I think they were concerned about the tourist crowding.

We enjoy a couple of extra beers and Jake hums a few bars of a familiar tune. It's my forty-ninth birthday.

Morning finds us climbing back up the road toward good old Highway 200. This section is fairly new and runs all the way to Mazatlán, our final destination. We're in some serious up and down climbs now over mountain ridges, in some places almost too steep to pedal. We gut it out. We're trying to top seventy miles today.

Rounding a curve, we see below us a coastal town the map calls Bahia Bufadero. I laugh because that translates to Blowhole Beach. I surmise they must have done some whale watching here. Jake can't believe I passed up the chance for some more bad jokes.

As we pedal down toward the water's edge, a picturesque little harbor sparkles in the morning sun, dotted with moored fishing boats and a crescent walkway packed with after-church strollers.

Not satisfied with our pilot's aerial navigation map, we go shopping for something with landmarks you recognize at bike level. A book store and a paper store come up zero but a customer overhears and suggests we try an American place up the beach. It turns out he is describing Playa Nexpa, the surfing school and resort we already knew about. We decide to try it.

Again, no maps. But we do burn up the rest of the morning eating lunch in a hammock and listening to burned-out surfer stories from an international collection of dropouts. The surf looks spectacular.

We've only done twenty-five miles for the day, so, we head out in the afternoon sun, climbing into the hills again, with dense jungle now on both sides of us. By 3:00 p.m., we've climbed over a dozen mountain ridges that run down to the coast and Jake has again pedaled ahead out of sight. All I can do is plug on. I notice yet another dead dog by the road which reminds me that there are no shoulders on this highway. I hear a shout and look up to spot Jake sitting on the porch of a store that marks the entrance to a tiny village. A dozen or so men are drinking beer after their siesta.

We ask everyone if they know how far it is to Maruata, the town where we plan to sleep. No one has a clue. We decide to push on. The highway is just a strip of asphalt with jungle on one edge and a cliff on the other.

Then we hear the bus. I'm trying to figure out where we can go to get out of the way when its brakes creak and it stops fifty feet behind us. Male passengers come climbing out, heading to the bushes. We walk down and talk to the driver. He thinks Maruata is at least sixty kilometers further but he's not sure. He is substituting for the regular driver, who failed to stop for banditos on his last trip and now fears they are laying for him.

The bus pulls away in a cloud of exhaust and I notice the sun is starting to set. Maruata is out of reach for tonight and we would need machetes we don't have in order to carve out a camping spot far enough off the highway for peace of mind. I'm trying to think of options when Jake taps my shoulder and says, "You gotta see this." He's pointing up the road to what looks like a mangy black kitten walking down the yellow line. Then I notice Kitty has too many legs. It's the biggest tarantula I've ever seen. Decision made.

Another hour of pedaling through the mountains has brought us to sunset. Unbelievably, the road suddenly bends and opens up over a river valley. Broad fields below us are cultivated and there are at least two houses or barns. Civilization! We hurtle down the road toward porch lights.

Which turn out to be lanterns. A large man, with a larger missing-teeth smile, greets us on his porch and welcomes us to sleep on the floor of his corn shed. He apologizes but his wife's family is visiting. But we are also welcome to join them for dinner.

In short order, we are feasting on fresh caught langostas from the river, downed with tortilla soup and warm beer. Everyone is smiling and laughing and not really believing we are riding bikes up their coastline.

We end up sharing the corn shed with a tranquil donkey, tightly zipped up in our bivvy sleeping sacks just in case any more of the local kitties are out wandering. Exhausted but full, we recall the day's events and decide it felt more like a week.

Everyone is up with the roosters in the morning, so we bike out in the dawn light with lots of gracias. Crossing two more ridges, we are shocked to arrive at the beachfront town of Maruata. We were that close.

We stop for a well-earned breakfast and stock up on our road menu of crackers, cheese, fruit, and juices. We come out of the store and a fellow gringo who is waiting for a bus asks if these are our bikes. He can't believe we just crossed the mountains and jungle but is happy to tell us the way ahead is much easier and open.

Three hours out of Maruata we are are looking down at what I imagine a California beach town would have looked like in the 1950s. Miles of broad, open beach sprinkled with rows of modest, low-slung motels in bright colors. It's called San Telmo and, of course, it's not on our crappy map and it's exactly what we crave on this Mexican coast. Low key, inexpensive, uncrowded—and an ambiance created by shady palm trees, fresh seafood, warm breezes, soothing surf and, of course, cheap beer. Our rooms are squeaky clean, the sheets are soft, and we each have a perfect reading hammock. Laundry and showers behind us, we wake up recharged and ready to roll.

Until Jake sticks his hand in the fan. He was standing by his bed, reaching up while putting his arm through his t-shirt sleeve when whack! Alerted by his cursing and the suddenly wobbly ceiling fan, I see blood gushing everywhere and I leap into paramedic mode. I stem the bleeding with a wad of toilet paper, one of my favorite T-shirts, and a belt tourniquet. Then I run for help.

The motel proprietor brings her first-aid kit, expecting a near-amputation. Her diagnosis includes the word pequito and a nodding smile. Jake will live and he has a nice bandage.

Just to be safe, I insist we stop at the next town we bike through and look up a local medico. We locate the nearest one in a small town called Cerro de Ortega, about four miles inland from the beach at Boca de Apiza where we are now arguing. Jake relents, we stash our bikes, and we go get him three stitches from Dr. Rutierruiz, late of the Guadalajara School of Medicine, along with a supply of antibiotics. Total bill: $18.

Jake and I hitch a pickup truck ride back to the beach for us and our bikes and we decamp at the lovely Hotel Solar, last remodeled just before the Great War. Jake can't go in the ocean or drink beer but I take care of his share and show a few local girls the fine art of bodysurfing, Utah style.

We wake up the next day with a Manzanillo-or-bust attitude since we'd loafed the last few days. It's a pretty flat seventy-mile run, so, we hit it hard. Jake hits it even harder. He is waiting for me for breakfast in the town of Tecomán in the middle of intensively farmed fields that stretch to the horizon.

After breakfast, Jake begins to pour it on again. But an old wolf is a canny wolf. And I decide to show him how to draft. No matter what he does, he can't pull away from me. He pedals faster and faster but I'm right on his wheel. He stands up and power pedals. I'm still there. He keeps looking back at me in amazement. Finally, after three hours and almost sixty miles, I wave him over to the side with a big smile. He gives me a WTF and I say, "You ever heard of drafting?" Jake says something about race cars and I say, "Not quite.

Here's the explanation. Pedaling faster increases your speed but it also increases your wind resistance. You're trying to go faster than the air flowing around you. When you ride closely behind someone, they are doing all the work. They are breaking the wind for you and you actually get pulled along by their slipstream. If you've ever followed someone in a boat, you can see the effect on the water where their wake flattens the sea in front of you.

Drafting pulls you along so well on your bike it has been proven that you use 20–40 percent less energy to maintain the same speed as the rider in front of you. If you ever watch Tour de France races, you see riders on the same team taking turns to draft for their teammates. Every time Jake stood up to power pedal, he was actually increasing his wind profile and pulling me along even more.

Jake and I get back on our bikes and I have him follow me to demonstrate. He becomes a believer. Then he starts thinking back to the puzzled looks he kept giving me, my fiendish smiles, and how hard he kept pedaling. He starts laughing, I start laughing, and soon we are can't-stand-up laughing together. I can't recall a better feeling after a long bike ride to somewhere.

A few hours later, we ride in together to Manzanillo. Jake's part of the trip ends here near the airport, so, we celebrate with a night in a luxury hotel. We are both very glad to have shared the trip.

The next morning Jake is away early but not before leaving me a note. "Tio, Thanks for the company. Great trip. On to Mazatlán! Love, Sabrino."

Pedaling in the pre-dawn darkness, I am thinking about more tarantulas and more steep mountain roads like I have already seen and I realize I am lonely. I miss my partner. I don't really care about Mazatlán. A mile later, I spot the turn for the airport. I mentally toss a coin. I may have cheated. I opt for duo instead of solo. A short while later, I am sitting on the plane next to a surprised nephew, laughing again.

CHAPTER 26
March 2, 1999—Salt Lake City, Utah

"Junk food and a man to man."

I am at the University of Utah for my workup which is the preamble to my first external beam radiation (EBR) session in five days. I'm nervous and morose and veteran nurse, Dottie Green, forever after known as Angel, sees my discomfort and takes me in hand. Literally.

One of Nurse Green's jobs is to rub a numbing salve on my penis and then insert a catheter up my urethra, through my prostate, and into my bladder. It looks and feels just like you are imagining. And I am convinced the salve isn't working. Dottie assures me it usually does. Usually ?

EBR side effects include fatigue, depleted stamina, weight gain, and hair loss. Which leaves me wondering what the hell are the good effects! Nurse Dottie is candid — I may also have bladder and even anus after-effects. And you know what that means —diapers and pads.

The reason for the tube highway through my body is so they can pump a dye in me which guides them in marking the axis from hip to hip and then the one from belly to butt . . . all centered through my prostate. These are matched to laser light tattoo dots on my skin which will, hopefully, accurately target the radiation pulses.

I ask Dottie what I can do to improve my odds here and she looks at me with a straight face and says that I need to eat more junk food. She says the radiation needs to target unhealthy cells and eating junk food will give me more of those to shoot. She waits for me to laugh at her joke but then she laughs herself at my stupefied expression. I am still not sure if that is a theory or not.

Dottie now realizes she has a basket case on her hands. She counsels me to call her friend, Gary Hustead, who is the coordinator of an American Cancer Society self-counseling group for prostate patients called Man to Man.

I don't know it yet but Dottie just gave me my lifeline.

CHAPTER 27
March 2, 1999—Park City, Utah

"There's this doctor named Bob . . . "

Gary Hustead returns my call that evening. He had prostate surgery two years earlier. The first thing he tells me is, "If I had it to do over again, I would look at hormone therapy. Check out the web page for a Los Angeles oncologist named Dr. Bob Leibowitz. He's a little controversial and maybe ahead of his time but I think he makes sense."

By the time Gary and I end our call, I am already devouring Dr. Bob's website. And I am getting excited. By the time I fall asleep that night, I have absorbed these amazing observations from Dr. Bob's six years of innovative treatment:

- You probably do not need to radiate, freeze, or surgically remove your prostate.
- Your prostate may be one of your body's producers of natural angiostatins or endostatins, one of your best protections against cancer growth, and you don't want to lose it.
- Since cancer cells grow from the nutrition provided by new blood vessels, angiogenesis, blocking their formation is critical and that may be what the statins produced by your prostate are doing for you.
- Prostate cancer cells can be starved by blocking the two crucial hormones they feed on, testosterone and dihydrotestosterone ,which is a metabolite your body creates from testosterone using an enzyme called 5a-reductase**.

Dr. Bob has been using what he calls triple androgen* blockade (TAB) to reduce testosterone* and its conversion to dihydrotestosterone. It's a combination of drugs that has worked for 110 men over a six-year period without a problem. And without any need for surgery or radiation. Or need to be retreated.

Can Dr. Bob be my answer?

For the first time since my doomsday call on January 26, I am honestly looking forward to the rest of my life.

CHAPTER 28
March 3, 1999—Park City, Utah

"My name is Jim and I have prostate cancer."

I've been waiting all day to attend my first Man to Man meeting at Gary Hustead's invitation. These meetings are kind of like AA meetings but for prostate cancer patients.

For the next two hours, I listen to men who went through their own decision process and the side effects they've been living with since. It's the same litany of sad bathroom and failed sex stories I've been reading about, but here are all these survivors telling me in person about their life after treatment.

The temporary euphoria I felt from studying Dr. Bob's website is now tempered by the hard realization that nothing else is going to work to give me that second chance at a normal life.
My yo-yo thought process gets jerked around again and again over the next few days.

The process starts with a conversation with a highly-recommended brachytherapist named Dr. Jim Haynes. After the usual invasive but now routine exam and the evaluation of my less than impressive scores, Dr. Haynes is blunt. Either I should get the treatment I need which, in his mind, is of course the seed implant process he does, or I will be facing serious consequences in a few years.

A few hours later, I am on the phone with Dr. Lowell Vance, a brilliant New England internist who happens to be my the widowed husband of my sister who died a few years earlier from ovarian cancer. Lowell is one of the smartest guys I've ever met and a distinguished doctor in his own right, so I sent him one of the videos describing Dr. Bob's TAB treatment and asked him for comment.

To make a long discussion short, my conservative and careful doctor friend thinks Dr. Bob could "be on to something . . . his ideas make a lot of sense." Up. Down. Down. Up. Time to call Dr. Bob.

CHAPTER 29
March 4, 1999—Park City, Utah

"An appointment with destiny?"

I call Dr. Bob's office first thing, expecting to beg, send roses, camp on his doorstep, whatever. He can see me next week. I am shocked. And right away the doubts creep in.

Why isn't the world beating down his door? How could he have an opening so soon?

My naivete about the world of doctor referrals is about to end. And I am about to meet the doctor I really want to believe is my salvation.

CHAPTER 30
March 10, 1999—Los Angeles, California

"My Doc Hollywood?"

I am in Los Angeles to meet with Dr. Bob. And, yes, that's what he tells me to call him. Driving through Beverly Hills I arrive at his office in next-door Century City. There on his door is Dr. Robert L. Leibowitz. It's official—he has a last name. And I note his practice has an official name, too: Compassionate Oncology Medical Group.

In short order, Dr. Bob's secretary has handed me a book of patient testimonials while his office manager walks me through the inevitable insurance forms. The nurse and medical assistant follow up with vitals, measures, and blood samples and I am ushered in to meet Dr. Bob. He quickly puts me at ease with his gentle smile, compassionate nature, and calm but serious inquiries.

"Tell me everything you can ever remember about urinary problems."

"Who else have you seen and what did they tell you?"

"You have a list of our patients. Feel free to call any of them."

"Do you understand that all of the side effects of our treatment are reversible?"

"I am not the only one using hormone therapy but no one else does it like we do except a doctor in Utah who called me and said he treated four patients successfully using our protocol."

"Our results are there in that book. Nobody has matched them."

I thoroughly enjoy our conversation. Dr. Bob is promising what I have been looking for and what no one else has offered. But I tell him I need to think it through.

I am troubled that Dr. Bob's work lacks peer-review articles, which is a very big deal with new treatment protocols. I am puzzled that other doctors do not refer to him.

Dr. Bob encourages me to do all the research I can — on him and everyone. He points to his book of patients and says, "You are holding my peer reviews," and he sends me off with a smile.

I jump in the car for the drive back to the airport ,but first I call the University of Utah radiation team and delay my start of ERB for a week.

I have some thinking to do.

CHAPTER 31
March 12, 1999—Park City, Utah

"The only thing worse than a bad decision
is no decision."

I get a call from Dr. Bob's office. My blood work showed my PSA is now at 6.8! Seven months ago it was 4.0. Three months ago it was 5.1. It's getting aggressive and accelerating. I thank them for the call and promise a quick call back. Time's up.

The debate in my head is getting louder. And it goes on all weekend.

I don't want to do surgery or radiation, even if I thought it would work. But every study or anecdotal information I can find says the end doesn't justify the means. And I don't want to be a D.U.P.E. with all the bathroom and bedroom aftereffects.

I am too young to gamble on the watch and wait theory—all the odds are against me.

Nobody has died from Dr. Bob's treatment. In fact, they are all alive—and I have talked with many of them at Dr. Bob's urging.

There are side effects but all are easily reversible and short-term. *I can live with that*, I think, enjoying the irony.

I have never been afraid to take the path off the map. I always look for opportunities, not guarantees.

CHAPTER 32
March 15, 1999—Park City, Utah

"I believe in you."

I wake up and sit down at my computer. I type out this short note and fax it to Dr. Bob's office:

> Dear Dr. Leibowitz,
>
> I want to be your patient. You believe TAB works and I believe you.
>
> I will be calling Zena shortly for my next appointment.
>
> Jim Doilney

A few minutes later, I am talking with Zena as she books me in for my appointment in Los Angeles two days from now. Path taken.

CHAPTER 33
March 17, 1999—Los Angeles, California

"I finally made it to Hollywood."

So, there I was cruising down Sunset Boulevard, soon to be empty of male hormones but full of pills and hope. My first treatment with Dr. Bob went great and I was literally stuffed with a massive dose of pills I would take each day for the next year or so.

I was also leaning to one side thanks to a shot in the butt of Lupron Depot—sort of a chemical castrator—which would repeat every ninety days.

WTF? Well, the pills were twenty-one vitamins and supplements I would need to keep up my male strength and stamina in the face of hormone deprivation. Then there were the three 50 mg capsules of Casodex and a single 5 mg of Finasteride. Bob was using 150 mg of Casodex, not the 50 mg other PCa docs prescribed.

It will take me several minutes every morning to wash everything down—who has time for breakfast?

In a medical nutshell, here's what's going to happen to my body and my PC every day:

The Lupron Depot is a potent hormone suppressor. Pediatricians use it to block the premature onset of puberty in young children, a condition called CCP. In me, it would suppress my natural production of testosterone, turning me into a temporary woman, at least in my mind. The Casodex was the daily partner to the quarterly Lupron shot.

The Finasteride was an equally important soldier in my army because it blocked the action of the devilish 5 alpha reductase enzyme, which splits my testosterone into two probable cancer catalyst components: DHT and estradiol, a form of estrogen found in men.

The brilliant Dr. Bob's revolutionary and evolutionary theory is that this naturally occurring split of testosterone provides the fuel for cancer cell growth and tumors. By blocking the production of the hormone and preventing the split of any remainder, I would be starving my cancer cells into submission.

Decades ago, a Nobel Prize winner, Charles Huggins, had declared that testosterone was the cause of PCa. His testosterone conclusion was text book stuff for med school students. To this day, testosterone supplements carry the warning that T can cause PCa.

Dr. Bob's mission was to prove that it wasn't the testosterone primarily at fault, it was the enzyme that split it apart and created new hormone fuels.

Blocking all three male hormones, or androgens, is Dr. Bob's Triple Androgen Blockade (TAB) treatment.

CHAPTER 34
October 2, 1999—Park City, Utah

"Hear me roar . . . "

I'm glad I won't have to be a woman much longer. If you ever had any doubt about the effect of hormones on personality, mood or basic desires, trying going without them. And if anyone ever suggests you're acting like your hormones are over-active, tell them you are just warming up.

For six months, my TAB treatment has knocked any vestige of male sex drive right out of my head and my shorts. I could swear I've had hot flashes and mood swings. I've even cried , shocking myself over small emotional outbursts.

My co-workers at my homebuilding company are glad to have me back and seemingly healthy, but more than a few have commented that I am acting "differently." And my beautiful, dutiful wife has noticed too. It won't be enough to save our marriage from an impending divorce, but she likes this side of me.

I know that all sounds like a male chauvinist fantasy….but remarkably, that is exactly what it feels like. And I am stuck here for at least the rest of the year. By Spring, if all goes well, I can begin planning on trips and romance again. Until then, I can't even have good fantasies.

CHAPTER 35
April 5, 2000—Park City, Utah

"Something's working."

Twelve months ago, I began what I thought was Dr. Bob's long-shot thirteen-month TAB treatment. After hundreds of pills swallowed and five painful butt shots endured, I am headed back to LA one more time to visit with Dr. Bob and get my scorecard filled out.

My TAB treatment was designed to focus on testosterone deprivation. Damn, it did work.

When I started in March of 1999, my testosterone level was at 300—about average. Three months later, I was down to 37! Just barely male. By July, I had dropped to 23 and that Fall I was basically off the chart. It's stayed there for the next eight months. My testosterone today is under 10!

One of the key trackers of prostate cancer is the PSA level (Prostate Specific Antigen *. Every American male over sixty who gets a physical at some point will be aware of or asked about his PSA level number. The commonly used magic number is 4. If yours is under 4.0, you'll likely be told no sweat. If you're over, you're usually on the road to long discussions about treatment consequences and being D.U.P.E.'d!

None of the answers are pretty. Here's why:

    1. Because no one has yet discovered the definite cause or a permanent cure for prostate cancer. All we have are treatments trying to manage it.

    2. Every mainstream treatment has really unpleasant consequences. You may end up with nasty bathroom problems . . . you know, the bag. Or worse, your ability to fully enjoy regular sex ending in ejaculation is over. And so on.

3. No one has yet shown that any of the mainstream treatments with their unfortunate side effects yield a better life expectancy or quality of life than simply watching and waiting.

4. The only reason you subject yourself and your beleaguered prostate to all the surgery, radiation, or chemo is because you are afraid it will spread and you'll die sooner than you deserve. But remember, even when they tell you "we think we got it all," there's no such thing as a 100 precent cure**. And there you are, living that greatly diminished life, changing your bag and watching porn, hoping you didn't do it all for nothing.

If you have any doubt why I was eager to jump on the Dr. Bob bandwagon, there it is.

When I started my TAB treatment in March of 1999, my PSA level was 6.8 and getting higher faster and faster. And I was sweating bullets.

Dr. Bob's team will now be monitoring me like a moon rocket on the launch pad. MRI's, bone scans, PT scans—and the always thrilling trans-rectal ultrasound wand, which feels just like you think it would.

The good news is that my PSA level dropped like a rock every month. Eventually, as low as 0.1. When you consider that the median level for men my age was 0.9, I was a star.

PSA is almost universally regarded as our most useful indicator of prostate cancer. It is only produced by the prostate gland, whose main purpose is to produce liquid for your semen and pressure it for ejaculation. But some PSA leaks into your bloodstream and these minute amounts are what they measure. More leaks indicate more cancer in your prostate gland.

While they are most often indicators of PCa risk, PSA changes can result from many other causes: prostatitis*, biopsies*, DREs*, age, enlarged prostate, benign tumors, urinary tract infections, vigorous exercise, medications, and even ejaculation. All PCa patients need to have an informed doctor-gatekeeper to avoid being D.U.P.E.'d.

PSA doesn't detect cancer—only a biopsy can confirm that—but it is the best warning light we have. And there are many arguments about how good

83

it is or whether it should even be tested. The risk of D.U.P.E.ing is so great that the American Academy of Family Physicians advises member doctors to not even run patients' PSA tests unless they also commit to serve as patients' treatment gatekeepers, so they can safeguard patients against unwarranted treatments that prostate specialist doctors commonly propose.

The score nobody argues about is your Gleason*. This is the one they give you once they have analyzed your biopsy. Patients with a Gleason of 6 or under usually have a good prognosis but often endure serious and immediate discussions of treatment options. If your Gleason is 7 or higher, your prognosis is far less certain.

When I met Dr. Bob, my Gleason was at 7. World-famous surgeons routinely only accept patients with Gleason 6 or under. These are the guys Dr. Bob would likely advise to manage their PCa with TAB, but most definitely not by butchering or baking their prostates via mainstream PCa doctors.

Think of it all this way. Your Gleason says yup, you got this much of it. Your PSA tells you how it's behaving.

After twelve months of TAB, we didn't think my cancer had gone away. But with my PSA down to almost zero and staying there, it was no longer a looming threat.

My macho would be coming back soon.

Thank you, Dr. Bob. I hope to get back in the saddle, literally, and soon.

TAB had left me weakened and with zero libido, but my wanderlust was strong and my testosterone was, I felt, coming back. I would not let cancer end my life.

CHAPTER 36
June 22, 2000—Mt. Elbrus, Russia

"Seven bishops go up a mountain . . . "

It was a beautiful summer day back home in Park City when I ran into my good friend and banker, Stan Jenkins. Stan has been a trusted advisor for nearly a decade and is also a respected member of the Mormon Church.

Here in Utah, we say with affection there are two things you will see every day—a mountain and a Mormon. Stan combined the best of both since he was already a bishop in the Church and a very accomplished mountain climber.

The first time Stan and I met, I noticed a photo on his desk of him standing on Aconcagua, the tallest peak in the Americas and one of the famed Seven Summits. I've done a bit of climbing myself, so, having a banker who's trekked to Argentina to master that 22,838-foot monster felt very cool.

Imagine my shock and delight when Stan's first comment, after I mentioned a few recent trips, was an invite to join his group that was off to climb Mount Elbrus in southern Russia's Caucasus mountains ,just east of the Black Sea.

Was I in their league? Well, my testosterone was now back to my old normal of 400. I was not without experience of my own on mountains, with lots of backcountry skiing, volcano climbing, and a couple of Grand Teton summits. But I wondered if I could keep up with climbers in the class of Stan's group.

Here it was, however, the day of departure. I was packed and as ready as I was going to be. Along with a new ice ax and my well-used climbing harness, I packed some rented ice cleats and an ultra-warm down jacket borrowed from local climbing legend, Charley Sturgis. I didn't know much about Russian mountains but I was pretty certain a glacier-covered dormant volcano in the Caucasus mountains would be brisk.

Mount Elbrus has been famous for a long time. To the ancient Greeks, it was the peak where Zeus chained Prometheus for stealing fire from the Gods and giving its secret to men. As the tallest peak in Russia, as well as in Europe, it has been attracting climbers for centuries. But it wasn't until 1874 that a British team finally claimed the summit.

I almost missed my chance. The day of departure, I realized I had forgotten to purchase a proper mountain expedition bag, so, I frantically scrounged around until I came up with a bright red bike touring bag. I was the last one to board, walking past six new climbing teammates I had yet to meet, but already making an impression upon. One of them later told me he had never seen anyone bring a bike bag to climb a mountain but it must be a good way to save money.

The next day—three flights, an ocean, and a continent away from home—I woke up over Russia. It looked empty and bleak. At Moscow's international airport we are met by Natasha who will be our chaperone in the city. We discover that a dozen years ago she was one of Russia's ten-man national climbing team.

Arriving at Red Square, I fascinate Natasha by telling her it looks just like the photographs as she ushers us into the mammoth Rossiya Hotel. Built during the Cold War to be the world's largest hotel, it has over 3,000 rooms and suites and, of course, its own police station and jail. It takes over an hour to check in, while we stand gawking at the huge lobby filled with people who look like they've never been to Park City. We finally head up to our rooms and there we meet our "Bacha."

On every floor of the Rossiya Hotel, there is a central desk with a commanding view of the entire hallway and room entries. Each desk is manned 24/7 by solidly-built, no-nonsense, stern-faced matrons. "Bacha" is an affectionate Russian term like grandma, but Natasha explained that the matrons are only called that behind their backs. When you leave your room, you give her your key. When you want to return to your room, you politely ask for your key. And you don't mess around with your Bacha.

The next day, my roommate Jeff Harmer and I toured around Moscow. Coming back to our room, we dutifully asked for our key from our Bacha when suddenly a part of the wall behind her sprang open, revealing a hidden passageway. A man walked out, gave us a little nonplussed nod, and walked away. Nobody said a word.

The next morning, our ancient Tupolev plane took off for Mineralnye Vody in the Caucasus mountains. By now, I knew my seven fellow climbers were all experienced way beyond me, as well as the fact that all of them were already or almost appointed as bishops in the Mormon Church. The Seven Bishops and Jim became our unofficial team name. We should have had tee-shirts made.

The airport town of Stavropol is typical last-century Soviet Union, done up in the official state color of dingy gray. We meet up with our lead guide Yuri, and his sidekick, Eugene, who is a doctor back home in the Crimea. That gave us a full party of ten, perfect for our six-passenger van plus our luggage and climbing gear.

Four intimate hours later, we have steadily driven south through a series of look-alike impoverished villages lined with mid-rise concrete apartment buildings. The unchanging landscape melds with scruffy dogs, hungry-looking children, and more bachas. At one point, we stop where someone has tied a rope across the road. Yuri gets out and has a chat with the local "tax collector" and we proceed after a generous donation.

Finally, we come to a steep turnoff that winds up to a large lodge . . . by far the nicest building we have seen. Yuri explains this was formerly a famous hunting lodge for important Politburo members, now past the good old days. We stumble off to what turn out to be pleasantly nice rooms decorated with the height of 1950's lodge kitsch. No matter. The beds are good.

The next morning, we are up early for our shakedown and orientation day. Yuri is going to test us and evaluate our skills versus the mountain. But first we start with a robust Russian climber's breakfast of cucumbers, tomatoes, salami, and cheese . . . followed by courses of eggs and oatmeal. Generally, I like to start a climb feeling lighter rather than bloated but Yuri says we need the fuel.

Hiking up the valley of the Adyl-Su River, we stay to the right side and cross the Kashkhatau glacier. It's broken by large crevasses, perfect for our training.

Once we've climbed 3,000 feet of vertical, Yuri announces the glissade. This is how climbers descend a glacier when the way down is not too steep or broken up. You can do it standing up—kind of a clumsy skiing where you balance on your boots and glide down the slope carefully holding your ice ax out in front across your body. If you fall, and you usually do, the trick is to quickly twist so you're facing uphill and then you slam your ax into the snow. Hopefully, you stop.

The alternate glissade method is to slide down on your butt with your ax held to your side and you drag the handle in the snow like a rudder. Once again, if you lose control, you twist to face uphill and slam the ax pick into the snow to stop.

Today, we all glissade down a smooth stretch of glacier about 1,000 feet long. A couple of our group show off their skiing skills by standing up for a few hundred feet before the predictable crash and drag. The rest of us butt flop down the ice, digging our axes in the snow to avoid what Yuri calls a very exciting and painful shortcut. If we go past the end of the glacier. It's a long rocky drop.

The next day, we climb and hike all the way to the end of the valley, over 7,000 feet up. It's time for another Soviet time warp. Fifteen years ago, the campsite we are in would have been a climber's paradise. There is a no-longer-heated swimming pool, overgrown tennis courts, and the unique barrel huts. These are created by helicoptering in giant concrete drain pipes over 10 feet in diameter.
The Soviet engineers laid the drain pipes in the snow, dropped in a rough wood floor, and then closed off the ends with a wood frame for windows and doors. Dry, safe, and relatively warm . . . a few even had metal pipe chimneys drilled in for wood stoves.

Amazingly, this little resort still had local hawkers pedaling beer, soda, rough-woven sweaters, and Soviet-era candy bars to passing campers. I guess nobody told them the season was never coming back.

Now, it's time for the tough side of the glacier. We start off roped together as we head up in a 45 degree chute lined with ice, grass, and rocks. We see plaques memorializing climbers who died from falls and, sadly, rock slides dislodged by climbers ahead of them. Not thirty minutes after Yuri translates this for us, a softball size rock comes hurling down from above. Yuri swings away to dodge the rock but still takes a painful hit. There were no climbers above us.

Our third day of climbing begins in a truck. We stand clutching the rails of an open flatbed as it rumbles through the mountains. In my imagination, I am standing next to David Niven and Gregory Peck with our fellow commandos as our hugely-mustachioed driver takes us to meet the partisans and surprise the Nazis in a daring raid.

Instead, we leave our truck at the railhead and a modest hike along a roaring glacier-fed stream brings us to a grassy meadow and our remote campsite. Which is already alive with forty teenagers and their two teachers. The huts are rentable for anyone, so, it's not like they don't belong. But now my commando illusion is completely blown.

My illusion shatters even further when the teenagers note we are American and they insist on serenading us with the Russian version of "Home, Home on the Range." We try to whistle Lara's Theme from Dr. Zhivago and when that fails one of our guys pantomimes ballet. In a blink, two of the Russian girls perform an exquisite pas de deux as we stand there dumbstruck. Not to be outdone, one of our bishops quickly forms all fifty of us in a circle and leads the group through an energetically-inept rendition of the hokey-pokey. Remember "put your right leg in and shake it all about?"

Now the teenagers are getting warmed up and some of the girls start showing their American dance moves when the teachers step in and hustle them all off to their campsite. Leaving us standing around with stupid grins, feeling like failed UN cultural advisors.

Yuri and Eugene decide we must have plenty of energy, so, they announce a cliff-face climb before supper. We hike and climb about 300 meters and there it is—a rock wall that I would never even consider back home in Utah.

Eugene says we will all climb one pitch, which is basically the length of a 50 meter rope or about 165 feet. Eugene and Josh use an overhead route and quickly clamber up like spiders. Aaron, who owns a climbing gym, easily follows. Jeff falls but recovers and makes it another way. Joe, Craig, and Mark follow Jeff's route which they self-grade at the hard end of the easy scale.

I was the last to go, as usual. I was also the first to fall twice which prompted Stan to yell out that three falls committed me to becoming Mormon. I make it to the top, still a fallen Catholic, and gratefully rappel down ready to hit my pillow in the dacha.

The next morning, we could feel the clouds of a storm system wrapping around us. Three days of weather delay set in, broken by the unexpected arrival of a large and mysterious Russian party.

We stepped out from breakfast to see the entire lodge staff lined up in greeting as a parade of twenty black limos wound up the long entrance drive. Machine-gun-toting guards were the first to disembark followed by a succession of politician-types wrapped in overcoats. One of the staff answered my whispered WTF question with a surprised look and the words, "Sergei Yushenkov."

Remember, this was 2000. Yushenkov back then was a popular member of the Russian parliament, a leader for military reforms, and had just begun to raise questions about a string of Moscow apartment bombings designed to turn public opinion in favor of the wars in Chechnya. Three years later, Yushenkov was the leading candidate against Putin when he was shot and killed outside his home.

We could never find out who all the people with Yushenkov were or why they were here in this remote mountain lodge. The only interaction we had was during a large dinner celebration one night when we were allowed to observe from our table in the corner. There was a lot of drinking, a lot of dancing with the hotel female staff, a lot more drinking, and of course the guy who always jumps out in the circle and does that crazy crouching kick dance. At one point, Sergei himself looked over at us as someone pointed to our table. He nodded at my wave. Three years later, I read the headlines and remembered him.

The weather refused to clear for our summit climb, so, we hopped in the truck and rumbled over to a nearby glacier peak called Gum A Chee. We camp at the bottom of the glacier, attractively called the tongue, and are up early to try and reach the 12,400-foot peak.

This is icy-dicey time. We are roped together in groups of five, everyone ready to plant an ice ax if anyone slips or falls into a crevasse. Sure enough,

Craig drops through snow up to his chest but scrambles out on his own. After an hour, we reach a 45-degree slope that will require careful coordination between each roped-together team. This brings us almost to the top.

Now, we are facing a 200-foot horizontal traverse across a 30-degree rock face. I am contemplating this when guide Eugene suddenly launches a free climb across. He makes it with no problem and sets climbing friends and a horizontal rope lead for safety.

I realize that if I slip here, the rope will set me into a pendulum across the rock face, ending in an unpleasant splat. They don't let me go last here and I reward their faith with perilous success and a near bladder failure.

Now, we are standing on the summit and turn toward a rumbling sound. We watch a 50-foot wide avalanche sweep down part of the mountain where we had seen other climbers maybe twenty minutes ago. When it settles, we are happy to see tracks where they had left the scene in plenty of time.

We pose for all-purpose summit photos—who can really tell where you were—and then climb to a rock saddle where Yuri has set a fixed line which we use to rappel down about two pitches . . . ready for lunch and a truck-ride home.

It's time for the summit of Mount Elbrus.
The next day starts with a surprise. Unlike a Mount Everest, which is a trek just to reach the base, Mount Elbrus is relatively accessible. Basically, just a couple of cable cars and some chair lifts is all it takes to reach your summit base camp at around 14,000 feet. Not bad. But once again, I learn the old lesson about the devil in the details.

To get to the aerial cable-car station at the foot of the mountain, we need to stand in our old familiar flatbed truck for a fifteen kilometer ride to the village of Terskal. There we meet Anatoly who looks like a poster boy for the Russian Mafia. He is there to collect an environmental donation of about $10 per climber—no paper work necessary, cash only. He smiles us on our way and we crowd onto our first cable car which will take us up about 10,000 feet to the Stari Krugozor Station. There are too many clouds for a view, so, we pile into our next car and ride up to 11,500 feet and Mir Station. Now comes the fun.

Our final stage will be by single-chair chairlift. If you've ever wondered where American ski resorts dump their old lifts when they install new ones, I can tell you. Every part of the lifts we are about to ride wobbles.

The plastic chairs feel like they will break in half any moment, the overhead cable looks more like a laundry line, and the towers holding us above the crevasses on crumbling concrete platforms actually sway in the wind.

We make it across and up the final 1,500 feet and finally reach the official base camp. You will never see it on postcards. It's affectionally known as Barrel Camp. That's because, except for two wooden huts and a storage shed, the accommodations are nine old oil tanks lined up like fat cigars in a box. Each cylinder is big enough to stand in, there are windows at each end, and the iron bed frames were rescued from a nearby abandoned insane asylum.

There is a single electric heater on the floor that sparks and crackles but never turns off.

Regrettably, we never got to enjoy a heater. Yuri informs us that our hut reservations have been countermanded by a team of Russian glaciologists and there is no appeal. Regrettably, all of the pipe lodgings are filled with climbers from Japan and Korea plus a party of wealthy St. Petersburg students who are enjoying glacier skiing with their own snowcat towing.

No one is about to share. So we turn to an abandoned, snow-filled wreck of a giant wooden crate. We have no choice and we begin to shovel it out. As we get it almost empty, the unmistakable aroma of stale piss preserved by the cold is overwhelming. It turns out we are next to the Priut, the camp's only outhouse. Inside a leaning shack is a broad horizontal board with a single hole, overhanging sheer vertical. The winds are fierce and so is the blowback, so it seems a lot of campers had used our crate as the safer alternative. Stan quickly dubs our place, A Sewer Runs Through It.

We would probably have been OK, but damn cold, and the crate was so narrow we had to sleep stretched out head to toe. But sleep was quickly out of the question.

First, it was the distant thumping of artillery bombs in Chechnya. Then the Russian students got so drunk they were soon prancing on top of their trailers in speedos and bikinis, shrieking American rock songs, oblivious to the biting weather. We all groggily agreed you couldn't ask for better preparation to climb the highest peak in Europe.

We woke up to a sunrise blown in on near gale-force winds. No climbing on the schedule. All we could do was hunker down and hope they would relent. So, Yuri challenged us to a training climb up the first stage—a two-hour hike up a 20-degree slope which we decided to take roped in line—to a stop called the Pastukhov Rocks. Along the way, teams of exhausted climbers pass us going down, turned back by the winds and weather at the summit. There had already been two snowcat rescues.

The next day, the weather clears just enough to give us a window for the East Summit. We have so little time that we can't hike Stage One again, so, Yuri hires the snowcat to get us back up to the Rocks. Stage Two begins here, a 40-degree climb up the glacier-covered shoulder between the East and West Summits. It gets steeper and tougher as you go. It's a garden of huge boulders and a remorseless, will-it-ever-end climb that leaves you exhausted after four hours of one step at a time. When we stopped, we had reached the famous Saddle . . . and I felt like a real mountain climber.

We were standing next to a ruined wooden hut at just over 16,000 feet and the winds were blowing so strong we couldn't even reach for a camera. I wondered about the final stage.

It was steeper. And windier. But since we were now traversing across the slope, my crampons got a better grip and I felt more confident and stronger. Also, much slower.

Finally, just over seven hours on the mountain, we made it to the East Summit of Mount Elbrus.

Looking over at the slightly higher West Summit, we knew the winds were too strong. In fact, no one else reached the West for the next three days. We posed for the it-could-be-anybody-behind-those-goggles photo and almost saw our cameraman become the flying bishop. After a much too short rest, we started down. We wanted to get off the slope before dark. And there was a rumor that the Russian scientists were vacating our huts. Victory is sweet. And maybe it won't smell like urine.

CHAPTER 37
August 10, 2001—Fairbanks, Alaska

"Bears, mosquitos, and guys who hate ponytails."

Two years ago, I was a long-time married guy with a short-time prostate prognosis. Now I'm a divorced guy with an outlier doctor and a lot of hope.

It's time to catch up with my western hemisphere dream. I'm in reasonable shape and I've knocked off enough interesting side trips from Russia and Corsica to Australia and New Zealand . . . so, back to that main dream. I've done legs on both continents. Here I am in Fairbanks, Alaska, ready for more. Time to get on with it.

At the airport baggage area, I retrieve the crushed box that holds my bike. Looming over me is an eleven-foot tall taxidermist's preservation of an awesome polar bear. I should have known.

I'm going to ride about 600 miles south from Fairbanks through Denali National Park, around Anchorage, and finally catch a ferry in Seward that will take me down the Inland Passage another 1,500 miles to Bellingham.

After an overnight rest and a stop to grab supplies, I'll bike south on the famed George Parks Highway, Alaska Route 3. It winds down through Denali State Park and the Alaskan Range, eventually ending in Anchorage.

Time to go . . .

I'm headed to the town of Nenana, about sixty miles away. Brutal headwinds and driving rain in my face welcome me for the first half. There's nothing in sight but forests on both sides and a couple of dirt road farm gates for the next thirty miles. That's when I spot a log cabin set back off the highway with a glowing red neon sign appropriately reading, Skinny Dick's Halfway Inn.

I'm in. I make my usual cheapskate request to sleep on the bar floor or pitch my tent in the backyard. Proprietor Debbie, belly-laughs and says she can let me have the last available room for $50. I decide to have a beer at the bar and think about it.

The bartender is Pete and he's been there sixteen years. There really is a Skinny Dick and the back wall is filled with photos of his years of ownership. Yep, he was skinny. He sold out last year and retired somewhere south. Debbie and husband Dennis are the new owners and they do a nice business selling cold beer, microwaved burgers, and expensive rooms. Nothing helps business like no competition for thirty miles in either direction. After many beers and countless stories about the legendary Dick, I no longer object to renting a bed.

Sunrise finds me wide awake and hauling down the highway. The air is cool enough to tear up my eyes and tame my headache. I pull into Nenana, a century-old coal mining town named after the unique Nenana River which I cross on a long bridge. The Nenana River is one of only three rivers in North America that flow north. It's also one of the most famous whitewater rafting runs on the continent.

I stop for breakfast at the Two Choices Café. A coin flip brings me a plate full of Belgian waffles. I ask for some fresh fruit and get only one choice, a bowl full of the best blueberries I have ever tasted. Fresh anything is rare in Alaska—it's not exactly farm country—but my waitress tells me they also have fresh bananas in season, grown in the central part of the state. I believed her.

The weather is good and the highway is smooth. With the tailwinds, I'm making such good time that I decide to try an overnight in Healy, eighty miles away. Signs tell me I'm in Golden Valley but the only color in sight is the deep green of endless pine forests.

I stop to read another sign with an image of a missile on it. I'm just a few miles away from Clear Air Force Base, an ICBM Early Warning Station and launch point built at the height of the Cold War fifty years ago. I recall the air raid drills from elementary school.

A few empty miles further, I see another rare sign of life, the roadside Tatlanika store and campground. More out of boredom than need, I pull in

96

and buy junk food snacks and a surprise bottle of Mondavi wine. Out in the parking lot, I stop to chat with Ross, who tells me he is a bush pilot. When I say Healy is my overnight camp, he recommends I ride a little further and detour west to Otto Lake. It's a fourteen mile there-and-back detour off the highway but his description persuades me to think about it.

Crossing the bridge puts me on the west side of the river but everything looks exactly the same. Forest on both sides occasionally broken by glimpses of wide, empty meadows. I see a yellow warning sign for a Dog Sled Crossing ahead. I'm not sure I believe it.

Sure enough, I come to a cleared area and there is the sign that marks the spot. I smile to myself, wondering what time of year busy motorists and dog sledders have to yield to each other.

Ten miles later, there's another dog sled crossing. These cleared areas by the road make a nice, sort of safe spot for me to pull over and rest. I'm worried about bears.

Anywhere in the Alaska wilderness, and a lot of places not so wild, everyone worries about bears. They are very big, very fast, and sometimes very hungry. Normally, they won't bother us if we don't bother them. But a lot of things—like the smell of food, or an unwashed biker, or an unwelcome trespassing—can make them act, well, not normal.

I have seen three or four large bears back in the trees as I've been riding. My regular cruising speed along here is around fifteen miles per hour . . . slower than the slowest bear.

My lunchtime junk food is starting to back up in me and I know I'm going to need to stop before long. I laugh out loud when I see a state highway sign that says Bear Rest Stop. Really? When I get close, I see some wit has spray-painted out the word, Creek, after Bear.

A few hundred yards further, I'm crossing over gurgling Bear Creek and there is my salvation. An honest-to-good official state highway rest stop with two enclosed toilets. I lean my bike against the wall and enter my sanctuary. A few minutes later, I regret my bike carelessness when I hear the tires of a car pulling in and stopping. Visions of my bike being tossed in a pickup bed run through my mind. I fumble to pull myself together and rush out the door. There's no one in sight, just an old green Subaru. And my bike, untouched. I yell out, "Have a great day," mount up, and roll on.

The next thirty miles were uneventful. Passed another dog sled crossing as I approached Healy and the mountains just beyond. I decided I would try Otto Lake, so I crossed over Dry Creek to the west of town and started looking for my turn a few miles further south.

Otto Lake Road was marked by the Denali Park Hotel, a definitely optimistic name for a collection of trailers around a parking lot. Probably booked all summer by the whitewater folks. Seven miles later, I was at the gate of my lakeside campsite, talking to a cheerful guard—a young lady from Utah! Five bucks got me a spot on the lake for my tent and also a stern warning.

Very seriously, she reminded me to sleep upwind from my cooking fire, hang my food supplies and clothes full of smelly biker stuff downwind and at least twelve feet above ground, and not to forget to wash myself all over before getting in my tent. Bears follow their noses.

The lake setting was beautiful. Sunset reflected off the still water with an image of the snow-capped mountains. I set up my tent, then built a nice big fire. Dinner was just-add-boiling-water Chili Mac from Mary Janes, my favorite organic camping food vendor. I finished off the Mondavi as well.

That got me bold enough to stick my naked body into Otto Lake where I lathered up head to toe and even shaved. Got to get the stink off!

Sweet as a baby, I confidently slid into my sleeping bag and zipped up my tent. And then lay wide awake all night. Every sound was a sniffing grizzly. Sometime before dawn, I gave in and slept .

Breakfast that morning was not me. Great! Guess my bear precautions worked. I stepped out of the tent for a desperate pee and was immediately swarmed by two million mosquitos. Howling and swatting, I threw myself back in the tent. And then swabbed every inch of me with the seriously lethal mosquito lotion I had bought at the store where I bought the wine.

I poke my head out and . . . it worked! Lots of buzzing but minimal biting. I build my fire, boil more water, and treat myself to Jim's Lakeside Mocha

. . . instant coffee and cocoa powder. The rest of the water goes into a bowl with Mary Jane's famous oatmeal and I relax for a few minutes and enjoy the mist over the tranquil lake. I can see my breath. The temperature dropped overnight.

Back on the road, seven miles to the highway. Then south, paralleling the river. I'm starting to get into the mountains now and the river valley is becoming a gorge. The kayaking and rafting must be awesome. My next stop will be in Denali National Park, home of Mount McKinley.

I have to get a backcountry camping permit in the park, so, I head to the Visitor Center. Permits are first come-first served. To get to the Park Center, I have to cross the river again. But first I have to ride through Glitter Gulch.

Picture the ugliest collection of no taste strip mall stores and that's what the highway is lined with. Liquor stores and bars, coffee shops, pizzerias, burger joints, Chinese and Thai takeout, trailers and cheap motels, gas stations, gift shops, and . . . ah ha . . . a bike rental. I love it!

I can't wait to stop and buy stuff. I choose a fancy coffee and donut, some takeout for lunch, and a Denali T-shirt. Appetite sated, I ride on to the Visitor Center and score one of the few remaining permits. But only after I watch the mandatory bear safety video!

I'm pointed west toward a must-see place called Wonder Lake. Part of its wonder is that it offers one of the best views of North America's tallest mountain, Denali. You may know it by its lower forty-eight name of Mount McKinley. The local natives and most Alaskans have always called it Denali, which in the straightforward native language means high, but lower forty-eight politicians have been arguing about who to name it for since the 1830s.

To get to Wonder Lake, I have to travel the mostly dirt Park Road. It corkscrews around mountains and through valleys for almost ninety miles. With my camping gear and permit, plus my required bearproof food container, I'm excited to be off the highway and backcountry biking again.

The afternoon passes in solitude and the sound of my tires. I see distant wolves, moose, and bears. My thoughts wander in a way only this kind of off-with-myself travel can induce.

Almost thirty miles in, a herd of caribou—that are bigger than you think and boast incredibly long antlers—migrate across the road and I stop to wave them on their way. Just beyond their now well-marked passing, the paved section of road ends. Trying not to run over piles of caribou shit, I didn't notice the pothole.

My seat post connector snapped from the hard bounce. And that was it for riding. I sat by the side of the road until one of the many camper connector buses came my way, and headed back east to the highway. Back at the Visitor Center, I walked my bike over to a nearby campground called Riley's. It was full up but an unexpectedly kind couple from Maryland noticed my aimless wandering and asked if I needed help. Ten minutes later, I was pitching my tent in the far corner of their campsite. They even offered to watch my gear while I jogged into Glitter Gulch.

The lone bike shop I had spotted coming in was my hope for a replacement connector part. They wouldn't sell me a spare part but were happy to rent me a bike for a couple of days for their $100 minimum.

Walking out empty-handed and pissed, I almost ran in to another guy in biker gear. His casual question of, "What's up," led to my rant about opportunistic bike mongers. He offered a solution. I could call a popular bike shop in Fairbanks that often shipped in parts via the daily Gray Lines Bus. "Give them a try."

I did and they did. They sold me my part over the phone via credit card and dropped the package off at the bus line's express office. The bus driver would leave my package at the door of the bike rental shop around 3:00 a.m. that night.

I was awake at 2:00 a.m. and foot racing with a squadron of mosquitos into town. At 2:55 the bus pulled up, the driver handed me my package, and I raced back under the northern lights while trying to minimize the insect blood loss and scooting into my tent. Problem solved.

The next morning, I decided to wait for one of the camper buses which my permit allowed me to ride all the way to Wonder Lake. The part I didn't get to on my bike would have been long, tiring, and probably wonderful. But I was happy to make it in two hours instead of six.

Wonder Lake is so popular with campers that everyone knows people make reservations almost a year in advance. Which the campground managers testily advise me. They tell me I should catch the bus back. But my backcountry permit allows me to pick my own wild spot almost anywhere—there just won't be any facilities and I am totally on my own.

As the last bus pulls out, I walk my bike across a meadow and over a hill, out of the sight of the suspicious camp managers. The lake is surrounded by taiga, thick pine forests broken by meadows. From the top of the hill, I look due north up the long expanse of the lake. To the south is the McKinley River, rushing east along the foot of the mountains. And above that is the grandaddy of them all—Denali—climbing to 20,310 feet in the clouds almost two miles away.

It's early autumn in this part of Alaska and the higher trees on the slopes are already turning red and gold. Above the tree line, snow covers everything. The last rays of the setting sun make the snow glisten and the trees look on fire.

There's a big boulder sitting south of the campground. I stay to the far side of it so the pesky managers don't see me. I watch the sun finally set after covering every inch of my skin with the deadliest repellant known. Once it's dusk, I figure the late-flying mosquitos and early prowling bears will have the managers enjoying cocktails in their snug tent. I grab my bike and sneak to the far end of the grounds where picnic tables are set up for day trippers.

At this point, I've gone full outlaw. I pull up a couple of tables on their side and create a fort with my tent in the middle. My Jetboil Mini Stove fire heats the water for my Mary Janes camp dinner. Then I put my smelly clothes and packed food in one of the campground's bear-proof containers. There's no lake to rinse off the day's stink. Oh well! I crawl into my tent, slathered in more mosquito repellant under my clothes. Not very comfy but life-saving, I figure.

Next morning, by the time the 8:00 a.m. camper bus has arrived and loaded up all the returning campers, the tables are back in place, my bike and gear are stowed on board, and I'm sitting in a nice window seat feeling more than a little smug and victorious.

As we pull out, we pass my sunset boulder and around the corner walks a bear the driver points out with a, "Look at the size of that motherfucker . . . he's over ten feet easy!"

I'm rethinking my solo camping plans for the next ninety miles.

I get off in Glitter Gulch and am back on my bike heading south in a matter of minutes. Next stop, Cantwell. Less than thirty miles down the highway with what I'm told is a nice campground and a got-everything store.

It's not quite lunchtime when I turn off the highway to Cantwell. The first things I see are two gas stations, a bible church, and a lady selling what looks like raw beef out of her parked car. I peddle on looking for downtown but instead end up at a large breeding kennel for sled dogs by the Windy Creek Trailhead. Every dog in the place greets me from a hundred yards away. I turn around and soon find the Cantwell Lodge and its Longhorn Saloon.

I lock my bike and walk into the suddenly quiet bar. I think it seems early in the day for so many drinkers. And then I look in the mirror behind the bar and remember that I am wearing a bandana tied over my head with my ponytail drooping down the back. Not to mention the spandex bike shorts. I drop any thought of asking for the latte I was planning on.

There's a menu behind the bar and the top item reads, "Spotted Owl Stew— Get some before it's all gone." At the end of the bar is a dartboard with a Bill Clinton photo as the target. I decide to order a hamburger, rare, with a pint of Jack Daniels to go. I decide to skip the trip to the men's room and intently study a map from my pocket for what feels like ninety minutes. I leave too much tip with my order and head out to my bike. I force myself to pedal slowly and nonchalantly all the way to the campground. I don't even turn on my bike light.

I am really glad to be two miles away from the saloon, sitting by a fire with company. I'm chatting with Sam and Claudia, a thirty-something English couple. I'm impressed when they describe the 6,400 miles they have already biked in a three-year tour of the Americas. They've already been across the continent once. I lament my generally too short bike tours, then realize I'm just a home builder who gets breaks that allow this kind of travel. I can't afford to quit the real world but I can take modestly short and weird vacations.

The next day, curiosity led me once again to a place I shouldn't have been.

I was a couple of hours south of the charms of Cantwell when I saw the poster child for the Eyesore Hall of Fame—a three-story, blotchy grey igloo, squatting on the side of the road like a huge poisonous mushroom, with dozens of oddly placed dormer windows jutting from the dome. Rounding a curve I spot the real thing, a single truck parked outside a next-door shack. Welcome to " Igloo City". There was even a sign declaring it an historic landmark.

I peeked inside an open door to the Igloo and saw mostly framing studs for unfinished walls and floors. Some were covered in chicken wire, creating cages for God knows what. Just inside the door was a counter with an ancient cash register and a rifle on top. Behind it sat a frowning skinhead couple who stared balefully at my arrival.

"You want somethin'?" Conscious that my head kerchief, ponytail, and shorts are an invitation to provoke, I said I was just passing and wondering about the history of the Igloo. The current owners, or maybe squatters, said it was a future resort hotel that was currently stalled by a governor who was happy to waste resort tax money on crap like bike lanes. They stared pointedly at my bike outside. I empathized and wished them luck as I backed out the door. I decided I would tuck my ponytail under a baseball cap for the rest of the trip.

After the glamour and excitement of Cantwell and Igloo City, I was glad for a long, quiet stretch of cruising down the highway, enjoying the simple beauty of the river valley as it wound between mountains. And always over my right shoulder, the solitary peak of Denali. It's not just one of the Seven Summits—the world's highest mountains on seven continents—it's also officially the world's most solitary peak, meaning the one farthest from any associated peaks of similar height. It stands alone.

At milepost 134, I arrived at the McKinley View Lodge. I was ready for a bed and a shower, both indoors.

The lodge is owned by Mary Carey, who came to Alaska thirty years ago to homestead and be a school teacher. She also wanted to be a journalist and pestered a local bush pilot to take her up in flights while she wrote down his stories. One of the spots they flew over looked so beautiful to Mary that she decided to build a lodge. It got off to a rough start when she lost all her building supplies trying to cross the river. It took her another eight years to persuade the governor to complete the Parks Highway between Fairbanks and Anchorage and then she finally had access.

I learned all this sitting by the fire for two nights while eighty-eight-year-old Mary and her daughter, Jean, a children's book author, told tales from Mary's famous biography, *Alaska, Not for a Woman.*

The next morning, I'm refreshed and ready to ride my final leg down to Anchorage, still about ninety miles to go. I won't make it all in one day but I'm optimistic about finding another great camping place before I'm out of Denali State Park.

When a bike wheel spoke breaks, you usually don't hear the sound. You feel something is not right all of a sudden. I was getting close to a likely campsite on the Susitna River, not far off the highway, when I felt a spoke break on my rear tire. I've been through this before, so, I just cut the broken one out, adjusted the others, and rode on. Within a hundred yards, four more spokes broke, the rear wheel cracked, and the tire went flat. Game. Set. Match.

I'm on the side of a pretty empty highway, it's getting colder, and all I can do is try to flag down a passing vehicle. If there are any. I don't want to be here after dark. My hopes lift when a red pickup slows down on my side and I'm glad I'm wearing the baseball cap when I see the driver is wearing his. But just as I start to wheel my bike up, he looks at me, grins, and throws an empty beer can out the window. He yells, " Bear bait," as he spits gravel and pulls away.

I decide to walk awhile, just to warm up. I come to one of those cleared areas where cars can pull over but it's closed off with yellow warning tape and signs on sawhorses that say, "Caution, Bears Active." Almost two hours later, only two semis and one motorcycle have passed me. I am seriously worried.

A green VW finally appears in the distance and . . . holy shit! . . . it's slowing down. The lady driving looks me over as she stops. "We'll have to figure some way to get you in here because you can't be out here after dark with food and smell. Didn't you see the bear signs?"

God bless you, Marlene. We get everything in and my bike tied on the back. Marlene is a massage therapist commuting between Glitter Gulch and Anchorage and she will take me all the way.

Ninety minutes of conversation later with a lot of Marlene's "Why would you ever want to do that?" she drops me off at an Anchorage bike shop cleverly named, The Bike Shop. Owners Ray and Cliff will fix me up with a new wheel and tire overnight and direct me to the Qupqugiaq Inn. Locals call it Suzy's.

I decide to go for an evening walk and take in the Anchorage sights. At the harbor, I look out at mud flats that seem to extend out for miles. How could this be a deep water port? A heavy fog is drifting, so that's the end of my strolling.

I sleep in next morning because I only have a short forty-mile leg to my next stop, Girdwood. Ultimately, I'll end up in Seward where I hop a ship. But for now, I'm happy with the biking on Alyeska Highway , hugging the shore of the Turnagain Arm, a long inlet off the larger Cook Inlet that ends at Anchorage. It's a beautiful ride with snowy mountains over my left shoulder.

Girdwood is an old railroad town turned into an upscale resort bordering the Alyeska Lodge and ski trails. I ride through town and further up the gorge formed by glacier creeks to the 125-year-old Crow Creek Mine. It's now a tourist stop where families come to pan for gold and attend outdoor concerts. I pitch my tent up the hill in the woods and head back down to a place I had marked for dinner, The Double Musky Inn.

It's crowded, but I grab the last stool at the bar. Several hours later, I've dined well and been overserved by an increasingly beautiful bartender. I force myself to bid her goodnight and stumble back up the three-mile trail to my tent.

Next morning, I wake up early if not alert and bike down to the Alaska River Class V Rapids reservation office. I'm hoping for a last-minute cancellation. My luck holds. One opening just came up on the Six Mile River run. Guide Kim tells me, "Most folks say it's invigorating."

We bus around the end of the Arm to the south bank where Six Mile River runs into the sea. I am reading a pamphlet that tells me, "Six Mile River is 12 miles of the most exciting whitewater rafting in Alaska." I read it again. I wonder who measured it and who named it.

At the raft launch, we get thirty minutes of intense pay-attention instruction from our guides, then push off. Guide Tom, who spoke to us on the dangers of the currents, rock walls and inattention, follows in the rescue kayak. At a set of Class III rapids, we are all required to get in the water for swim tests to prove we can handle any mistakes. A little further on, we pull over to the bank and climb out. It's time for our Class V test.

Five of us walk up to an overhang. Fifteen feet below, Tom is holding his kayak in front of an eddy on the other side of some rocks. Our test is to jump down into the water and swim past the eddy without getting swept away. Four of us make it. Tom grabs the fifth one with seconds to spare.

A new guide, Diana, is waiting to lead us through the Class V. I remember that this class of rapids is defined as extremely difficult. There is only one class rated more dangerous ---waterfalls. To add to my confidence, when I ask Diana about the fresh stitches on her forehead and chin, she tells me she was thrown out on her last run through here. It's like getting back on a horse. Kim tells Diana not to feel bad, that only one group has gone through successfully so far this season.

Diana handles the long stretch perfectly this time. And, by some miracle, so do three of the tourists. I am one of them. I sleep well in my tent that night.

The next day's ride is a piece of cake. Seward Highway continues to be a sparsely traveled, smooth asphalt run between mountains. The cool air and the beauty of the mountains buoys my spirits as I climb up towards Summit Lake.

Forty miles later, I pull into the rustic and handsome Summit Lake Lodge. A seaplane is taking off over the lake, a reminder of another adventure I need to try one day. The next day is just like yesterday and the final forty-five miles around Kenai Lake and on down to Seward pass quickly.

Seward sits at the top of Resurrection Bay and is one of those Alaska towns that have got everything you want to do. Mountain hiking and climbing, rafting, fishing, boating, and so on. It also marks the end of my biking tour.

I check into The Sourdough B&B and chat with manager Gordon, about how to fill my free day. I take in the Seward Museum for details I never knew about the 1964 earthquake and the 1989 Valdez Oil Spill. A half- day boat tour around the bay is highlighted by tail-whomp showers from breeching humpback whales.

It's day seventeen. I switch from Alaska's scenic roads to the Alaska Marine Highway, a system of state-subsidized ferries that connect its ports to Bellingham, Washington. I'll be spending the next week on a series of short hauls down the Gulf of Alaska along the coastal fjords and through the Inland Passage. About 1,500 nautical miles total.

I didn't reserve a stateroom, opting instead for pitching my tent under an overhang on the open aft deck. Duct tape substitutes for tent pegs. No problem. I'm soon surrounded by tents of fellow packers and bikers, most about half my age.

Ah, the impatience of youth. The minute we cast off, my neighbors are all lighting up joints and hash pipes. Their happy laughs turn to groans and complaints as the ferry crew quickly confiscates all the illegal substances clearly banned by signs all over the boat. I figure the staff regularly resupplies this way.

An hour later, we're crossing Prince William Sound and I'm pleased to be visited by Claudia and Sam, my British friends from Cantwell. They've brought along Dale, a forty-ish bike tourer I'd drunk with in Girdwood who had spotted me on the aft deck. We spend the next few hours as the adults, enjoying our legal alcohol.

The ferry captain frequently interrupts with bullhorn observations. "There are three orcas off our starboard side . . . watch for nuclear subs that sometimes pass here on our port side" . . . and so on.

107

We detour up through the fjords to reach the town of Valdez. This is a local ferry, so, there will be several out-of-the-way stops. It's dinner time as we dock, so, I walk my bike to the ramp and am rolling into town while most passengers are still standing around. This will be my habit at every port.

In Valdez, I step in to a cheery looking bar and diner. I'm soon talking with Dennis, the cook and bartender, who tells me he's a "spillionaire" in waiting. It seems the 1989 oil spill killed the fishing business for 30,000 Alaskan fishermen, so all they do is wait for the expected class action settlement which everyone's math works out to millions for each. My neighbor at the bar adds that he hasn't even taken his boat out in the twelve years since. It's getting close to the ferry's 10:00 p.m. departure, so I have to hustle back.

A sad note: Although Exxon was initially ordered to pay over $5 billion in damages to those 30,000 fishing folk who lost their livelihood, twenty years of court battles ended in a payout of only $507 million . . . an average of well under $20,000 each. The guys I met in Valdez had probably gone broke waiting.

I spent my first night on deck pretty snug and dry in my tent, fresh from my twenty-five cent shower and towel. Overnight, our long, roundabout route takes us out of the Sound and into the Gulf of Alaska which is also the north arm of the Pacific Ocean. Everything to our left is snow and ice mountains with glaciers and rivers spilling into the sea. Everything to our right is endless blue water . . . somehow, it looks even colder.

A long day passes with more whale sightings and by late afternoon we are pulling into the town of Yakutat, population 700 . . . but I see a plane taking off from its airport. Once again, I'm first off on my bike for a quick tour before we depart in two hours.

There's always a bar and there's always a story. This time I meet Abel Stugies, a local who runs a very successful roofing company owned by his wife. His wife is Inuit and, by making her the company owner, they qualified for Native American preferential biding on everything from public schools to a CIA listening post. They are both well-fed and forty-ish and, with all their big income, their idea of a high time is a visit down the coast to Washington, their first. Their truck almost runs me over as we board the ferry.

It's Sunday morning as we dock in Juneau after a slow, winding path picking our way between mountains, glaciers, and fjords as we come in from the open sea, crossing through Glacier Bay.

Juneau is Alaska's capital city. It straddles both sides of the long, narrow Gastineau Channel. It is also the second largest city by area in the United States. Since we are going to lay over here for two days, I decide to hop my bike again and pedal the fourteen miles into the historic downtown. I even check in for a nice hotel room with a soft bed.

A visit to the nearby Mendenhall Glacier captures some memorable images. The waterfall roaring out of the mist and throwing a rainbow over a brilliant blue pond. The way the sunlight bounces through the intricate cuts of the glacier ice, giving it the feel of a giant diamond worked on by a mad cutter. I am amazed to see local Eskimo kids swimming in an icy lake a few hundred yards away.

I have to get up out of that soft bed at 5:30 a.m. Tuesday morning. The ferry dock is fourteen miles away and it leaves at 7:15 sharp. I make it with two minutes to spare, cheered by fellow passengers who have seen me do this before.

Pat is a retired Army helicopter pilot who saw me race down the dock and up the ramp just in time. He comes over to introduce himself and in a few minutes I know I am talking to a former US Army Warrant Officer. We hit it off even though I confess I managed not to be drafted. We're about the same age and he smiles, "College boy, eh?"

Pat has just completed a solo wilderness kayak trip 900 miles down a bunch of rivers I never heard of. He is more than just fit for his age. As we talk, I volunteer my quest to beat the prostate cancer I'm carrying. In a few minutes, this tough-as-nails leader of men is quietly weeping as we share the terrible fears. While I am bragging about my no-surgery PSA and testosterone levels, Pat reveals he went under the knife and had his prostate removed. I don't need to be told that he had to wear a bag on that entire kayak trip, probably diapers, and that sex is a memory. I cry with him.

The ferry stopped in Sitka for a three-hour layover that afternoon. I was back on my bike for my usual tour. I ended up at a touristy café and coffee shop, sharing a booth with an Indian-looking young mother and her daughter.

They were paging through some kind of picture book while the mother patiently answered many questions.

The little girl, maybe four or five, had black hair and big brown eyes. She seemed puzzled about the colors of the other children in the pictures. The mother explained that different people in different countries came in many colors but they were all the same inside. The girl asked, "What color are we?"

I didn't understand the mother's answer. "We are Yuk'ip."

The daughter accepted that with, "Oh . . . I like ours the best."

The mother, who knew all along I was eavesdropping, glanced up at me and smiled proudly.

I rushed back to the ferry dock, once again cheered to a down-to-the-wire finish. Hey, boats are like buses. There's always the next one.

When we were underway, I went to find the captain and asked him what it means when you say you are Yuk'ip.

The captain seemed surprised. "Those are one of the Alaska native original tribes. They don't call themselves Indians. Usually they don't say much to lower forty-eight-types."

You never know when you'll learn something about people.

The next day, we stopped a few hours south in Petersburg. Then we had to swing out to sea and go around Prince of Wales Island because the inland passage to Ketchikan was frozen over.

I was looking forward to Ketchikan because it is home to an amazing totem pole collection. Eighty-two of them—some as tall as sixty feet—are scattered around the town, at the dock, and also in a temperature-controlled lodge. Some are more than a century old.

Ketchikan means "thundering wings of the eagle" in Tlingit which is the language of the original inhabitants. The first pole you see on arrival is a totem with a giant eagle, wings spread. Each of the totems recounts a different legend or family history. I only had seventy-five minutes but I think I saw them all.

The next two days were uneventful with 700 miles of cruising south along British Columbia, around Vancouver Island, and then a sharp turn up the Salish Sea to the little bay where we docked in Bellingham. My 1,500 miles at sea were done. The next day, I caught a ride to the airport and flew home.

These trips are great for my soul but I know they are really only side trips from this journey I'm on to defeat this cancer. Meeting people like ex-warrant officer, Pat, along the way reminds me that every year another 190,000** or more guys are getting mowed down by the effects of this deforming killer. I am going to find the way we can all beat this.

CHAPTER 38
February 19, 2003—Los Angeles, California

"Everybody in Hollywood has a dream . . . "

I am on a plane flying into Los Angeles where I will soon again be in the hands of Dr. Bob and team as I begin my great leap forward to Testosterone Replacement Therapy (TRT).

One of the best after-effects of my TAB hormone blocking treatment over 1999 and 2000 was that my testosterone levels had eventually climbed back to the lower-average range and stayed there, giving me back the stamina and strength that were a major part of my adventure-travel lifestyle.

But lower average was not what I was looking for these days. I wanted to get to the fountain of youth levels of the 600's and beyond. In addition to the enhanced athleticism I hoped to rejuvenate, I was hoping my libido and sex drive would also return to my normal.

Walking into Dr. Bob's office building in Century City, I glance at the directory and note a full roster of plastic surgeons and other specialists in the world of making us into our fantasized selves. Guilty. Been there, done that. But conversation about testosterone and prostate cancer is not a fantasy. Because it really is a serious issue.

Back in 1966, Charles Huggins won a Nobel Prize for his work that said testosterone enhanced the growth of prostate cancer cells. Over thirty-five years later, the medical world is still stuck on that claim. But Dr. Bob and a few other brave souls have looked closer and have said, "Not so fast."

The theories and empirical studies of Dr. Bob and others have proposed that, while testosterone is present, it's actually what happens to it that contributes to cancer growth. And what happens is that it gets split by an enzyme into two other forms of hormones and these are what fuel the cancer. Hormone therapy can control this. Testosterone, by itself, is not only not the culprit — it is critical for optimal living. And to me, increasing my Testosterone level was part of how I maximized living. That is a very simplistic version of the actual science.

112

CHAPTER 39
April 20, 2003—Kathmandu, Nepal

"Chasing the snow leopard."

With my TRT program working, I was thinking big. Like Himalayas big. Which got me thinking about Nepal.

Years ago, I read a book called *The Snow Leopard* by an adventure traveler named Peter Matthiessen. It was about an expedition he made across the Himalayas with a fellow naturalist. Peter was a mystical sort and he was searching for the mythical snow leopards only found there. He never saw one.

Matthiessen's book became famous as a spiritual journey, only possible in mountains like those in the Himalayas. And I was hooked. So, I convinced my just-turned twenty-five-year-old son, Max, that we ought to go check it out, coincidentally on the twenty-five-year anniversary of the publication of *The Snow Leopard*.

That was our whole plan. We packed up all of our cold weather camping and hiking gear and booked a flight to Bangkok with a connection to Kathmandu, Nepal.

If you don't know Nepal, it doesn't take long to describe it. It's kind of a fat sausage of a country, tucked into the southern edge of the Himalayas with China just over the mountains to the north and India all along the border to the south. The people are simple and agrarian with most of them living along the fertile plains to the south and the foothills and forests just above. It's one of the least-developed countries in Asia. Someday, they may harness the mighty rivers that run down the gorges from the north and then they will have small head, hydro-electric power to spare.

But in 2003, Kathmandu is still definitely third world, stuffed with half a million residents and centuries of dusty history. It's also an uneasy place thanks to Maoist rebels and the royal murders that took out the king and crown prince two years ago. On our cab ride to our hotel, the driver advises that a big smile and a $10 tip will appease most rebels you meet on the roads. We make sure to tip him when we get out.

We're staying at the lovely Excelsior Annex, the cheapest tourist hotel in Kathmandu's Thamel neighborhood. Everywhere are nameless alleys stuffed with hole-in-the-wall shops that are shoe-horned into and under latter-day apartments and ancient temples. Max is starting to wonder about my planning.

It's smelly, ugly, and overrun by rickshaws, maimed beggars, wandering babas, and peddlers selling things we can't identify. Next to outdoor stands featuring strange animal parts and prayer wheels are cyber cafes. There are Buddhist flags everywhere, rippling in the stinking breeze. Kathmandu has no sewer system unless you call its river an open sewer main.

We round a corner and almost walk into the middle of a riverside mass cremation ceremony. Indescribable.

Max and I take the next day for tourist things, starting with a visit to the famous monkey temple at Swayambhunath. A rickshaw ride drops us at the bottom of 350 steps swarming with monkeys that regard us as trespassers. Bald monks of all ages are everywhere . . . chanting, blowing trumpets, and waving those flags. It feels like halftime at a Utah football game. The beggars are relentless. Back in our room, the paper-thin walls make sleep elusive. We can't wait to hit the trail.

Morning finds us on a five-hour bus ride across the foothills to Nepal's second biggest city, Pokhara. It's a welcome change. Still crowded with a quarter-million people but relieved by the beautiful adjacent Phewa Lake, and the majestic Annapurna, the mountains we came to see.

Pokhara is where Peter Matthiessen began his snow leopard expedition and I've told Max we will follow his path. Turns out I underestimated what it takes. Like a team of guides and porters, tents, and lots of cash for bribes. I'm figuring out how to break it to Max when the coffee shop we're sitting in is brightened by the arrival of a trio of American voices. A couple from San Francisco and their ex-pat friend are soon regaling us with stories about their just-completed hike around the famous Annapurna Circuit—a two to three-week trek that starts four bus hours from here. I smile and turn to Max with our new plan.

The Annapurna Circuit follows an ancient trade route that connected India to Mongolia. It was opened to trekkers after a peace treaty between Khampa guerrillas and Nepal in the late 1970s. The original 200 mile, twenty-three-day trek has now been shortened to more like 150 miles and fourteen days but it's still considered the best long-distance trek in the world with thousands of visitors every year. We have to get going because May blizzards make the higher sections impassable.

We're off on our first leg the next day on the bus to our starting point, Besishahar. It was quite a ride.

I share my undersized seat with passengers who come and go . . . in my case, a pair of ninety-year-olds followed by a breastfeeding young mother, a lady muffled in scarves holding a caged chicken, and yet another breastfeeding mother. Max thinks he's lucked out with a middle seat next to a pretty German girl at the window. But three times during our ride his fellow aisle passenger has to lean across both of them to projectile vomit ,mostly out the window.

We get off in the square of Besishahar where there is a chaos of porters, packhorses, and truck exhaust. Everything from here on must be carried across the Himalayas on foot. We backpack down a steep stone path to the Marsyangdi River. It is a deafening torrent of white and brown water poring over house size boulders. Our path will follow this river into the mountains.

Our trek will climb from tropic to near arctic climates, from altitudes of 600 meters to nearly 6,000 meters or 18,000 feet as we circle the Annapurna massif in an east to west, counterclockwise progression over river gorges and deep valleys.

Our first river crossing is a flimsy-looking suspension bridge with rusting cables and many broken or missing footboards. I let Max insist on going first. We make it with only a few heart-stopping slips and then notice a sign that points to a new bridge upstream. The one we just crossed is condemned.

The path crosses and recrosses the river at least a dozen times over the next 15 kilometers, and after twelve more suspension bridges we're feeling cocky. The sun disappears early in the mountains, so we stop in a small village called Ngadi . . . really just a cluster of hostels and tea houses catering to trekkers. We check-in to the Sky High Hotel, a thatch-walled, tin-roofed,

115

dirt-floored, five-star collection of four cubicle rooms . . . each about seven feet square. Beds are plywood platforms with foam pads and our terrace is a few plastic chairs under the roof overhang.

Dinner is included, served in a tiny central courtyard. We are delighted to be joined by Tina . . . Max's German bus companion . . . and her friends, Yoyo and Angie. They have just finished a three-month stint as volunteer nurses in Kathmandu and will be on the trail with us. The last room belongs to Namu, a Korean schoolteacher and marathon runner.

As everyone laughs and chats over what will be our standard meal of Dal Bhat . . . rice, lentil soup, curried vegetables, and crisp wafer bread. I'm wondering how my fifty-five-year-old legs will keep up with these twenty-somethings. I have another fifty cent beer.

The next day, we continue our steady climb along and above the river. The roar of the rushing, tumbling river . . . even when we're 400 feet above it makes conversation a challenge. We settle into a routine of carefully stepping along the wet and slippery trail, frequently crossed by mountain streams and occasional muddy boulders. Waterfalls trickle down sheer cliffs and rice fields appear along terraces carved out of mountainsides.

Every hour, we hear the clop of hooves and then the shouts of porters as caravans of packhorses pass us, coming and going as we squeeze to the side. Everything along this trail moves on foot including the propane and beer that will enable our dinner that night.

We hear tales of hikers who died on the trail. One hiker fell only twenty feet down a cliff with a badly sprained ankle. For three days, no one could hear his cries over the noise of the river until finally a packhorse stopped above him, smelling his scent. He lived. But many others didn't.

We've made another 18 km and reached the village of Chamje. The last few miles, we caught up with Naomi, the only American we've seen. She is a twenty-one-year-old solo traveler and confirms that, yes, all those green terraces we see along the slopes below us are marijuana patches. We are staying the night at Chamje's finest, the Tibetan Hotel, where ten of us gather around the after-Dal Bhat fire. Beer is the universal language for our group of Israeli, German, Swiss, Korean, English, and Nepalese speakers.

Morning finds us happily walking our first stretch of flat ground in days. The village of Tal even has a soccer field with Nepalese kids wearing Manchester United shirts. We walk under a large Chorten, a carved stone arch over the road that announces entry into a new territory. Cresting a ridge, we can look down into what's known as Mustang territory which has nothing to do with horses and is sort of a high plains that stretches for miles.

The villages we pass are slowly becoming less of the Hindu culture of the lowlands and more of the high altitude Tibetan culture of the mountains. But we still see prayer wheels in every village.

A word here about these prayer wheels. Imagine a cylinder about the size of a large soup can, usually made of metal or carved wood stuck on a stick. It spins as you turn it. All around the outside are layers of written prayers or mantras. Spinning the wheel is the equivalent of repeating all of the prayers and blessings, bringing you good karma. Wheels can also be spun by water, wind, or light and the blessings pass through them.

It's a lot more complicated and spiritual than that but you get the idea. Never hurts to keep the wheels spinning.

Another 20 km day brings us into Danaque and the Trekkers Hotel. Max and I are the only guests in the ten rooms, so, we get the special Dal Bhat with tomatoes and fancy curry. A lot of these villages and hotels seem almost deserted. Tourism has dropped way down since 9/11. Most of the hikers we see are intrepid young people, leaving a worried world behind for a few weeks or months of escape. The bottom line for me is lots of time spent with my son. I'm learning a lot from him.

There's nothing on the trail better than a clear, sunny day. We start out for Chame, our lunch destination, with the snowy peak of Manaslu . . . 8,156 meters . . . glistening high above us against a perfect blue sky. We're walking now through forests of pine and fir that feel and smell like back home on the Wasatch. Caught up in the tranquility of the undisturbed nature, it's even more jarring when we crest a ridge overlooking a bustling lumber operation.

Hundreds of large trees have been felled and are being milled into foot square timbers thirty feet long. There's no electricity or power, so, it's all done by manpower. A half dozen two-man teams are busily pulling long saws back and forth, working without a break as curious trekkers with sad faces pause to watch. A hillside across from us is already denuded of everything but stumps. In the rainy season, the hillside will turn to dangerous mud but the lumber teams will have moved on. We are not surprised when a few miles on we have to cross a huge old mudslide that took out everything in its path.

Chame is a large village of about a hundred buildings. We are clearly in Tibetan Buddhist country now. People greet us with, "Namaste." "I salute you." Flags and prayer wheels are everywhere. Our New Tibet Hotel sits on the river bank. A few hundred meters up the slope, we find a rumored hot spring and decide to build our own hot tub. Carefully stacking the flat rocks we find scattered across the slope, we dam up the flow and build a bowl-shaped enclosure that slowly starts to fill its six-foot diameter. A half-hour later, we are enjoying victory beers as we sink into heated bliss.

That night after dinner, we invite our friends of the road—Tina, Yoyo, Angie, Namu, and a few others—to join us in our mountain tub. We are legends.

The weather holds and the day is bright and beautiful. This morning's hero view is a mountain called Lamjung Himal, almost 7,000 meters high and blindingly white in the snow high above us. We stop for lunch on a terrace above the Marsyangdi River and look across in awe at a sheer cliff over 4,000 feet high and at least three miles long. You could fit a half dozen El Capitans along it but I doubt you could climb it.

Next, we cross one of the longest, oldest suspension bridges we've seen yet. We're told it will lead us to a more serene, scenic area near upper Pisang. We heard right. It's maybe the most authentic Tibetan village on the Circuit. The buildings are all stacked stone walls with flat timber roofs. The breeze blows across a sea of Buddhist flags. The prayer wheel wall is at least thirty yards long but I spin every wheel, using the correct counterclockwise turn to ensure whatever. Meanwhile, Max has walked on ahead and I look up to spot him about half a mile in front of me.

I also spot three young men bursting out of some bushes and running down the slope toward Max.

My heart is pounding with thoughts of the guerrillas we've heard about but never seen. I start running as two of the men cut in front of Max and one drops behind. I'm thinking ambush as they round a curve out of my sight. I am shouting, "Max, Max," at the top of my voice.

I reach the bend, sweating and out of breath, and Max is sitting against a Chorten next to a mani wall. He is alone and with a puzzled expression as he spots me. He didn't see any men. I tell him my worries and he looks at me like so many sons have looked at needlessly-worried fathers.

I change the subject, asking about the mani wall. Like prayer walls, these are everywhere in Buddhist country. A mani is a stone tablet, hand carved with a prayer. Priests do them and then they get stacked in walls along roads or pathways to temples. You'll see them ten, twenty, and fifty feet long . . . with prayers surely hundreds of years old . . . sitting in the sun and rain in some kind of eternal limbo, waiting to bless you. I'm not sure I understand any more than that. But that day I was wondering if some of those prayers helped protect my son.

Mani walls usually mean you're near a village and we were supposed to be near Ghyaru, our stop for the night. There was nothing in sight but another suspension bridge over a raging creek. Beyond it was a switchback trail that very steeply climbed up into some mist.

Our constant companions have caught up with us and we all debate where the village has gone. No one wants to believe we have to make that climb into the clouds. Ever resilient, Max shrugs, bounces across the bridge, and heads up. No choice. I follow him. After an hour's steep climb, the mist is below us and we are in bright sunlight. Another postcard Buddhist village is before us and we turn to get our first glimpse of the legendary Annapurna peaks, known simply as II, III and IV.

Our lodge is the Yakru Mount Resort and, though it has not a single resort quality, the view is worth the highest prices yet. It will cost us nearly $30 for a double room with a full meal plan. This includes the luxury of a floor area made private by curtains, two plywood platforms with foam pads, a private water hose, and a toilet hole in the floor. Breakfast and dinner include a coffee and a beer plus a Snickers bar.

Our host explains the reason for the luxury pricing is the high cost he pays to bring all these luxuries up so high. The porters are constantly asking for higher wages. We all understand and agree it's absolutely worth it.

Max and I reluctantly leave our posh retreat in Ghyaru and hike back down the switchback to pick up our path along the Marsyangdi. We're heading due west toward Manang at the bottom of a huge river gorge. Side trips and detours are usually a bad idea in wild country but Max and I decide to climb up to see another ancient temple.

We learn three important lessons.

The first is about prayer wheels, those beautifully carved and decorated cylinders we are careful to spin. Here at the old and nearly deserted temple in Ngowal, improvisation is the order of the day. Where prayer wheels have gone missing along the wall, the monks have substituted colorfully painted soup and coffee cans. Buddhists are all about the intent, not the execution.
Second, we discover a prayer wheel under a stupa, kind of a shrine, where the wheels are turned by a flowing stream. In this way, everyone downstream receives the spiritual benefits of the blessed water. In the temple itself are small individual prayer wheels that turn from the heat of a strategically placed candle, casting a blessed light on those passing by.

Third, most practical of all, are the duties of the key monk. We learned this after finding the best parts of many temples are behind locked doors. Only toward the end of our trek did we find out we are supposed to seek the key monk out and, for a kind donation, he unlocks the doors.

Our next stretch is across a surprisingly flat bottom along the river. And, unbelievably, we see a runway for an airport.

You have to imagine standing in the bottom of a valley gorge with 6,000-foot-high mountains walling you off on the right and freaking huge mountains on your left like Annapurna II and III. Then add the wind that comes whistling down the valley. We asked when flights go in and out of Humde Airport. The answer was, "When they can."

By lunchtime, we have reached a village called Braga. Once again, curiosity has us climbing up to see a 500-year-old Gompa, or monastery.

We spot a monk perched on the roof staring into the sun. We're embarrassed when he turns toward us and, as we start to apologize, he says in clear English, "Don't miss the Buddha in the foyer," and turns back towards the sun. The Buddha sculpture is impressive with incredibly detailed carving, lifelike eyes, and what looks like a gold lamb wrapped around his torso. We skipped the locked doors.

As we leave Braga, we are told about a famous lama who occupies a mountaintop hermitage just up the path. Tibetans hold him in great reverence and seek out his blessing and visions. We can speak with him after making the customary 100 rupees donation. Max does some quick math. "I guess that makes him the Dollar Lama," he grins. And we decide to pass. Who knows how our lives might have changed for the price of a beer?

We reach Manang in time for dinner at our Hotel Himalaya. At three stories, it's the tallest building we have seen since Pokhara. Our priciest room yet offers both a double and single plywood platform with foam pads, a private toilet hole, and a cold water shower. Namu has joined us on the path and will share the room. We split the $5 cost.
The next morning, I walk out on the sun deck and am stunned by the awesome view and the deadly drop—there is no rail. Can you imagine an American hotel with no deck rail, no warning signs, and no personal injury lawyers in sight? This is typical throughout Nepal. Safety is a private issue. You do what you think you need, no one will advise you or restrict you. Dying is part of living. Etc.

We stop by the local mountain rescue center to meet an American doctor from Colorado Springs. He is retired and he and his wife are volunteers here. His priority is warning hikers about altitude sickness and the need to acclimate here in Manang for a day or two before attempting Thorong La Pass. It's a very big deal.

Manang is around 3,500 meters or nearly 11,700 feet. But Thorong La pass, where we are climbing, is 17,700 feet. So, imagine an elevator ride that takes you up over a mile! Now, try doing it on foot. And then think that at the top of the pass you have only half the oxygen that is available to your lungs at sea level.

Altitude sickness means severe headaches, weakness, and real trouble breathing. We heed the doctor's advice and take a day to acclimate. We keep measuring our oxygen saturation with one of those thumb devices. You need to be well over 90 percent to be safe. I'm at 93 percent. Max seems unaffected.

Sitting around the hotel, we catch up with Tina, Yuri, Alon, Namu, and other trekkers we have shared the trail with. Our hotel host tells us he is about to close for the season because the pass will soon close with snow. In his excellent English, he explains how here in Manang he is a faithful Buddhist but, once he returns to Pokhara for the season, he will be a practicing Hindu. He says no one minds and the cultures mix peacefully. We dub him the Summer Buddhist.

We finally leave Manang and head up the trail toward Yak Kharka, our next stop that is another 1,000 meters higher. We are well above the timberline, so, it's nothing but stones and rushing streams at our feet. But every time we look up, there are the Himalayas perched above us. The aptly named Yak Hotel greets us after a necessarily short day of only four hours. We're exhausted even though we stopped every few minutes to breath and drink lots of water.

Our welcoming hotel room is an eight-foot square of dry-stacked stone with a leaky tin roof. The community bathroom is a three-foot stone wall square. A gushing stream runs through it, providing the water you scoop into an empty coffee can for showering and flushing. We're too cold and tired to shower, so, we collapse for a nap before dinner.

No one else dressed for dinner that night . . . or any other one. We sat around a yak dung stove, shoveling the usual Dal Bhat, gulping hot tea, and farting. Max and I warm some water on the stove and retreat to the bathroom to sponge off some of the grime. Oddly refreshed, we sit on our sleeping platforms, talk quietly, and write in our journals.

It's a strange kind of peacefulness that only seems to come from surviving the exertion, deprivation, and disconnect that I always promise myself I won't do again. But how great to be sharing it all with my son. He gets it.

Morning comes with tea from our host and his assistant. Their toothless smiles and encouraging words send us on our way. There is no one in sight but us and a herd of yaks. Most people don't know that a yak is the male of the species, the female is a nak. So, go for the nak milk, not the yak stuff.

They cannot survive below 10,000 feet altitude, so not many travelers have actually seen one. They are hairy, ugly, scraggly, and cow-like creatures and those who have been around a wet one say the smell will choke you. Nonetheless, we are grateful for their dung to build our fire and put nak butter on our toast.

We're now walking uphill toward the Thorong La High Camp at 4,800 meters and our last overnight before the pass. This is one of the hardest parts. The air is very thin and everything is gray rock and a little snow. As usual, Max has hiked ahead with Peter, a Swiss mountain guide scouting trips for future clients, and Max has parlayed his thirty-year age advantage into a sizeable lead. I assume we'll meet again at the High Camp.

Rounding a bend, I notice there are pebbles everywhere, evidence of an old rock slide. Then I hear Max shouting and I look up to see him emphatically waving me forward. At the same time, a team of Nepalese porters, laden with their huge backpacks, come running past me headed downhill and talking excitedly. Whatever everyone is excited about, I don't wait to find out. I run the next thirty yards to Max. He grabs my arm to keep going and tells me he was standing where I was when a yak-sized boulder came bouncing down the slope right toward him. Not knowing which way to run, he waited until the last second and then jumped left. The boulder went to his right.

Peter, who was ahead and didn't see Max jump, told us how a boulder like that took out a trekker couple at that exact spot two years ago.

An hour later, legs trembling and lungs pumping, we reach High Camp. It will be our last night in the high Himalayas. We share dinner with Christina, a Canadian ICU nurse whose lifelong friend had died of ovarian cancer, so she decided it was time to catch up on seeing the world. She took a leave of absence and hired a porter and guide to get her over the Himalayas. She's already done Thailand, Cambodia, and Vietnam. She is sixty-one and undaunted. I'm fifty-six and impressed. We share a lukewarm meal and a cold hut.

We have to be up and hiking by 5:00 a.m. because high, cold winds sweep through the pass by mid-morning. We could only manage a slow pace but we reached the top of the pass by 8:00 a.m.—we could tell by all the Buddhist flags and a nice sign. I look around at a sea of whitecaps, only these are snowcapped summits of the highest mountains on earth. We really are on the roof of the world.

Waterfalls sprout from glacier faces, misting into steam and splashing on rocks a thousand feet below. Flanking us are two 21,000 foot peaks, Yakawkang and Khatung Kang. Max and I decide to climb up Yakawkang another 300 feet so we can say we have stood at 18,000 feet. Home in Park City is 7,000. And we say we live in mountains!

Going down the other side was harder than going up. We're dropping down 1,600 meters to the village of Muktinath but it's a constant switchback and a killer on my knees. Max, of course, was way ahead.

Three hours later, I hobble into our hotel, the Bob Marley. What else would you expect to find in a Tibetan village in Nepal? The owner is a very large Rasta lady whose age and origin I cannot determine. But she cleverly combined a sacred spring and a natural gas-seep flame into a hot tub experience I've never forgotten.

The Circuit was, at least symbolically, complete.

CHAPTER 40
July 5, 2003—Park City, Utah

"Thalidomide?"

After nearly three years of TAB, I was cruising along pretty much free of cancer symptoms. I was able to lead a fairly normal lifestyle and resume much of the hiking, biking, and outdoor activity I loved.

Now, with my TRT program launched, I was expecting a major boost to every part of my physical program. Dr. Bob had also decided that taking my regular dose of AndroGel—the testosterone replacement gel applied on the skin—along with the countering drugs that prevented the split into cancer feeders, should be supplemented by another version of cancer cell deprivation.

Remember Thalidomide? Back in the 1960s, it became the source of horror stories about birth defects and deformities. What doctors and the drug companies didn't know then was that the very reason Thalidomide was hailed as a sedative made it lethal for pregnant women and fetuses.

Thalidomide worked by inhibiting the formation of new blood vessels to feed growth. It did not discriminate. It killed all the new blood vessels including the ones needed by a fetus to properly grow its body and limbs. The results were tragic.

By 1998, Thalidomide was back from decades of banishment, allowing doctors' carefully controlled off-label use to target leprosy and certain cancers. Prostate cancer was one of them. Dr. Bob was one of the first to prescribe it. And I was one of the first of his patients who tried it.

Thalidomide worked for me. For well over a year. I was extensively monitored all through my treatment with regular PSA readings, MRI and CT scans, blood tests, and the ever-wonderful transrectal ultrasound wand. Then one day in August of that year, Dr. Bob noticed a slight numbness in my toes that did not go away. Exit Thalidomide.

Fortunately, there were no lasting effects and all continued on course. All I wanted was more testosterone!

CHAPTER 41
April 2, 2004—San Jose, Costa Rica

"Where the asphalt ends . . . "

As I have written before, one of my long-term travel goals was to bike from Alaska to Patagonia, following the Pacific coasts of North and South America.

I had no illusions about a non-stop continuous trek but I figured I would take some bite-sized chunks over the years until I had it covered, in no particular order.

So, somehow in the spring of 2004, it was Costa Rica's turn with maybe a piece of Panama thrown in. A 4,000 mile flight from Park City landed me in San Jose, Costa Rica. From the air, it could have been San Jose, California, with lots of high-rises and freeways.

Following my usual habit, I unpacked my bike in the luggage claim area, loaded my gear, and pedaled out the terminal door. To my shock, I am hailed by my ex-brother-in-law, Victor. I had not seen him in five years but had emailed about my planned visit. He never answered but here he was. In short order, we have covered the events of his new wife and a pending birth as we share a few beers in his home.

I leave Victor and his wife with thanks the next morning, full of that first-day confidence and enthusiasm. But it only takes about twenty miles of insanely steep hills to remind me to check a contour map next time. The busy highways west of San Jose have given way to country roads, lazy rivers, rain forests, and small farms. Unlike most of Central America at the time, you don't see a lot of armed police and soldiers. The Ticos are a laid-back people and it seems they are not plagued with the oppressive federales and pervasive poverty I'd seen everywhere else.

Another thirty miles of the same up and down extra-humid biking finally brings me to the end of a too-long first day and into Orotina, a small highway-junction town with general stores, gas stations right out of the

1950s, and dirt floor cafes and bars. I welcome my $6 dollar a night room, a fresh fish dinner, and cold cervezas.

The next morning, a thirty-mile run away from the morning sun brings me to my first destination, a coastal town called Puntarenas.

To get to the town, I bike out along a seven-mile causeway into the Gulf of Nicoya. Apparently, this needle of land thrust out into the bay was established as a port by a pirate in the early 1700s. Eventually, the dirt road to the mainland was joined by a railroad and it's still a major port today. But for me, this is where the asphalt ends.

I pull my bike onto the busy ferry and pay the man $1.60 for the ten-mile trip across the bay to the Nicoya Peninsula. Every shaded seat was taken or saved,or else my fellow passengers didn't care for my sweaty, stinking, shirtless, carcass sitting beside them. So I curled up under some shaded stairs and slept.

Some people call Nicoya the hidden paradise of Costa Rica, an eighty-mile-long thumb of land sticking off Costa Rica's northwest coast. My plan was to ride around its southern tip and then up the Pacific Ocean beaches. But first, I had to cross the thirty-one miles from the Gulf to the ocean, to a legendary surfing town called Malpais.

Imagine my surprise at yet another sweaty day of steep, rutted, washboard roads baking in the sun. I never saw another bike tourer. But I'm glad I had decided that my Santa Cruz Blurr bike with smooth-center, tread-edge tires was the right combo for this terrain.

This first segment already gave me a clue why this part of Costa Rica is what would eventually be labeled a Blue Zone—a special region on the earth where people proved to lead longer, healthier, and more stress-free lives. The natural beauty of the environment with its rainforests, beaches, waterfalls, rivers, and mountains was obvious. But the friendly, unworried smiles of the families I met were genuine even when they warned me about armed thieves near most resorts.

By the time I got to Montezuma that night, I was in love with the country. The posh resort atmosphere of the town, however, put me quickly on my way the next day. Next stop, Malpais.

Malpais is a nice little beach town but the name is known throughout the surfing world for the string of pristine beaches and awesome Pacific waves that never seem to quit all along this southern tip of the peninsula. Although I had surfed a bit in my younger years as a beach town cook, I knew when I was overmatched. The guys at the local surf shop told me the right place for me was a resort further north called Tamarindo. Little did they know . . .

I spent a wonderfully restful night in my tent on the beach just above the high tide mark. Now, I was finally riding on the Pacific coast with sunset on my left and nothing but a hundred miles of beaches in front of my handlebars.

The next two days are kind of a blissful blur of endless white beach, pounding green surf, repeated wrong guesses that the sand was firm enough to bike, and two fateful decisions.

The first decision came about halfway when I chose to forego the long detour to cross over the Rio Bongo by bridge. Instead, I hefted my bike and packs over my head and waded through the waist-deep muddy current to the other side.

The second decision was when I biked up after dark to a tiny roadside hotel in Playa Ostional. The dinner hour had passed but they offered me a basket of fresh-picked mangos and a cubbyhole cot for the off-season rate of $3 dollars.

Over the next morning's coffee, I regaled the owner couple with tales of my trip along the coast. When I mentioned the ford across Rio Bongo, their eyes bulged and they gasped. An old man pointed to a large set of toothed jaws hanging on the wall and sputtered, "Cocodrilo! Muy grande!"

Yep, turns out the river I waded through has some very large saltwater crocodiles. The breakfast group decided I must be blessed.

Later that day, along yet another oceanfront wildlife refuge, I finally hit a long stretch of hard-packed sand. I decided to let it all out.

Pedaling furiously with the salt wind in my eyes, I thought I heard clapping and cheering. I slowed up and there to my left, a hundred feet out to sea, was a lineup of maybe twenty surfers waiting for a wave. I don't know if they were cheering my speed or whether it was a break in boredom, but if you remember the theme music from the movie *Chariots of Fire* you know what I was playing in my head as I smiled and waved.

At the end of that very long day, I had reached Tamarindo, your basic upscale Latin resort town. I quickly rode through to catch a short boat ride out to an even more lush private resort called Playa Grande. And that's where I met my good friend Marc from back home, along with his wife, daughter, and a lady friend.

Grunge Jim cleaned up to become Resort Jim and I welcomed a three-day break with showers, air-conditioning, real food, and fruit-filled resort drinks.

Vacation break over, I say goodbye to Marc and family and bus and bike to some volcano watching. It's an all-day ride due east to the mountains around Lake Arenal far into the interior mainland. This is the home of Volcan Arenal, Central America's most active volcano which consistently spits up lava flows and fiery rocks though rarely killing locals. It's almost always cloud covered but you can hear it occasionally.

When I get to the closest hotel that night, I can hear rocks falling in the distance and and I can feel the tremors. Bad luck, the hotel office has closed but a friendly night watchman directs me to a tent site near the hot springs. By midnight, I am settled in my bivvy tent.

Typically, I get out of my sweaty clothes before I sleep and pull out the next day's shorts and tee to use as a pillow. In an inner tent pocket, I stash my passport, credit card, and a split of my cash. That night I am barely asleep when I hear footsteps outside my tent. Thinking it's my watchman friend, I call out, "Hola! Los Maderos," which is slang Spanish for cops. I hear a surprised grunt and then someone very smelly is grabbing at my head and arms, trying to pull me out of my tent. We struggle and he loses his grip as I come spilling out of the tent. I can see a dark, bulky shape as he runs toward another and then both disappear into the dark and silence. No sign of the watchman. I stand there confused, naked and panting. I can't help but notice that the promised volcano eruption is now at full force, shooting fireballs visible over an unclouded peak. I'd never have seen it had I not been robbed!

I reach back in my tent, grab my shorts and a headlight. Thankfully, I see my bike still chained to a tree but my two large bike packs with all my gear and the rest of my money are gone.

My yelling finally brings the watchman and he calls the local police station. Three officers show up quickly and their flashlights reveal a large jagged rock dropped at the opening of my tent. They are great guys and eager to help. We spend the next two hours driving the surrounding dirt roads, picking up thrown away pieces of my gear.

Eventually, I recover my now empty bike packs, my shaving kit with my stash of crucial medications and, by some great stroke, a folding bike tool which has a cache where I keep much of my cash and credit cards. The apparently fashion-savvy robbers got my clothes, my shoes, my camera, and my sunglasses . . . but I had enough bike gear to carry on. I must admit, however, like on many other trips . . . that quitting and going home crossed my mind.

I spend the rest of the night in the police station bunk room in Fortuna, the closest town. It's the first time I've been robbed on a trip but far from the scariest moment.

The next morning, the cops help me arrange a seat on a van transport heading south to San Jose. I have called Victor again and I asked for a few days' asylum. They couldn't be nicer even though they have just welcomed a new baby.

I begin my second week of Central America travel heading back to the coast with a four-hour bus ride and a twenty-five-mile bike ride and hike to the south and a beach town called Dominical. The hike part came when the downhills were so steep and long that my brake pads were red-hot and overheating my rims, a sure recipe for disaster. So, I got off and walked.

Have you ever wished, like me, that you could speak decent Spanish? Have you ever promised to someday learn how to really surf? Then you know why I ended up at the Dominical Spanish and Surfing School. Even better, I am staying at the world-famous Tortilla Flats —the iconic bar, restaurant, and hotel known to surfers the world over.

No longer a homeless robbery victim, no longer a grungy biker, I am now Diego the Spanish surf bum . . . and it's great to rub elbows with the real surfers. I am also ten to thirty years older than my fellow surfers and linguists but that's never a problem with my kind of travel.

When you're all on the same level and sharing the same good, bad, and thrilling experience spectrum, it evens out. You're neither old nor young, wealthy or not.

Everyone is interesting, everyone has a story or two, and no one is looking for an edge. We're all just travelers on the road. No wonder Willie Nelson can't do without it. Dominical is clearly one of the regular way-stops for this crowd.

I spend a languid week with fellow surf students who include a two-time world champion snowboarder; a three-time Boston Marathoner; a questing couple who sold it all to look for something different; a delightful young lady who manages the Monterrey, California Marina Dunes resort; and a young New England rock climber who sees himself in my later-year writer/wanderer incarnation. We just all fit, somehow.

But I am a travelin' man and at the end of the week it's time to get back on the bike and leave the coast for a forty-mile trek through the rain forest to an overnight in Palmar Norte. It's basically a boring farm town and the local joke is something like, "Wait till you see Palmar South!"

Today, I have to do another sixty miles through the rain forest but this stretch is largely shaded thanks to the narrow, shoulder-less road. The numerous carcasses of poisonous roadkill snakes are offset by the flicker of brilliantly-colored parrots and hummingbirds and the calls of monkeys . . . I think.

There is almost no traffic as I near the Panama border.

The border crossing here at Paso Canoas is like borders all through Central America . . . lots of selling, begging, noise, and confusion. And fees. But one of the roadside vendors sells me the most impossibly delicious concoction of papaya and ice-cold milk that I have ever poured down my throat.

I have come to Panama because I want to stand on the only place in the world where you can see both the Atlantic and Pacific Oceans at the same time . . . only at dawn. It's called Volcán Barú.

My first stop, however, is an alluring pension just over the border run by an attractive mother and daughter team. Mom lets me know she is only forty and her daughter only nineteen but that sadly both are without current boyfriends. I am starting to wonder if a red road bike is equivalent to a red Ferrari for bachelors in Paso Canoas.

The warm friendliness of the mother and daughter extends to a late dinner invitation in their apartment but I beg off due to a dawn departure. When I inquire about a store to buy some road supplies, the daughter quickly volunteers to drive me to the mercado. She seems let down at my choice of sausages, crackers, and apples without even a bottle of wine. The ride back was quiet and no one offered to fix me a dawn breakfast. Women can be so fickle.

Next day is an uneventful thirty-mile glide way out of my way to David, Panama's third-largest city. It's probably equally high on the boredom scale. But I have to go here because it has the only express bus that runs up north to the town of Boquete where you find the only trail up to the summit of Volcán Barú.

After my $2 bus ride to Boquete, I am out of the tropic lowlands and into the popular green mountain highlands. This is coffee land where the 3,900 foot elevation creates a beautifully temperate climate beloved by English-speaking ex-pats.

In the distance, shrouded in clouds, is the mysterious Volcán Barú.

I am looking for an ex-pat explorer of sorts named Livingston . . . first name, Richard.

I spot his flyers posted around the town square. I call him and, after a few qualifying questions, he tells me, "Meet in front of the post office at four. I'll be wearing a straw hat with a red bandana."

Feeling like a drug dealer, I am there at the appointed rendezvous. He explains he will provide all of the outfitting gear and equipment I will need.

133

All I have to do is buy my provisions now and he shepherds me around the mercado. He is not surprised at my reliance on lots of peanut butter and jelly sandwiches but insists I supplement what he calls my American menu with a pint of rum. "You will be glad." He hustles off, admonishing me to get plenty of sleep and be back here at our spot at 6:00 a.m. sharp. I take his advice to heart and cut back on that night's tortillas and beer

Dawn comes and there is Richard in the square with a twenty-year-old backpack, sleeping bag, rain gear, warm jacket, and fire starter . . . all so heavy and old any US army surplus store would be embarrassed to give it away. But it all works. He has done such outfitting before. Within the hour, I am climbing up the off-road-vehicle (OVR) trail he has put me on.

It is tortuous. There is a fog that doesn't want to lift and I think that I am hiking at around 4,000 feet and the summit is over 11,000 feet—the tallest peak in Panama. There is no sound but the laughing call of the quetzal, a small local bird famous for its very long tail feathers—and apparently little variety in its calls.

Did I mention this is an overnight climb? About halfway, the growl of a laboring engine breaks up the bird symphony and an ugly but workable utility vehicle is making its way up the trail.
The driver stops and smiles. He is a TV tower technician and he has seen this before. He offers me a ride. I quickly accept. And quickly regret.

Now, instead of aching calves, I have bruised knees and tender elbows from bouncing side to side in the cab. It's actually a relief to get out every hundred yards or so and use the winch to get us up and over an otherwise impassable runoff or ditch.

At the end of a very long ride and day, my driver friend drops me off at a dilapidated wooden platform with a sagging roof. This will be my summit camp for the push to the top. Hopefully, in the morning.
I have seen plenty of summit photos showing the incredible early morning views of the sun sparkling on both oceans. I've also read all the warnings about clouds that surround the peak which is why dawn offers the highest odds for viewing.

I am thinking of this as I dine on my P&J cuisine. I fall into fitful, shivering sleep, thinking about the mountain pumas Richard warned about. It would be just my luck. The rum is a godsend. I hope my watch alarm will not fail me.

The alarm does not fail. Nor does the weather. By 6:00 a.m., I have hiked the last kilometer to the summit under clear skies and a rising sun. Swiveling my head, I can see the dawn sunrise tracking a golden highway from the horizon all the way across the Atlantic to the shores of Panama. Then I turn and watch the first rays touch the sparkles on the still misty Pacific. The last time I felt this religious was when I was a twelve-year-old altar boy.

The rest of the morning was a hateful hike down to reality. I'm at the trailhead by 1:00 p.m., greeted by a skeptical Richard. We jump in his truck and he congratulates me on my weather luck. Surprisingly, he invites me to dinner in Boquete.

I have a week left until I fly home out of Panama City. In the morning, Richard is kind enough to drive me to the bus station in David. On the way, he counsels me about life, bragging about his beautiful Latina wife. "Never marry an American girl. By age three, they are spoiled. Get a Latina!" I explain I'm not in the market.

From there, I am thinking about more surfing in the renowned surfers paradise around Santa Catalina. I get off the bus when I see the sign.

What I didn't see was the worn-off part that said, "200 k." That's about 125 miles out of my way and I just don't have the time. Or, honestly, the will. I bike over to a nearby agricultural inspection station and luck out with an English-speaking policeman. I have to get this right and I don't trust my Spanish.

The policeman smiles, says no problem, and flags down the next passing express bus. Soon my bike and packs and me are on our way toward Panama City, next stop unknown.

Turns out there's another sign. This one says, "Rio Mar Surf & Skate School." I can't resist. And once again me and bike are standing by the side of the highway.

In just over an hour, I am happily pedaling along the Rio Calabazo on the outskirts of the town of San Carlos. And I come to a you-can't-miss-it bright

135

red motel sort of place with surfboards stacked everywhere and the sounds of skateboards on a ramp. As I check in to a $10 a night room, I ask where we surf and the answer is, "Right out front." For the next three days, I am glued to instructor Mike . . . a fifty-ish ex-pat now considered a Zonie because he has been here so long . . . along with camp owner, Alan, and fellow students, Lisa and Stash. The latter are a thirty-ish couple from Telluride. He's a music techie who works with the Sundance festival and also custom renovates old homes. Lisa is a freelance editor. Alan has a special surprise in his background.

On my third and last day, Alan is sitting on his board next to me when he says he has to leave tomorrow for his other gig as a tugboat captain on the Panama Canal! He wonders if I would like to tag along. When my loud, "Yes!" spooks Lisa and Stash right off their boards, he extends the invite to them.

The next day, we are at Canal headquarters and heading out with senior captain Aleman, so nicknamed because somebody said he looks German. We watch as he ties up his tug to a huge Danish flag freighter and begins to push it into the Pacific entry lock. From there, it goes into the mouth of the Miraflores lock where six huge locomotives on rails, three to a side, tie up with the freighter and gently keep it moving and centered through the lock. The lock is like a 1,000 foot by 110 foot bathtub that slowly fills with millions of gallons, gradually lifting tug and ship. This gets repeated, lock after lock, all day. The amount of tonnage and water involved to create this moving river of ships and freight is awesome to think about. And it's forty-eight miles long! You can stand on the banks and watch what looks like moving buildings gliding by, stacked six stories high with shipping containers.

This amazing system of locks required diverting local rivers and the huge Gatun Lake as a basic pump for the dam and lock system, lifting and lowering these huge ships to different levels on the Atlantic and Pacific sides.

The French unsuccessfully tried a simpler straight canal cut, not realizing that the task was so huge that not even a group of nations would have the time, resources, and manpower to achieve it.

I still think the Panama Canal ranks right up there with putting a man on the moon.

Two days later, I am on the plane home. I have seen why so many Americans and Brits end up moving to Costa Rica and Panama, to enjoy a lifestyle that to me combines some of the best things you can hope for.

CHAPTER 42
August 7, 2004—Fernie, British Columbia

"It took me five months to get this high."

People are cheering for me. Hundreds of them, lining the street. I'm in Fernie, British Columbia, high up in the Canadian Rockies, furiously pedaling away from the starting line of the toughest mountain bike race in the world. The Trans Rockies.

Five months ago, I signed up unprepared and under-trained but I was in lust.

Years before, I rode from Prince Rupert, British Columbia, to Banff, Alberta, the whole time looking up at the Rockies and wondering if I would ever get up there. All I knew was that you couldn't just go on your own . . . you needed access permits and a lot of support.

Back in February, I was coming off a knee injury from a trail run.

There were four other riders from Park City who were also entered in the race. None of them gave me good odds of being ready for the race by August.

By May, I was proving those riders wrong. Not beating them but lagging behind just fine. Then came the deadline week to sign up with a partner, race safety rules require one. I logged in to the race site and eventually met and liked a Canadian Kiwi named Lee Boswell. He was clearly a free spirit, a different path kind of guy, and we quickly agreed we didn't give a shit about winning . . . we just wanted to do it all the way.

All the way is a big deal. Nearly half the riders who enter the race don't finish. And Lee and I would be in the old farts' Master Class where our combined ages must exceed eighty. Even younger riders don't make it the 370 miles to the end.

My training kicks into high gear. In April, I spend several weeks biking through Costa Rica and Panama, averaging over fifty miles a day. In June, I ride down the Pacific coast from San Francisco to Santa Barbara in five days. I crisscross the 250 miles of trails around Park City, frequently spotting Marc and Kurt, neighbors and friends who are also entered. They are still too fast for me. The other two local entrants are Lynn and Carolyn. I don't ride with them because I don't want to know. I become obsessed with four-day training cycles and five-hour rides.

Despite all of that, I'm just focused on finishing. Not willing to give up good food and drink, I won't adopt the monk-like existence of the serious racers.

Today, we'll see if that works. At the race start point, I finally meet Lee in person. You'd never guess he is a former corporate computer systems manager. But his current business is a dead giveaway. He has more body piercings than I can count, including one through his nose between his eyes. He has closed his local shop here in Fernie for the race, so, I guess his customers will just have to get by with the piercings they have.

Over a bag of beers in the parking lot, we quickly bond and reaffirm our a-finish-is-a-win philosophy. Our only difference is budget.

The Trans Rockies is not a free event nor is it cheap to enter. You are required to pay for the infrastructure and safety support you will need as well as room and board on the trail for seven nights. The minimum of $1,100 gets you a tent and a meal when you finish every night, aid stations and medical staff, as well as bike mechanics who keep you going through all the falls and breakdowns.

Lee is fine with the minimum. I opt for the upgrade. For an additional $1,200, Park City buddy Marc and I will share an RV driven by race staff, waiting each night with soft beds and plenty of hot water. Marc's partner, Kurt, sticks with the minimum.

It's a pretty intimidating atmosphere in Fernie for the races. Everyone is swapping stories about famous past crashes, lost bikers, bear encounters, and the effects of 40,000 vertical feet over seven days. And everyone is buff, young, good-looking, and absolutely confident. They are from all over the world and one out of four are women who could pass for the kind of swimsuit models that moves my blood.

I go to sleep that night wondering what I thought when I signed up for this.

The sun comes up, however, along with my confidence and I meet up with Lee at the starting lot where 230 riders mill around. Over a thousand spectators line the streets as we head out. The start is like a cattle stampede, so Lee and I hang back. We laugh as we pedal out in last place and we get the biggest cheers . . . obviously, Lee's piercing fans.

We are riding to Crows Nest Pass, ninety-five kilometers away—up, down, and up to 1,600 vertical feet. We pedal, admire the views, and pedal some more. Unlike my solo bike trips, where I just camp when I get tired, this is a race and we have to hit the landmarks and stops each night. So, sixty miles on our first day isn't a guideline. It's the rule.

Lee likes to stop for photos and snacks. A lot. I don't complain. But the price we pay that night is end of the line for pasta in the dinner tent and no hot water left in my expensive RV. My two buddies from Park City finished today in five hours. The two women from back home took just under six. Lee and I come in thirty-second out of thity-four in our Masters class, at over seven hours. Hey, we said we weren't out to win. And I am hammered.

Morning of day two seems to arrive about ten minutes after I fell asleep. On paper, our route from Crows Nest to Dutch Creek Camp looks about the same —84 up and down kilometers to another net of up 1,700 vertical feet. And again, 230 riders assemble in the start corral for the stampede start. But it quickly gets very different.

The first ten klicks follow a gravel road of roller-coaster ups and downs. From our now familiar trailing position, we follow a route marked by broken tape markers. We try not to slip off narrow tracks that run along high riverbank cliffs. Surprisingly, there are a lot of mud-filled holes on the track and no two have the same depth. We ford rushing streams where ice-cold mountain water climbs over your thighs.

Hours of grinding climbs and downhill plunges exhaust and frustrate what little judgement I have. I fight to pedal up inclines I normally walk. I fly recklessly on the downhill side, ecstatic to feel any speed. I risk suicidal flings over my handlebars and pedal furiously along skinny trails that barely hang on the mountainside.

Miraculously, Lee and I are now sometimes passing other riders . . . victims of failing bikes and muscles.

As we hike our bikes up a last ascent, we pause at the crest for another incredible mountain vista. We grin. Before us is a twenty kilometer downhill to the camp. We can do this.

We roll into camp under the stage finish banner, down a lane lined by tents in military precision with the massive dining tent at the end. The ten RVs known as Plutocrats Row are just beyond near the medical stations and all-night bike mechanics shops. These last two are busy all hours. Bikers are already being medically released because of injuries, and the bikes take such a beating they are almost rebuilt overnight.

After everyone has washed down their bikes and scrubbed off the mud, dinner is an orgy of carbs and lies with everyone stuffing their faces in-between tales of incredible runs and near-death falls. Video clips on the big screen show the truth and the stage winners go on top of the leader boards. A speaker blares Queen's "We are the champions! " I sing along with 230 others!

Marc and Kurt are now in ninth place among the Masters Class. Carolyn and Lynn are fifth among the women. And Lee and I have a lot of nice photos.

Day three is where attrition begins. Our pack of twenty pairs who started together and who maintained a back-of-the-pack camaraderie are now reduced to sixteen. New pairs form as partners drop out from injury or equipment failure. There is an ironic tradition that riders who drop out parcel out their equipment to those still going on. So, Lee now sports new sunglasses from a Mexican airline pilot who charged him with getting them over the line.

The strangers have become characters.

Eric is the French Canadian body builder and bike mechanic who gallantly carries both his and his girlfriend's bike up any climb she can't pedal. Liz is the stylish chick from Vancouver who patiently waits along the trail for her older partner, a guy who is never going to finish. Rochelle is the tattooed young red-haired singer for an all-girl rock band called Panting Daisies. She never loses her infectious grin no matter how long her partner has to fidget and wait for her.

141

And then there is Brett Wolfe, a legendary figure in bike races because he competes and wins on one leg. I hear how he lost his leg in a motorcycle crash twelve years ago and then simply switched to mountain bike racing. A slight Alaskan with a slim beard, he doesn't look like the toughest man on the mountain. But ask anyone who's raced with him from Costa Rica to the Alps and they will tell you he can do anything. Including the world speed record for one-legged track racing.

We all set out for the third stage from our Dutch Creek camp to Etherington Creek, ninety-six k's away. It's not long before our double-track gravel trail turns into a hellish bog. As far ahead as we can see, it's nothing but a sunken meadow buried under thick, squishy, knee-high mud.

It's impossible to pedal or ride. Mud cakes my derailleur and chain. It takes huge effort to alternately lift and push my bike forward. After the fourth slip and fall, I am equally smothered in thick brown goo. Somewhere above us, unexpected rain has flooded the mountain streams and to me it looks like they all drain into this one damn bog.

About 1,500 meters in, a quirk in the landscape plunges me into a clear-running stream. All around me, bikers are cursing the freezing cold while blessing the chance to wash off pounds of mud. By mid-afternoon, Lee and I emerge onto dry land in proud possession of last place. We know that because the only people in sight are an injured biker and a helicopter crew about to lift him out. Luckily for me . . .

. . . because under all the mud, the plate on one of my toe cleats has ripped out the bottom of my shoe and there's no way I can go on. The dropping-out biker, however, honors our strange tradition, takes off his shoes, and tosses them to me. Lee and I pull it together and pedal on. Shit. Just when I was hoping for an equipment failure so I could drop out with honor.

Two hours later we are starting to lose the light. We haven't seen a trail marker or biker for awhile. We realize we have missed a crucial turn and are now lost in the Canadian Rockies with no food and wearing nothing but stinky wet spandex underwear and plastic helmets.

We don't panic. Because just as we have figured it out, we hear a shout. Rolling up the trail behind us is one of the race sweep riders—guardian angels who trail behind and pick up all the lost, forlorn, and beaten riders like us.

It's already dark as we reach Etherington Creek camp. We'd been on the trail for just under twelve hours, having barely beaten the official stage deadline. I don't remember anything except pulling off my clothes and falling into bed.

Day four feels like day forty. I wake up exhausted. All I have to do today is climb to another net up 1,600 feet over sixty-three kilometers and get to Sandy McNabb camp before nightfall. And they tell us we are out of the mud. The crowd at the start definitely feels smaller. Among the missing is Carolyn from Park City, who wrenched her knee after her brakes gave out on a downhill. When she waves, I almost want to join her. But there's Rochelle, the rock singer, wearing a new knee brace, gingerly pedaling up to the start. The bike mechanics have again worked their all-night magic, rebuilding bikes from swapped parts to keep us going. We are all crazy.

Today's course goes up and up. We climb along misty trails that suddenly open above beautiful cirques . . . deep mountain amphitheaters formed by glaciers into valleys and sometimes lakes. The weather is crystal clear and the air tastes just like the Rockies are supposed to. It's glorious. What a difference a few hours can make.

A couple of times today, I catch up and ride a bit with Brett Wolfe. He uses his bike like a crutch to walk up the steep climbs, going twice as fast as I can walk along pushing my bike. Then he rips down the pitched trails like the racer he is. Lee tries to stay with him. We are back to our frequent stops for snacks and photo ops and an occasional shared joint with Team 93. Lee and I had named our team the Rough Riders, but we stopped mentioning that after the first day.

My years of marathon runs now give me an edge. I have counting and breathing exercises to stretch out my stamina. I keep my head down and use mental blocks to ignore exhaustion and keep my feet pushing pedals one more time, then one more time.

We finish among the middle of today's riders. Or, as we call it, "No longer last for the first time." That night in the dining tent I silently ask myself again if I really belong here but then there on the big screen is a group of racers on one of the panoramic cirques and I am among them! I'm feeling high.

Day five is our longest stage yet . . . 106 kilometers up, down and around to a killer 2,248 vertical feet rise getting to Bragg Creek. Our Masters division is dwindling, not surprising when you know that the two partners' ages must exceed a combined eighty. Marc and Kurt from Park City have slipped down to thirteenth place. Lee and I are hanging on to twenty-eighth, up from the thirty-fourth where we started. Honesty forces me to add that five teams have been forced out. My friend Lynn, has lost her partner Carolyn but gamely pedals on near the front of the women's pack.

Lee now wants to drop our your turn- my turn strategy and pass some people. He is encouraged by our pace and his impatience gradually goads me into a pace influenced more by pride than ability.

I become a downhill blur, abandoning brakes on the downhills and swooping by packs of wiser bikers, then pedaling furiously up the next climb, gaining ground and position. Eventually, I cut one of my downhill swoops a bit too close, scraping a hapless biker and pulling us into a sliding pile of bikes and riders. The justifiably-enraged biker pushes off of me, ready to coldcock the idiot who was out of control.

It's Lee. He can't believe it. He forgets his anger as he realizes I have caught and almost passed him. Adjusting his nose piercing, he grunts, "It's about time." For the last five miles, we take turns drafting each other, then shamelessly draft a couple a few yards from the finish and leapfrog past them. As I roll to a stop, I smell my sizzling front axle bearing ,which has almost disintegrated from the heat friction of all the mud ground into it.

But we made it. Two more days. I think we are going to finish this thing.

The next morning leaving Bragg Creek, we roll out our new strategy. It's eighty-five k's to Rafter Six Dude Camp and though we'll climb over 2,000 vertical feet, the first ten k's today are on pavement. We are going to fly.

Less than 200 bikers reach the line now and the start is like one huge peloton. Lee and I are in front of a twenty-six rider pack and just ahead are two groups of about forty. The lead group is quickly out of sight.

As we crest with a long downhill run ahead, I sling out and go for it. Two other guys go with me and we trade wind breaks until we catch the third group. I am now riding with the big dogs.

Not for long. The pace is crushing. I soon slide back with Lee and buddies, tired but exhilarated. We reach camp by mid-afternoon with our best stage finish yet. My confidence is growing.

I'm stretched out on the grass by our RV. All around me people are celebrating Last Stage Eve with songs, beer, weed, and stories in ten different languages . . . but the pride all translates. Like them, I finally believe I just might finish this epic. Lee, Marc, and I share a joint.

Day seven is the last stage and the shortest yet . . . only fifty-two k's and an ending with an easier 353 net down vertical feet. That's an excellent bike day back home. And that's where I made my big mistake.

Marathon runners all tell you the worst thing you can do is look for the finish line. Same for bike racers. I'm quickly exhausted because I am no longer in grinder mode. I'm trying to finish this f-ing thing off before it finishes me. I start taking chances on downhills and curves. And, like a skier who can't hold his form and balance, I am trying to muscle where I should be gliding. I'm suddenly doubting I can make it.

I roll down the last downhill to the slight slope that leads up to the finish. It looks like a mountain to me. I am pedaling so slow I can barely keep my balance. Lee comes running down the slope to help and I snarl, "Fuck off! I'm doing this!" He stands back and urges me on.

Numb with blisters and exhaustion, wracked by cramps, I'm sure I look pathetic as I crawl under the finish banner. But I did it. For the rest of my life, that's all I have to say.

For the record, Lee and I finished twenty-fourth in our Master division of thirty-six starters, only twenty-four hours behind the best in the world. You can look it up. We're the Rough Riders.

CHAPTER 43
September 8, 2005—Los Angeles, California

"You may need to borrow a bra"

For over two years, my TRT program has brought the joys of outdoor adventure and everyday sex back into my life. I must also give my wife Michelle, a lot of credit on both fronts. I hoped it would never end but, of course, Dr. Bob had cautioned me that TRT was not a permanent treatment ,just like my TAB program.

TRT ended much sooner than I expected. One September day I was at the LA airport, ready to fly home after a routine visit to Dr. Bob. My phone rang. It was Mary Duong, the brilliant NP from Dr. Bob's office who I had come to trust like my personal angel.

Mary said, "Your PSA was 9.21 just seven days ago at your regular blood test. Today's test showed a climb to 12.7. You need to stop the AndroGel right now and take some of those special Estrogen capsules."

"I don't have any of those left."

"Don't worry. We'll call the compounding lab in New Jersey and have some rushed to you overnight."

My flight home was not a relaxed one.

So, about the Estrogen. What I was taking was actually Estinyl in a Dr. Bob custom-estrogen compound he had formulated to have specific protection for prostate cancer patients. Specifically, it suppresses testosterone generation and also inhibits free testosterone. Remember, I had long been taking drugs to prevent testosterone from splitting into those two suspected cancer nutrients, estradiol and DHT.
Within weeks, we were watching the Dr. Bob's magic Estinyl mix drop my PSA back to safe levels. Unfortunately, I was also growing lovely breasts.

146

CHAPTER 44
October 21, 2005—Los Angeles, California

"An effect no one expected . . . "

People were starting to notice my chest or at least my paranoid macho mind thought so. Dr. Bob has previously warned me about some of the estrogen side effects which seemed acceptable to get the benefits. we had arranged a series of visits with a Utah oncologist, Dr. Nitin Chandramouli, who was not bothered that Utah's Huntsman Cancer Institute turned me down, and three small radiation doses soon restored my desired chest profile.

Today, Michelle has accompanied me on a follow-up visit to Dr. Bob in LA and we learn about an effect no one expected.

After a routine blood draw, we are walked down and seated in Dr. Bob's office. A minute later, he walks in, closes the door, and looks me right in the eyes without his usual smile. "Your treatment is failing. Your PSA is up to 25.3. Your cancer is back and we are losing control."

I am stunned and momentarily speechless.

"We are going to start you on a chemo drug regimen right now and I'll explain as we go along."

Within a half hour, I am hooked up to an IV in COMG's infusion room. My head is spinning but Dr. Bob calmly walks me through the routine.

"This is similar to the standard regimen of chemo drug treatment, but instead of one big dose a month and all the unpleasant side effects you hear about, we'll give you one-third here the first week. Then you'll have the next two doses the next two weeks at your Utah clinic with Dr. Chandramouli. Then a week off. That will be your routine for the next six months until we can kick your prostate cancer back down and get it back in the box."

I won't walk you through all the tears and protests and shouts of unfairness along with the lack of testosterone that I went through. Michelle was our hero. When I got down, she brought me up and we made it through.

My worst and strongest chemotherapy memory was the difference between the hopeful and confident faces of the patients I saw each month in Dr. Bob's office contrasted with the gray, mournful, and often pained faces I saw in the Utah infusion clinic. Chemotherapy comes in all forms and conditions. I was lucky I got Dr. Bob's alternate regimen.

CHAPTER 45
August 6, 2006—Los Angeles, California

"Goodbye chemo . . . hello TRT."

Memory is a wonderful thing. And your mind tends to keep the happiest parts on the front page. Only a few months after my successful chemotherapy concluded, and the absence of testosterone was painfully obvious while traveling in Tibet and other places, I was again begging Dr. Bob to put me back on the TRT regimen. I remembered how I felt then, the intense joy, and I knew how I felt now with the intense longing.

Dr. Bob agreed. Again, for a limited run. And this time, with a full complement of our special Estinyl compound.

This time, the team has added the expert services of Dr. Duke Bahn, a nearby Ventura radiologist, who will track my tumor size and vascularity, i.e., blood flow, every six months using that good old transrectal ultrasound wand. Any increase in either variable will indicate more cancer activity. Dr. Bob will alternate this with bone scans and MRI testing.

I am off and, literally, running again. Slathered in AndroGel.

CHAPTER 46
April 22, 2011—Park City, Utah

"Why does too much of a good thing always end up being a bad thing?"

My TRT the second time around was a resounding success. For the past four years, my wife, Michelle, and I have enthusiastically enjoyed my fully-functional and energic lifestyle filled with travel and adventure. By the fifth year, however, cancer's continual roller coaster of good and bad PSA counts and never-ending testing and dose management has taken its toll and the wheels were starting to come off.

As I had been warned, the increased testosterone, necessarily combined with the PSA-reducing Estinyl, was leading to the overpopulation of red blood cells and high hematocrit (HCT) readings**. Twice, I had to undergo a Middle Ages process called a phlebotomy or bloodletting. I literally had too much blood in the tank.

We were trying to avoid the consequences of a deep-vein thrombosis (DVT) which would have seriously affected my successful protocols.

Michelle was also feeling the fatigue of the constant war in my body and, by the Spring of 2011, it was time for her to get off the front lines. And that was when all my careful monitoring and adjusting blew up with a double whammy.

In late winter, I suffered a frightening transient ischemic attack (TIA). Often called a ministroke, it has all the symptoms of the big one—a numbness or sudden weakness on one side of your body, slurred speech, blurred vision, and loss of balance. Though it sounds a lot like a good drunk, there is no hangover. My TIA was over in a few minutes and I felt completely recovered. As I found after I rushed myself to the ER, however, it was the real thing. And I was overcome with fear and sobbing. The injustice of all these years of fighting for my health, only to be suddenly threatened with an unrelated and shocking attack, was too much.

It got worse, in my mind, when I visited Dr. Bob in early April and he abruptly ended my TRT . . . mainly due to the increased risk indicated by the TIA.

In a matter of weeks, my halcyon days of a TRT high were over, my confidence was shattered, and Michelle and I were divorcing.

CHAPTER 47
July 25, 2011—Cape Town, South Africa

"I'm not getting into that thing."

By the summer of 2011, Michelle and I had already separated, amicably divorced, and reconciled . . . all in a matter of months. But that's another story.

We needed a break from Park City.

Earning her deserved place in the Ex-Wives Hall of Fame, Michelle announced that she would like to use the $10,000 cash I gifted her when I proposed—in lieu of an engagement ring but that's another story, as well—and use it to treat us to a month's expedition to Africa.

Michelle's only condition was that I join her in her long-held dream to cage dive with great white sharks off the coast of Cape Town.

With my usual mix of too much bravado, too little testosterone, and not enough foresight, I agreed.

The day after we arrived in Cape Town, we were on a boat out of Simon's Town with the crew of Apex Expeditions, owned and operated by shark swimmer-to-the-stars, Chris Fallows . . . you've seen him on National Geographic and the Discovery Channel, etc. Chris and his team are dedicated conservationists and they treat their ocean world and its apex predators with respect. They also give you a very close up and personal experience with hungry sharks.

The boat was heading out toward Seal Island in False Bay. Seal Island is where every winter thousands of Cape fur seals swim to breed and they will get there no matter what. But nature has played a cruel trick on them.

As the sex-starved seals churn their flippers and tails to race out to Seal Island, something deadly is waiting for them just a few fathoms below.

152

Great white sharks. Hundreds of them, surrounding the island in a ring of death, ready to launch like deadly missiles up to the sea's surface. Razor-sharp-toothed jaws gaping wide, they tear into the frantic seals on the surface in an orgy of feeding. It's only because there are tens of thousands of seals versus hundreds of sharks that the breeding of the seals succeeds.

Knowing this, we start preparations on our boat to get into the ocean with all of them. Fallows has warned us that these sightings don't happen every day. False Bay is big, so, when sharks are nearby, it's time to plunge in.

Luckily, we do that by stepping into a four foot by six foot by seven foot underwater cage floating a few feet below the water just off the boat's rail. Two of us at a time will then stand in this galvanized open cube, hoping the spaces between the protective rails are not too wide.

Hearts pounding, we will be sucking air out of a hose like marathon runners, wondering if our bodies wrapped in black wetsuits look too much like the tasty nearby seals.

Michelle drops in right away and I have no choice but to reluctantly follow her. Immediately, my head is swinging left to right. I am floating upright a few feet below the surface, encased in what feels like a flimsy wire frame box made out of old coat hangars.

More than a few of us forget to even take pictures as the first great whites swim by for a closer look. The blackest eyes I have ever seen scan me like a laser. Like ghosts, the sharks disappear in the murky water. When Michelle goes back down a second time, I decline. And, of course, feel immediately justified and regretful when a huge great white starts head-butting the cage a few inches from Michelle and a camera. Whenever she shared vacation snapshots, she loved to pull that one out. I rarely mention where I was when she took it.

We only see the above surface seal attacks a few times and our guides gently called them predations. They explain that much of the action takes place out of sight below us. It turns out that generations of seals have developed a defense strategy, so the smarter ones swim along the bottom where the water is less clear, only rushing up to the surface for a quick breath. The sharks have learned to prowl the bottom, spooking nervous seals up to the surface where waiting partners quickly spot them and launch.

It is horrifying but undeniably spectacular when you see the immense power of a twelve-foot great white explode completely out of the water, flying into the air with a hapless seal clutched in its jaws, before falling back into the sea with a cannonball splash.

For ten days, we tow our cage out to sea searching for these awesome predators. One day, I was lounging on the bow when a guide pointed to what looked like a single white-capped wave rushing toward us. In a few minutes, we gaped open-mouthed as a pod of hundreds of dolphins sprinted by, rushing to something or running from it, we never knew.

Every morning, Michelle is enthralled and enthusiastic. She is in the cage at every chance. My first time was heart-pounding and it was also my only time. My theory is that one time down is educational, any turns after that are bets of sharks versus cage, with me as the stakes.

Yet, it's hard not to admire the brutal, yet elegant, perfection of the great white. They are like the terminators of the ocean. Nothing can stop them and they just don't quit. Sadly, we learned years later that the great whites have mysteriously disappeared from the waters off Seal Island. Fear, overfishing, and hunting by humans . . . the true apex predator . . . have driven these magnificent creatures into hiding somewhere in the ocean wastes.

My years of adventure travel have put me in many tough spots and perilous situations, but nothing has ever induced such leg-shaking, heart-pounding trembling as sharing the sea with a so-close-I-can-touch-him great white. And yeah, you really do wish you had a bigger boat.

CHAPTER 48
December 20, 2011—Park City, Utah

"Taking stock of what I've learned."

L ooking back at the upheavals of the past year, plus the thirteen years of managing my cancer through the ups and downs of my unconventional methods, I decided it was time to flip back through the pages of my memory and take an inventory of what I had learned.

Two huge changes in my life prompted this inventory. The first was that Michelle and I had built a test reconciliation over the summer into what we hoped was again a stable and lasting relationship. Our love had never waivered.

The second change was an ultimatum from Dr. Bob and his team that my years of TRT dancing were coming to a halt. We had too many complications to manage safely. I had no choice but to accept a truce. But not a surrender. I would bide my time. Because I had learned too much to accept defeat. Here is just a small sample:

1. Established mainstream medical professionals were inescapably devoted to and captured by their own expertise, technology, and sub-specialty tribes. They are bands of brothers and sisters. If I talked to surgeons, each would emphatically promote his or her particular surgical technique, team, and specialized equipment—and nothing else. If I talked to a radiologist, only his particular form of radiation therapy was best, thanks to unique proprietary technique or equipment. Even more evangelical were the brachytherapists, those maestros of the long needle and radioactive seed implants.

But they all offered only a different path to get to the same place . . . a life where some or all bodily functions on the D.U.P.E. scale would likely be compromised or eliminated . . . with no evidence whatever that their cancer work would extend their patients' lives. "We know you'll never again ejaculate but let's take out your cancer and hope for the best." It was the most, after all, that they could offer.

155

Any mention of hormone therapy was quickly dismissed as a dangerous gamble, unproven theory, or only as a last resort. That changed somewhat over the years so that eventually the unproven part was dropped. But even in 2011, there were still Utah doctors who regarded me as having been misguided by quacks.

2. My priority from the start had been to refuse the consequences of D.U.P.E., a path no man would take voluntarily if he understood all the facts . . . especially if they were given another choice. But since D.U.P.E.'ing was the only path offered, and my cancer was at a point where I could not watch and wait, I had to find the path that few had taken, starting with Bob's TAB**.

3. I was warned time after time that my next step could be the disaster everyone predicted. When I began hormone therapy directed at testosterone, it was the demon behind prostate cancer. I found out it was not—which basically refuted a Nobel Laureate.

4. When I began to use thalidomide, people were shocked and horrified. They remembered the heartbreaking birth defects of forty years before. But the very effect that made thalidomide so dangerous to pregnant women, its ability to block the formation of new blood vessels, made it the logical answer to slow the growth of cancer cells by cutting their blood supply. It worked for me for awhile until we found something better. But ten years later, the anti-angiogenesis drugs that succeeded it were finally being accepted as important cancer fighters.

5. When I began to take a form of estrogen, a custom Estinyl compound, it was considered virtually poisonous for men and a cause of serious heart problems. Once again, I learned that the accepted wisdom often becomes yesterday's myth. And bioidentical Estinyl taken in a modified compound became another lifesaver for me. Not without its own complications, but with benefits that may make it mainstream years from now.

6. I learned to understand and sympathize with brilliant doctors whose experiences and practices—bound by accepted standards, a rigid referral network, and the threat of litigation or loss of insurance— left them nowhere to go. They had to defend what they practiced and preached.

156

7. I learned to understand but lament profit-above-all-else big pharmaceutical companies that, per stockholder directives. only worked to develop medicines they could patent and market for the highest margins. Their investors left them no choice. And, thus, they did not choose to redeploy or even produce older, less expensive, and out-of-patent drugs.

8. I learned to understand and sympathize with large hospitals and medical centers that struggle to maintain high levels, quality staff, and up-to-date technology . . . all the while convincing their directors and financiers to invest in new methods and equipment. Once they buy it, they are bound to use it and promote it. Imagine the threat Dr. Bob's simple hormone therapy would offer to a multimillion-dollar brachytherapy clinic.

9. I learned to understand and sympathize with all the urologists who are more and more forced to admit, even if only before they fall asleep at night, that the so-called gold standards—aka standards of care—of prostate cancer mitigation . . . the debilitating burn, bake, and butcher of radiation, chemo, and surgery are still painfully and woefully failing.

10. I learned to understand and empathize with all the men I met along the way who, facing such enormous internal pressure to "get the cancer out", succumbed to the only choices their doctors could give them. And they were now living the diminished lives resulting from their decisions . . . never having been told about the all-but-zero evidence that prescribed treatments would extend their lives.

11. I learned from the NEJM article of July 2012 that largely corroborated an earlier Swedish study, one of the few comparing mortality results from prostate surgery eight years later to the results from doing only watch and wait over the same time. At the end, there was no statistically significant difference between the two groups of men. The reported small 2.6 percent variance was only between those men who already had the most advanced cancer.

The conclusion of all this, combined with my ten years of anecdotal experience and patient interviews, supported by Dr. Bob's published clinical follow-up data, convinced me that his far superior mortality rates offered me my most promising path.

So I learned a lot. But what had I gained?

157

At that point, I could chalk up thirteen extra years of meeting my primary goal of a fully functional daily life and my treasured active lifestyle. Not always perfect, but I came close.

I could also add up thirteen years of up and down success, a continuous emotional roller coaster, unrelenting health management, exhaustive travel to and from doctors' offices and clinics, and a very fortunate medical insurance portfolio.

Along the way, I have put a lot of stress on everyone I love, gone through two divorces, and watched my careers as a successful builder and politician pass me by. But today, I could not have a more loving family, nor could I be here without their support. And I continue to travel, roughly and widely.

Add it all up. I did. And I gave myself a win.

I had earned every day I had gained and still wanted more. With score card in hand, I faced the New Year. Content for now but confident that somewhere down that unknown path, somehow, there were more TRT happy days in my future.

CHAPTER 49
September 9, 2012—Roncesvalles, Spain

"We find the way . . . "

No deadlines. No plans. No urgent goals. I was off the TRT. I was on with Michelle. I was bored with my local builder career. I didn't have an obsession for anything but the desire to enjoy life.

But I did have this itch from my twenty-five years of adventure travel. What was I doing just sitting on my ass in Park City?

Michelle knew it before I did. So when she suggested we take a shot at one of the oldest, most famous cross-country treks in the world, I said yes before I even knew what country.

It was the Camino de Santiago . . . a 1,200-year-old pilgrimage across Spain to a tomb of the apostle St. James in Santiago de Compostela.

Dozens of well-defined routes once wound across Europe but now most hikers took one of several trails across Spain to the northwest corner of the Iberian Peninsula. For over a thousand years, pilgrims had stopped at the many hostelries and inns along the route and we would do the same.

Michelle, "You want to go?"

"Sure, but I have a problem."

I'd endured psoriatic arthritis since 2010 and it was so bad I'd developed those clawed hands you see on arthritics.

I found a doctor who put me on a refrigerated weekly injection drug, Embrel, which quickly restored my grip on life. Weekly. Refrigerated. The Camino plan forced me to research since I couldn't hike with a refrigerator and couldn't know when we'd be where. Yes, there was a monthly injection option, Simponi. I got our Madrid hotel to store my Simponi. Then, thirty days into hiking, I caught a four-hour bus to Madrid, got my syringe out of

159

the hotel refrigerator, injected myself, and road four hours back to the Camino.

The Camino de Santiago has been a pilgrims' path since the eighth century. Millions of people have walked it over the centuries since. It is also known as the Way of St. James.

Originally, it was all part of the myth of the Apostle James whose body was brought back by sea to be buried in northern Spain because of a vision he had. The ship sank and his body was washed ashore covered in scallop shells. That's why, still today, scallops in France are called Coquilles St. Jacques. True story.

The body of James was entombed in a cathedral specifically built for him and a town grew up around it called Santiago de Compostela. Legend soon established that a visit to the Saint's shrine would grant pilgrims special relief in purgatory. And they came. Eventually, by the hundreds and thousands ,from all over Europe.

The pilgrims' original path was from their front door but, eventually, the easiest routes became focal points and by the nineth century Pope Callixtus II even published a travel guide. We Catholics don't miss a trick.

Over the next few centuries, the main Way came to be the one that started in France just over the Pyrenees border in a town called Saint-Jean-Pied-de-Port which translates as foot of the pass , and refers to the pass over the mountains about five hundred miles from Santiago.

In the Middle Ages, five hundred miles could take months to complete on foot with mountains, rivers, valleys, and wastelands to cross. So, naturally, the Church and its enterprising members began to build a series of rest stops for pilgrims.

Fast forward a thousand years and not a lot has changed. It's still a long hike across the countryside, there are more hikers than pilgrims but the paths haven't changed and, while a few still camp by the side of the paths, most stay in auberges or refugios which are basically hostels.

Our starting point is a small Spanish town south of a Pyrenees pass called Roncesvalles, famous in history for the legend "Song of Roland." We carry light backpacks with a minimal change of clothes and layers for rain or snow in the mountains. The most important items are our favorite shoes and double-layer socks which minimized blister risk.

We are seldom alone on Camino's mostly rural paths. A thousand years ago, various Camino Ways moved thousands of pilgrims across Europe. The throngs dwindled to a trickle over the centuries. Then, a few decades ago, a revival began and suddenly 10,000 or more a year made the walk. Now, the annual pilgrim count has 190,000 who hike the last hundred miles needed for dispensations and about 60,000 who walk the entire five hundred miles. It's the Middle Ages all over again, but now it's very few religious pilgrims. It's a broad mix of hikers, bikers, bird watchers, and loners looking for a different kind of redemption.

We hear many languages every day. Two Germans will be followed by a Dane and a Swede. French girls will be chatting with Italians. Russians with Latvians. And no one assumes you speak English. But everyone is friendly and somehow we all converse. Michelle and I use our Spanglish and we were always able to find a room and order a meal. Who knows what our listeners thought we were trying to say.

We cover about fifteen miles per day. The walking is fairly easy and linked by medieval villages, old castles, crumbling monasteries, and threadbare farms. We move and flow past it all like a river of wanderers.

If you've ever gone tubing down a lazy river on a hot summer day, you know the experience. You drift along, moving slower or faster with the current, first with one group and then another. Like random molecules, you bump and connect to others, starting and pausing conversations with fellow walkers as you go, to be resumed at the next stopping point. Or not.

We ramble through lush vineyards and cross desert wastes. One day, the sun was blocked by ten-story haystacks, another time we got stuck on an ancient castle drawbridge. We wandered through a real Templar castle, wondering about hidden mysteries. We paused in two small towns for their running of the bulls . . . not as much pageantry as nearby Pamplona but equally thrilling. We often pass long-abandoned shepherds' huts that once were used by pilgrims like us and that are now falling down. There are also stone chapels and churches where the stained-glass windows date back centuries.

161

Crossing an old Roman bridge or climbing a bell tower, you murmur, "Buena Camino" to your fellow peregrinos --- pilgrims --- as you pass. It's as ubiquitous as, "Have a nice day," but you feel a little pride and camaraderie each time.

Just to give you a feeling for who we met along the way, here is a small sample. A retired Interpol detective. A trauma surgeon from Texas. A lawyer from Korea. A German army colonel. A prosecutor from Madrid. An organic farmer from the Crimea. Four priests from Minnesota. College students from everywhere enjoying their gap year. A Canadian grandfather and granddaughter. Four middle-aged women from a California book club who read John Brierly's *A Pilgrim's Guide to Camino de Santiago* and were inspired to do it in person. And our favorite, Harold, eighty-two, a former professor and engineer who had just finished law school so he could do pro bono work for Mexican communities back in Texas.

Everyone has their own reasons to come spend a month in solitude and contemplation, in the midst of a moving community of strangers where everyone acts like a friend.

There's no agenda, no right or wrong way, no real rule but the Golden one. Go with the flow takes on another whole meaning. And then there are the stars.

Far from city lights and light pollution, the sky is immense and the Milky Way seems to run overhead like a giant light highway, leading you to the sea. It's the only guide you need.

As we got to the end of the Camino, we began to slow down, dropping our average daily miles from twelve to five. We stopped to smell more roses. We didn't want it to end. Or else we didn't want to rush back to rushing.

Forty days ago we began our journey with that single step.

Now, we are in Santiago de Compostela and have received our Compostela credentials, a kind of diploma for those who walk the Way and can show the all-important stamps from each official post along the path.

At noon, we assemble with over a thousand peregrinos at the Cathedral of St. James huge Parador Plaza for the blessing mass. As a former altar boy,

I can't help taking a little comfort that I am now covered for purgatory, just in case.

CHAPTER 50
January 4, 2013—Los Angeles, California

"I gotta be me . . . "

I am back in LA to visit Dr. Bob. Four months ago, I hiked five hundred miles across Spain with Michelle as we completed the ancient Camino de Santiago. It was hugely satisfying to check off one of my bucket list goals and even more gratifying to do it with my wife.

Spiritually and emotionally, it was a success. Physically, it was a reminder that my regimen of estrogen compound maintenance and very low testosterone was needed for my health but was a real damper on my strength and stamina.

I wanted to feel like my old self.

Then, I cajoled and pleaded with Dr. Bob and Sharooz and they consented, if there was a thorough round of tests to eliminate any pending problems.

And here I am. Ready to ride on with TRT #3!!!

CHAPTER 51
June 10, 2013—Park City, Utah

"My heart just isn't in it."

I admit I had some medical issues that my cancer treatments likely exacerbated. But I was almost always a fully functional male, no D.U.P.E. Not that summer.

I was feeling plain lousy and my home team doctor, Kim Scott, told me I had A-fib.

Atrial fibrillation is the medical term for an irregular and often rapid heart beat. Lots of people get it. Basically, the two upper chambers of your heart get out of sync with the two lower chambers and you get dizzy, tired, weak, and sometimes dead. But usually medication can get you back in sync. The big danger is blood clots, a risk exacerbated by my Estinyl use.

I had recently developed a violent bronchial cough. I used my research skills and developed a theory my cardiologist said was plausible and that my research deemed probable. It was this:

Violent coughing has been shown to crack and shake loose the arterial plaque that can line the walls of everyone's arteries, at least a bit. Plaque is made up of materials like fat, cholesterol, and other waste materials from your bloodstream. It can break loose and crack. Estinyl, one of COMG's management tools, can cause resulting blood cell debris which stick to arterial cracks.

This explanation seemed logical since only one of my three arteries was blocked.

It's one way you get A-fib. Because two of your arteries are pumping away full blast and the clogged one is not doing the job. So, the blood feed to your heart is no longer balanced and your drummer loses his beat.

At any rate, that was the diagnosis from the School of Jim, Medical Division.

My internist, Dr. Kim Scott, and my local heart surgeon, Dr. Anwar Tandar, agreed about my condition, if not my self-diagnosis, and recommended that I have a stent placed in the balky artery. A stent is basically a short length of repair tube that bridges the arterial block and restores the normal flow. Plumbing for your blood line.

If you can remember when cars had carburetors, you'll recall the amazing restored power for a car after a tune-up and a carburetor cleanup.

That was me. Clean pipes and turbocharged by my TRT.

CHAPTER 52
January 10, 2014—Park City, Utah

"Now I remember why I quit."

I had originally come to Park City as the owner and operator of a bar and deli at the base of the main ski lift. Business was good. So, of course, I got tired of it and sold it off and used the gains to get into developing real estate. Not a bad idea in a booming ski resort. And, like everyone else in the early 2000s, I was doing well.

Real estate development is a game of leverage and credit. And when the Great Recession of 2008 rolled in, the banks took their ball and went home. Suddenly, award-winning projects were being shut down in midstream and perfectly good loans were being withdrawn. Including mine.

It took a few years to rebuild my business and, once I had things stabilized, I kept it low-key while I tried other things. Including being an author.

At some point, I realized I had a lot to learn about writing but I knew a lot about developing. And I also like the money. So, I pulled out the plans for my last leftover parcel of land and put together the concept for a new apartment complex in Park City.

Newpark Flats got off to a rousing start but, once again, we ran into a changing credit market and, once again, I was forced to scrape and bow to banks while I looked for an investor or two.

The story eventually had a happy ending when I sold my majority interest in the partially completed project to new investors, made a nice profit, and swore I would never again put on my builder/developer hat.

I was ready to hit the road again. And already thinking about Portugal, Scotland, a fourth New Zealand adventure, even Iran, and maybe, just maybe, Cuba . . .

CHAPTER 53
November 16, 1992—Auckland, New Zealand

"A kiwi once again."

Back in my late twenties, my wife Diane and I vacationed in New Zealand and I swore I'd come back some day to do it on a non-tourist level. Almost twenty years later, I did. By myself.

On November 14, 1992 I lifted off on my west-bound flight over the Pacific headed for Auckland, New Zealand. Sometime around midnight, I was sound asleep when we flew across the International Date Line. When I woke up a few hours later, it was November 16. I never saw November 15. It's one of those arbitrary rules to account for twenty-four hours in a day, longitude, and something else I can't remember. But there it is—a permanent blank in my life, one whole day never lived.

New Zealand is actually a nation of two main islands plus some small ones and I landed on the North Island at Auckland. The North Island is the more populated and, in some ways, the more modern. I was headed to the South Island, settled for a longer time with a more rugged terrain and spectacular scenery. They film a lot of movies there.

My flight from Auckland deposited me, my bike, and my gear at the far end of the South Island, a place called Invercargill. My plan was to swim in the Pacific at the farthest point south—next stop Antarctica—and then bike up through the mountains along the coast to the farthest point north and jump in the Pacific there.

At the airport, I screwed around for an hour with my bike, trying to fix a bent seat post and some bad threads on my pedals. Finally, I got it together by late afternoon and headed to my overnight at Beach Road Camp.

I almost missed the place in the mist and fog. The office was dark and locked. A non-welcome note tersely sent me to Cabin #9. I was the only lodger in the camp.

Cabin #9 was bleak. A bare bulb with a pull-chain, a weak shower, old but clean sheets, a single sliver of soap, and a threadbare washcloth. No towels, no pillow. But it was dry. There was room to pull my loaded bike inside out of the rain. And the heater I plugged in made the cabin warm at just about the time my eyes closed.

The sun came up very early—it was almost the summer solstice—barely visible through the morning fog. I decided to accomplish one goal, so I ran down to the beach, plunged in to get my head wet, and ran back to the warmth of the cabin. The Pacific is always very cold and my only towel was yesterday's T-shirt.

I hung around long enough to boil water on my camp stove for my usual instant coffee and oatmeal. When I pushed my loaded bike out of the cabin, the fog had turned to a misty rain. The temperature had dropped at least ten degrees.

I admit despair was creeping in. My first night was a letdown, even for a devoted camper like me. My first morning ride didn't match my sunny New Zealand memories. I began to pedal north. Long way to go. At least I had a tailwind and pedaling got me warm.

The misting rain turns to fine sleet on my neck. I decide to stop under a highway overpass. Not a good idea. Without the warming effort of pedaling, I'm immediately cold. The wind reminds me how wet I am. Standing there shivering, I decide I'm better off to just keep going. I rummage in my bike panniers for something warm and dry to put on.

I might have mentioned before that I do not splurge on equipment and gear. I'm happy to borrow free stuff. I knew the panniers I borrowed for this trip were old and not waterproof but I cleverly packed everything in garbage bags to keep them dry. The secret to making garbage bags rainproof is to keep them sealed up. Mine were not.

I did rummage up an old fleece shirt that was mildly damp and enjoyed the warmth when I pulled it on. Maybe now that the rain was sleet, my weatherproof bike jacket would do better, as well.

My first-day trek across rolling farm land ended seventy-nine miles later near the town of Athol. I had a reservation for a free night in a luxury lodge courtesy of my buddy Steve, from back in Park City. Except this was off-season and the lodge wasn't officially open. I get the caretaker on the phone but he is an hour away and cannot pick me up. He had a note about me and left a key under a mat plus instructions for tuning on the water and lights. It's already dark and I am biked out. I imagine biking through the night and then not finding the key. I decide I should just tent where I am.

Then I hear faint but unmistakable voices singing Uncle John's Band. Following that old Grateful Dead tune, I come to a barn with a faded Bed & Breakfast sign painted on the side. I push my bike up to an open door and my future friend, Jem Pearse, looks up from his pottery wheel.

Jem later told me he was about to say, "Closed for the season," when he noticed how wet and cold and prayerful I looked. Instead, he said, "The rooms aren't made up but you can sleep on our floor and you can leave your bike in here."

Ten minutes later, I am sitting in Jem's warm and cozy cabin wrapped in a robe, wet clothes hanging everywhere, while his glorious wife Maureen is heating up leftover stew. After me, there were no leftovers.

Jem and Maureen asked me the usual incredulous questions as to why I want to bike across the entire South Island in this weather. In turn, I ply them with questions about their sort of aging hippy lifestyle. Turns out they are both fifty-ish and have lived here all their lives. Their three sons have grown and moved to the North Island and, between her school teaching and his pottery business, they are just fine. We talked long into the night and I have rarely met any couple I enjoyed so much.

Next day was a pleasant and sunny forty-eight-mile flatland run up to Queenstown. NZ6 was my road, paralleling the Mataura River. About halfway, the road started to climb as the mountains closed in and I stopped for a water break. Up rode a fellow bike tourer headed south. He stopped to chat as most of us do.

Heinrich left Germany almost a year ago and he's already traveled the entire Western Hemisphere from Newfoundland down to Tierra del Fuego, knocking off two continents. He came to New Zealand to bike the length of the islands as a warm-up for crossing Australia. I asked where he's headed next. He says, "Around." As in, you know, around the world. I realize I've just met one of the guys who will inspire me in years to come. As I travel around.

Back on my bike, I'm getting squeezed by mountains. On my left are the steep cliffs which mark The Remarkables and on my right is the Eyre. This stretch of road is called The Devil's Staircase. You get the idea.

Now Lake Wakatipu, which I can't resist calling kittypoo, is off the left edge of the road and I start to wind around Double Cone peak as Queenstown comes into sight.

I was looking forward to a night in a hotel. And after my pleasant encounters with Jem, Maureen, and Heinrich, I'm optimistic about meeting more new people.

Check-in at the Hulbert House starts off great as I am greeted by a stunning, twenty-something Norwegian girl named Cassy. She's very friendly and introduces me to the owner, Ted, a guy about my age. Ted suggests that the three of us share wine and cheese and the afternoon sun out on the lawn. An hour later, we're all mellow and I ask about dinner. Ted notes that he, Cassy, and her friend Ingrid are all going to the best place in town, The Flame Grill. Nobody suggests I come along.

Nonplussed but hungry, I head back to my room to shower and change. As I walk into town, I see a place with a line—always a good sign. I ask the guy at the door if there's room at the bar. He asks if I'd mind sharing a table for two with another single Yank instead. Welcome to The Flame Grill.

My luck holds when I sit down at a table by the window with Diane, a beautiful executive from Apple, who's a long way from Silicon Valley on a sabbatical. She is charming and full of laughter. At one point, we are toasting and I glance out the window. Standing there a few yards away are Ted, Cassy, and Ingrid waiting in line to be where I am. Do they think my smile is sincere? It was a great evening.

Next morning, Cassy served me breakfast and Ted walked by with a slight wave. I thanked them for the restaurant tip, and tried not to let them see me smirking.

Running west out of Queenstown, NZ6 winds around lakes and low hills until it swings south along the Kawarau River. About thirty miles out, the road runs through a deep gorge carved by the river and then over a bridge.

I made a detour before the Kawarau River bridge to take a side road to a place unique to modern history. It's an adjacent suspension bridg where bungy jumping was born ---and a worldwide craze began.

I think about it. Especially after chatting with three ladies from Bend, Oregon, who had just made the jump and were still wildly exhilarated.

A short time later, I was on my back in the rescue raft that picks you up when you stop bouncing. I had made the 134-foot drop to the river with my heart in my mouth and bb's in my shorts. But I did it.

As I biked off, the tailwinds picked up and I was soon covering the last forty miles at well over thirty-four miles per hour. My heart rate has seldom been so high for so long.

After running through the gorge, I had passed out to the Cardrona River valley that is lined with farms, vineyards, and lavender fields. Pulling into the lakeside ski resort town of Wanaka, I decided to cap off a great day with a night's stay at the luxurious Glen Ruth Hotel.

It's good that I did. The next day is a long eighty-mile run through the mountains along river gorges which eventually points me west to the sea. My destination is a beach town called Haast on the west coast, looking out on the Tasman Sea. The coast here is pierced by impassable fjords that run down to the sea, so, this was one of my few chances to get to the beach.

Legends call the Tasman the Sea of Man due to its very rough waters and a fierce unrelenting current that can and will sweep you west from the beach all the way across to Tasmania. The other half of the legend . . . resented by some . . . is that the ocean off the lower-lying opposite east coast is called the Sea of Woman, because the same westbound current brings you back to shore and hugs you safely close to land.

I set off with an easy fifteen-mile wake-up ride along the west shore of Lake Hawea, then across a narrow spit of land that dropped me on the east shore of Lake Wanaka, hopscotching the mountains. Fifteen miles further at the north end of the lake, I entered the Makarora River gorge which would take me by Mount Brewster and dump me into the Haast River valley.

When people ask me for a visual impression of New Zealand, I say, "Green, blue, and white." The deep emerald of the forests, the turquoise blue of the glacial rivers and streams, the snowy caps of the mountains. That's what I was riding through now for the next fifty miles. Until everything changed, right at the end.

As I neared the top of the pass that would drop me down to the sea, I was really looking forward to one of those long, gliding downhills where you effortlessly soar, enjoying the glorious view and maybe a sunset.

You should know that wind is a huge factor in long-distance bike touring. Tailwinds can make your day, headwinds can break you. Just as I left behind the quiet forest and gurgling river of the gorge, I went over the pass. Smack into a blinding, roaring headwind.

It was a salty gale, born of the warm sea waters rushing up to meet the cold mountain air, and it nearly pushed me over. Spray driven from the river next to me joined in the shower and the wind stung my eyes.

Instead of a two-hour coast down to the sea, I spent the next five hours balancing and weaving as the wind and gravity held me in an evil dance.

At one point, a group of luxury bike tourers, followed by their support Land Rovers, came riding up the hill pushed by their tailwind and sped by me with cheers. I wished I had claymores.

The sun did not set until very late thanks to the summer solstice, so at least I arrived with a sunset dimly seen in fog. I drank my dinner that night. And slept a long dream of windless roads.

Next morning, I share my breakfast table with a TV crew that is filming a documentary about the wild, sparsely populated west coast of South Island. They have just covered the same route I am following. Because there are so few roads, many travelers choose to join backpacking groups riding about in tour buses which stop at hostel-like places each night. My crew friends tell me they wish they could have filmed me---a rarely-seen oddity--- a solo traveler on a bike. That seems to be my role.

173

Haast sits on a broad river delta where the blue-water river pours into the emerald sea. To the east are green-shrouded mountains covered at the lower levels with what looks like tropical rainforest. Mixed with all kinds of evergreens are palms and ferns and hanging moss. It's a little surreal.

I am riding right beside the forest as the road barely fits between the forest edge and the beach on my left. I've got seventy-five miles to go to reach my next stop at Fox Glacier. It's all national parks and wilderness. It's also a lot of windy rain and swarms of no-see-ums.

The wind off the ocean usually keeps the bugs off me, but when the grade of the road slows me down to less than twelve miles per hour, the stingers attack. I can't figure out if one swarm is just following me or if they are just a continuous blanket over the coast.

The road takes a sharp turn to the east into the mountains and I leave my stinging friends behind. I cross the Whakapohai River and then come to the head of Lake Moeraki. Another deep blue wonder fed by a glacial river, reflecting the surrounding green mountains I'm climbing into.

An hour later, the road drops into a broad river valley and, as I cross the Paringa, I come to a large salmon farm. They have a café. I'm grateful for the fresh coffee but decide to pass on the salmon pancakes.

I'm crossing over rushing rivers regularly now, mostly on narrow wooden bridges with pull outs. The green mountains to the east are giving way to their taller snow-capped peaks, home of the glaciers that feed the rivers. But now the road swings back to the west and I'm running along the beach at Bruce Bay when disaster strikes.

Unknown to me, my left bike shoe has somehow lost a screw that holds a cleat in place. When I stop for a rest, that loose shoe cleat is hooked into the pedal and won't come lose. Result—I can't put my foot down when I stop and I fall over to my left and crash in the gravel still attached to my bike. Working my foot out of the shoe and releasing the shoe from my bike, I see the problem. I don't carry spare cleat screws. I have no choice but to get back on and ride with one foot attached and one not, a really awkward pedaling style.

After a few hundred yards, I don't think this is going to work. So by some kind of perverse reasoning, I decide this spot on the beach is perfect to try out the myth of the Sea of Man current. I drop my bike and slowly wade in.

Not so bad but ten yards out I can feel the current. As it gets up to my waist, I can really feel the pull. One more step and I'm a believer. Not yet ready to visit Tasmania, I dig in my feet and begin a slow slog back to shore. I keep my feet attached to the earth. No fool, I don't even try to swim.

Back on my bike in my one-shoe-attached-one-shoe-loose mode, I follow the road back up the mountains and down into river valleys before I finally reach the broad plain of the Cook River, also fed by plunging Fox River right off a huge glacier.

The guys in the gas station at Fox Glacier are like me. They don't carry spare shoe cleat screws. I'm out of luck. No choice but to keep going to the next town. A long, twisting, and now uncomfortable ride through more mountains and over more rivers finally dumps me out onto the Waiho River valley and the resort town of Franz Josef.

The snow-topped mountains above me are the Southern Alps of South Island and the source of the magnificent glaciers that draw tourists to this area.

The local glacier is immense, falling over ten miles from the mountains where it becomes a wide swath of gravel and rocks cut by the fast-running river of ice melt. I quickly find a bike shop where they can fix my shoe and tune my battered bike ,but not till the end of the day.

I've already clocked over ninety uncomfortable miles today and I'm ready to sit. I spot a bulletin board flyer about a glacier helicopter tour. With at least two hours to wait for my bike, I can't resist. I walk into the office but the tour is booked. I tell the guide I will give him half the cash now if he will let me sit here and read a book until it's time to go. If there are any no-shows, I get the seat. If not, he keeps the cash. An hour later, the guide grins and tells me I can sit in the co-pilot seat. Deal!

We fly over Mount Cook. At just over 12,000 feet, it's New Zealand's tallest. Then we land and walk across the snowfield where the glacier is born.

That night, I treat myself to a well-earned stay at the Franz Josef Lodge highlighted by perfectly done lamb, mint jelly, and an award-winning Syrah.

It's another morning of green mountains and crystal lakes but this time with both shoes working well. Once again, the mountain road drops me down into a broad plain scoured out by some ancient glacier and I am crossing farm fields when I come into the town of Whataroa. I spot a sign advertising jet boat tours of the last wild white heron grounds in New Zealand. Why not?

I try a repeat of my half-price offer. This time I don't have to wait. They're leaving now and I jump in. I immediately notice that every head on the boat is the same color as the herons. I am the youngest passenger by at least thirty years. Then the jet boat takes off.

We're flying up the Waitangitaona River, heading into the rain forest at the foot of the mountains. The last forty-three nesting pairs of New Zealand's great white herons live here. The boat flies over the water but makes very little sound as we glide into the forest. Suddenly, everything explodes in a blizzard of white. All the herons on earth seem to take off at once right under our nose. And settle down just as quickly. I think these birds have learned how to put on a show. In breeding season, we wouldn't get anywhere near this part of the river.

Back on my bike, I'm headed to Ross, an 1800s gold-mining town. Fifty miles of mountains, rivers, and valleys brings me into town just at dusk. Not wanting to search for campsites in the dark, I step into a likely-looking tavern in the 110-year-old Empire Hotel. The bar is jammed but I spot an empty stool next to a hippy-looking lady. I offer to buy her a beer for some camping advice.

Alice is a vagabond artist who travels the islands in her VW camper. She makes her comfy living selling sketches of historic places including old bars where she drinks for free. Six rounds later, we are great friends and she tells me to follow her. She is camped on the beach. I barely remember pitching my tent next to her VW.

Next morning, the heat of the sun and the sound of the surf wakes me up. Alone. Alice and her VW are gone without a story. I skip my stove, building a small fire and boiling water for my usual coffee and oatmeal. Followed by a cautious and quick head-clearing wade in my old friend, the Tasman Sea.

The rest of the morning is a long ride along the beach across miles of tidal flatlands. Until I come to a huge river delta at Hokitika. This is the biggest town I've been in since Queenstown and I'm uncomfortable in the congestion until I ride through it and stop for a quick roadside bite on the other side.

Back on the beach highway again, it's more miles of flat, easy riding with increasing oceanside development as I get farther north. By late afternoon, I reach another big river delta and a couple of good-sized towns, Graymouth and Blaketown. Same drill. Pedal through as fast as I can, stop, and grab a picnic to go.

Once I cross the Gray River, I'm in the Rapahoe Range Reserve. By late afternoon, I've followed a path out to the Point Elizabeth lookout. I'm just finishing my picnic and a long look at the calm-looking Tasman Sea when a local who says he's a miner sits down to chat.

Grif says he's never seen the sea look so still but warns me, "Don't even think about swimming." The currents, etc. I tell him I've been in twice already. He gives me a look that says I'm either a liar or a ghost and says goodbye.

I push on up the coast road which is getting much steeper and turning into more cliff than beach. If you've ever traveled California's Big Sur highway where the cliffs hang over the beaches, you know the feeling.

The sun is beginning it's long solstice set as I roll into Barrytown. Not wanting to miss out, I stop to buy a six-pack for tonight's camping. I'm headed another fifteen miles or so to a place called Punakaiki and it looks like I'll get there after dark. The beach here is famous for its blowholes and pancake rock formations.

Sure enough, I get to the beachside campground after everything is closed and pitch my tent between giant RVs, rustic cabins, and a few other tents. Dinner that night is beer and jerky, mostly beer.

177

At 8:00 a.m. I'm standing outside The Nifty Café waiting for its opening. Thirty minutes later, a ponytailed, hippy lady and her pre-teen daughter unlock the door. I am soon wrapped around two quiches and three coffees and eying a donut. As I'm describing my route to momma Toni, she fills me in on all the west coast hippy tribe I'll be meeting along the way. The first is at the studio next door. This is pretty normal on my bike trips where everyone finds the solo bike adventurer an oddity and somehow interesting to talk with.

I obligingly walk up the hill and meet Billy, another ponytail, sitting at his potter's wheel. Seems to be a recuring type. Behind the counter of his small shop is the alluring and mostly unbuttoned Rose. Somehow, I resist her sales pitch while admiring the views, one of which is miles of ocean from their 100-foot bluff.

Time to be on my way. I walk out and almost over a fellow bike tourer who was also steered to pottery by Toni's café. This is Bridget, a very fit-looking Kiwi from the North Island who is basically doing the reverse of my route. So, naturally, I ask her what to expect. Her reply, "Don't expect you'll make that, mate."

Now, I had planned just from reading to head north to Karamea and then cut east through the Tasman Reserve mountains along the famous Heaphy Track until I came out of the mountains on the east coast.

When I casually described that to Bridget, she just as casually replied, "I expect that's your road bike outside and it will never make a trail like that. Doubt you could do it on a mountain bike with big knobby tires. You'll be breaking spokes and mending flats every mile of the way. You ask me, you're only route across is Buller's Gorge."

I hate it when pretty girls are so much smarter than I am. But I usually listen. So, I decide to stay on the coast highway along Woodpecker Bay and then follow the highway east as I pass signs for Virgin's Flat and Cape Foulwind. Makes you wonder about local history. Now I'm going to be following the Buller River as it runs into the mountains. This is the lower Buller Gorge and I'll never forget it.

Remember when I came over a mountain pass on my way to Haast and got smacked down by headwinds? What goes around . . .

As I entered lower Buller Gorge, a tailwind like I'd never felt seemed to pick me up and push me up the grade. I was at twenty miles per hour and faster. Going uphill! An hour later, I hated to stop at Berlin's Café and Bar but it looked on my map like the only store for the next 100 miles and I needed supplies and beer for camp dinner that night.

I couldn't resist the smell of burgers and fries at the café grill, so, I sat at the bar for a late afternoon refuel. While I was asking the bartender about campsites between here and Inangahua Junction, where the mountain railroad crossed the river, an eavesdropper named Peter introduced himself and asked if that was my bike and tent parked by the door. Delighted to hear the affirmative, Peter told me his wife Joyce was an avid biker and I could come home with him, share some bike stories over supper, and sleep on their couch. He lived ten miles up the river.

I figured why not and bought two six-packs, one to share and one as a gift, and let Peter drop them in his truck. I started up the gorge to his place, expecting him to pass me along the way. I beat him home.

When I rolled in to Peter and Joyce's yard, Joyce came out with a question on her face. I explained I had met Peter and he invited me to dinner so we could talk biking. She was delighted and chatted away. Two hours later, I was running out of stories and interest in Joyce's when she asked me where I left Peter. When I said Berlin's bar, she got hysterical. Peter is an alcoholic and there's no telling where he might be with twelve beers in his truck. Just then, he pulled into the yard. He was fine. He threw the one remaining empty beer out his window.

It was quite a night. Peter insisted on sharing an old bottle of Tequila he had been saving and by then Joyce and I were both into her homemade wine and my beer. We all stumbled down to the Buller River to skinny dip, Peter swinging his naked butt on a rope swing over the Buller. We hiked back arm in arm, then scarfed down huge bowls of potato and wild onion homemade stew. I thought we had bonded but Joyce told Peter to show me where to pitch my tent in the yard.

Morning arrived with the noise of Peter's truck as he left for work. Joyce was up, too, with coffee and honey toast for my breakfast. Then she showed me her special railroad bike. It was an old ten-speed they'd rigged so it could run on one rail of a railroad track. They ran it up an abandoned rail line across the river where they maintained dozens of beehives in forest clearings bordered by manuka plants. The bees also pollinated the nearby fields of marijuana plants that Peter and Joyce harvested as well. The rail line was the only access in or out, so, their unique industry was well-hidden. I had to admire the ingenuity.

Joyce told me their weed was a popular product but their Manuka marijuana honey, thanks to the stoned bees, was the real cash cow. At that point, I was starting to feel the effect of the honey on my toast but couldn't resist when she offered me another slice. As well as a jar for the road.

If you ever wonder where all the hippies went, try South Island. They're all fine, living a sustainable life on the land. Pottery, carpentry, honey, weed, fishing, and guiding . . . somehow, they make it all work. And some, like Nadia, have an even better system.

I met Nadia the next day because I was looking for coffee. I was now on the upper Buller Gorge and enjoying my tailwind. Near a deserted town called Lyell, I spotted a lady feeding pigs in a pen near the road and stopped to ask her if there was anyplace up ahead for coffee and lunch. She told me I needed to see Nadia.

"About ten kilometers up, just after the big bend in the river, go over the iron bridge and look for a yellow farmhouse on the hill. That's Nadia's and she'll give you anything you want if you got cash."

Sure enough, I spotted the house and stopped at a gate. I didn't see anyone, so, I just yelled, "Nadia."

A young woman's voice answered, "What do you want?"

I answered, "Coffee and breakfast."

The reply was a simple, "Come on up." A beautiful college-age girl was waiting.

"Are you Nadia?"

"Nah, I'm BJ. Nadia's my mom. Come on in."

Sitting at a kitchen table are two forty-ish women, both breastfeeding babies. I recognized them because they were the same two who had been cruising in Berlin's Bar during happy hour two days before. Nadia introduces herself and I'm quickly seated at the table with a bowl of delicious granola and coffee with fresh-from-the-teat milk. I'm a little queasy at the description but I did see cows in the yard.

These ladies are real live-off-the-land farmers. There are chickens roaming everywhere. The roof is thatched with stalks. There are pigs and goats out in pens and BJ is home from a North Island ag school to work on fences during break. We're sitting on the porch and she explains Nadia's system.

"Mom's got nine babies so far and she's always laying for more. Each one brings a monthly welfare check and there's enough left over to keep the farm going. My payments stopped when I turned eighteen but this is still my home and I help out when I can. None of us is ever sure who the dad was but we've got a couple of moms here to raise us. You're a likely looking fellow. So. she'd probably give you a good price if you want to sleep over. I know she's got tonight open."

By now, I've finished two coffees with warm milk and I'm getting a little jumpy. Not just from the coffee. I smile at BJ and explain I've got to get to Picton on the coast to catch the ferry north by tomorrow and I'm running late already. I thank her and head to my bike before Nadia comes out to change my mind. I wondered if she would be trolling tonight at Berlin's.

Hippies. I don't think I could have been one. But then, I always regretted not going to Woodstock. I'm still thinking about Nadia and BJ as I passed through Murchison and on to a tavern in Owen River for lunch. I pulled out my map and realized I was going to be way ahead of schedule. I was running out of island. I had figured three additional days for the Heaphy Track crossing and now I was almost out of the mountains.

Still enjoying the friendly tailwind, I casually cruised to a pretty little alpine village called Saint Arnaud at the head of Lake Rotoiti. I splurged on another luxury room and dinner, celebrating one of my last nights.

I wake up regretting on starting my last leg ,an eighty-mile run to Picton where I will catch the Inter-Island Ferry to the North Island and my Auckland flight home. This top end of South Island is a broad peninsula split by coves and dead-end bays. At the end of one of these sits Picton, my ferry port.

The ride from Saint Arnaud is pleasant and uneventful, leaving the gorge at last and entering the Wairau River valley. Gradually, the mountains become low hills and I'm passing vineyards instead of glaciers but the biking gets easier and it's no less beautiful. All is well, the weather is lovely, and I'll probably make the noon ferry.

Just as I catch my first glimpse of the Sea of Woman, the rain begins. A few miles further and I get a flat tire. Patching in the rain is uncomfortable but I've done it before. A few miles more and I will do it again. Is my bike telling me we don't want to leave?

After my last patch, a young Maori guy pulls up on his bike. "Need any help, mate?"

" No, I've got plenty of time before I catch the five o'clock ferry and I have more patches." He smiles and waves. The sun comes out.

I will miss these Kiwis and their magical island.

I've done about 700 miles, biking a legitimate south end to north end from sea to sea, and someday I will come back to do the North Island.

See you then, mates.

CHAPTER 54
August 5, 2015—Newport, Oregon

"Dancing with loggers."

I was rolling pretty good the summer of 2015. Michelle and I spent some tourist weeks in the Middle East and then got back to the Iberian Peninsula to hike another part of the Camino de Santiago. But I was ready to hit the two-wheel road again.

My older friend Colin challenged me with a 300-mile ride down the Oregon Coast. If you've never seen it, a lot of people think it's the most spectacular coastline in the country.

The Oregon biking trail covers over 370 miles of long sandy beaches, tidal pools, capes, and headlands. The highlights are huge offshore rock formations called sea stacks that stand guard out in the waves like walls and turrets of ancient castles.

To hang out on these beaches, people in RVs and campers get to park in hotly-contested, reserved campsites. Amazingly, Oregon coastal parks all have unlimited hiker-biker campsites. Colin and I could just bike as far as our stamina allowed, then camp.

Colin was an accomplished biker but had never, as he said, tented. He's a city guy. I offered my hard-won experience plus my spare tent. We were ready to go. We met in Portland, then got a ride 130 miles west to the coast.

As we rode, Colin explained that if we could average fifty to sixty miles a day, we'd be in California in less than a week. I laughed and said that sounded easy. But thirty miles down the road, I was feeling weak and gassed. I should have admitted I hadn't trained. Instead, I made up some bullshit story about wanting to see Yachats, the next beach town, and suggested we knock off early.

We pulled in to the Yatel Motel, grabbed some Mexican food and beer, and enjoyed a sunset beach walk. I couldn't wait to hit my pillow.

Morning comes. I feel fine and shrug off my first day jitters. But I was wrong. Apparently, it's the multi-day jitters. Every day I struggle to make forty miles.

I wasn't sure I would even get to Florence, home of the famous Oregon Dunes with miles of sand-swept hills and valleys along the ocean. Ours was a parallel course of miles of hills along the ocean highway. It felt like the Tour de France but I wasn't wearing any yellow jersey.

I kept apologizing to Colin about my puzzling lack of fitness and he kept making jokes about me accidentally confusing my testosterone for estrogen. When we stopped to see the famous Three Sisters Rocks—those landmark sea stacks—Colin announced they now had a fourth sister . . . me! The next day, of course, begins a long, up and down section of highway that bikers call the Seven Devils. You can just imagine why and damned if it doesn't happen seven times.

A word here in my defense for anyone who thinks forty miles a day on Oregon 101 is easy. First of all, you share the road with everyone else. There is no bike lane and very little shoulder. Lots of huge logging trucks are in a big hurry. The wind blast when one of them sweeps by a foot from your left shoulder is an adventure by itself. But the highway is not the worst part.

The worst are the bridges and tunnels. Try riding your bike through a dark tunnel with no bike lane and all the trucks behind you pissed because you are not pedaling fifty miles an hour.

The bridges are a different challenge. Most have no bike lane, the shoulder just ends. Many are long, and some give you no choice but to get off and walk your bike along a drainage path. Or you can enjoy the affection you get on bridges that let bikers push a button and start yellow flashing lights that tell all the drivers to slow down for the bikers on bridge. Patience is not a virtue taught in Oregon schools.

But then, there are times like the day we pulled over in a place called the Samuel H. Boardman State Scenic Corridor. Twelve miles of pristine beach and coastline with a sample of everything from whale watching to the Devil's Punch Bowl—a natural, lava rock, infinity edge pool—and a little chunk of paradise called Secret Beach.

You hike down a thickly forested trail where you hear gulls and surf but you only get isolated rays of sun. Suddenly, it opens up and you are standing among sea stack rocks four stories tall. Turn a corner and Millers Creek is tumbling down a cliff in a spectacular waterfall into the ocean and the surf looks like ripples from where it falls. If you ran into hobbits or elves, they wouldn't seem out of place.

The days roll by in bursts of muscle agony and short breath but I keep pushing. Who needs to train?

A couple of nights we camp out on the beach, mindful that many of the beaches are open to buggies and jeeps driving through. We also enjoy campfires on the sand but are careful not to burn any of the legally-protected driftwood. We never saw any patrolling rangers.

We meet a wild assortment of bikers and hikers in our campsites each night. One of my favorites was a new college grad named Mike who was hiking the entire 370-mile Oregon stretch—more than 300 miles of which are on the beach with only about sixty or so forced on to roads by forests and cliffs. So Mike had to carefully time the high tides to plot his hiking and sleeping times. He said he'd made a few miscalculations, blocked from walking for a few hours until the tide receded. He was going to publish a guide for future tide walkers.

One morning in Coos Bay, we woke up to the smell of pancakes. Following our noses, we walked in to Mom's Kitchen where Mom herself took our order. Since Mom was a very fit-looking thirty-ish, I asked her about the name. That brought out an older Mom from the kitchen who said she'd been there thirty years and brought her daughter into the business. And then they both started chuckling when a round little gray-haired lady pushed through the kitchen door and asked, "Who wants to meet Mom?" Three generations and over fifty years, they've been greeting hikers and bikers coming down the trail. Simple story but a nice one.

By the time we passed through Brookings, we had been on the road for a week and just over 250 miles. Colin finally took mercy and told me I was done.

We pushed on over the California border and rolled into our final stop at Jedediah Smith Redwoods State Park. That last night we slept under trees over a thousand years old and I swore to Colin I'd never again subject him to such weak biking. Cocky, he said he didn't expect much from me. I had no comeback . . until I would school him in Cuba three years later.

We biked into Crescent City, California , sent our bikes home by UPS and drove a rental car to San Francisco. Someday I'm going back to that coast to do it right.

CHAPTER 55
October 28, 2015—Park City, Utah

"My heart knew before I did."

For nearly three years, I had once again enjoyed the benefits and enjoyment of my testosterone replacement treatment . . . and they were many.

But then I learned the term " congestive heart failure," or CHF.

Now as bad as that sounds, it doesn't mean your heart stops working. In fact, it means your heart is working much harder. Usually because there is something restricting the flow of blood. As your heart responds, the kidney joins in and retains more water and salt which builds up in your limbs and throughout your body. You become congested.

So here I was, Mr. TRT at the top of my game, notwithstanding my lack of exercise and suddenly I was getting short of breath, weak in the knees, swollen legs and, again, the urgent need to pee during the night.

My internist, Kim Scott, took about five minutes to diagnose me with CHF and put me to bed. Obviously, as I am writing this, I recovered. But this episode called in a full review of my somewhat exotic regimen of prescribed drugs and a few days later Dr. Bob asked me to come see him for a serious talk.

I had a feeling . . .

CHAPTER 56
February 1, 1987—Quito, Ecuador

"Skiing on lava."

J ust before Christmas in 1987, I was looking through a collection of old travel photos when I flipped over a shot of a beautiful snow-capped mountain with a perfect cone shape. I knew it immediately as Cotopaxi.

An icon in Ecuador. A landmark for the capital city of Quito. Not yet a clothing brand. One of the highest active volcanos in the world. It erupted for the first time in a century just a few months ago.

There was a time when I was one of the handful of people in the world who had climbed to the top of Cotopaxi and skied down.

It was the winter of 1987. I and two Park City buddies, Steve and Mike, decided for reasons I can't even remember that we were ready to climb mountains in the Andes that we could ski down. Naturally, we picked an active volcano.

Our planned first climb was Chimborazo. At more than 20,000 feet, it was actually the highest point on earth closest to the sun—and from the center of the earth--- thanks to proximity to the equator and the earth's somewhat elliptical shape. Our choice for skiing down, Cotopaxi, was a volcano often seen on postcards . . . one of more than fifty volcanos scattered across the Andes and all part of the legendary Ring of Fire.

We flew into Quito late on February 2. A taxi ride to our overnight hotel ---$3.50 a night with private bath and mattresses --- made us decide to skip dinner and, instead, opt for lots of hydration and sleep.

Quito's 9,500 feet altitude put a quick end to the sleeping as did the raucous early-morning noise of 2 million citizens ---apparently all walking below our windows.

The day in Ecuador starts at dawn for the overwhelmingly Indian population, all of them wearing bright colored ponchos and derby hats and most of them carrying goods to sell or just bought at the endless outdoor markets. Quito is so hilly it makes San Francisco seem flat and, combined with the altitude, it made a casual stroll to breakfast more like an expedition climb.

Guide companies with experience in Quito were tough to locate. A call to the best known, American Alpine Institute, got us a cordial recommendation to go away. There was no one available. So, we decided to self-guide. We had a few concerns.

There was no transportation to the mountains available. There was a real danger of altitude sickness and tainted water. These were the days when you dropped iodine in your water to make it safe. We had the shots and pills for malaria, typhoid, yellow fever, and everything else. Ecuador had just gone through a failed military coup and we weren't sure about the roads in the mountains. We had no maps.

I sat down with Mike and Steve and we made a plan. Twenty-four hours later we had rented a four-wheel drive Isuzu Trooper and packed it with food, climbing gear and our skis, and were on the road.

We decided to skip Chimborazo when we heard the roads were impassable, so, we drove thirty some miles south to Cotopaxi. Even with the four-wheel, we barely made it to the foot of the mountain. Now, we had to climb with all our gear up a thousand vertical feet to reach the Refuge. This was the mountain hut named for Jose Rivas—although we never learned why—built in 1971 at 15,800 feet to serve as a base camp for climbers before the final 4,000 feet climb to the summit.

We hike through fog, sleet, and snow and the altitude effects are brutal. We muscle and struggle to the Refuge and the first people we meet are three guides from the friendly American Alpine Institute enjoying some days off. They are amazed we came without a guide.

That night we can barely get through dinner before Mike is having a very rough time with altitude sickness. Pounding headaches, aching joints, and a racing pulse that's up over 105. His normal rate is mid-50s. Anything over 110 gets you rushed to lower altitude before you risk pulmonary or cerebral edema. My normal 60 is up to 100 but I have no aches and no pounding heart. Steve is at 85 and okay.

Nonetheless, we do some ratchet assist training at the Refuge. If one of us falls into a crevasse, such skill could prove the difference between life and death.

Hydration intensity is the only way to counter the altitude sickness effects other than retreating to lower altitudes. The lack of oxygen at high altitudes literally makes your blood run thicker. That's what causes the dizziness and joint aches. Drinking a lot of water, constantly, alleviates the problem somewhat.

That night we toss restlessly in our freezing sleeping bags. I now have the same headache as Mike.

The next two days, Friday and Saturday, we hydrate and acclimate as we practice glacier climbing. Although the climb to the summit is not especially steep, it's lots of ice and snow and crevasses. We use ice axes, crampons, and stay roped together as we cross deep cuts in the ice.

Sunday at midnight we begin the final ascent. We have to reach the top by dawn and then start down right away. The morning sun is hot and the snow gets loose and sloppy in a matter of hours. Nobody tries to hike down later in the day . . . and we are going to ski it.

I'm the third man on a three-man rope and there is no moon. As we cross the first glacier crevasse, I'm hyperventilating like no forty-year-old should.

It's pitch black except for the stars overhead and the lights of Quito off to the north. All I can see is our headlamps reflecting off the ice path for twenty feet ahead. I'm glad the other two are leading me up.

Six hours later—I know that because I've checked my watch every twenty minutes or so—we must be coming close to the last leg. It's a 400 -foot climb up the 70+ degree vertical, mixed ice and exposed rock of Yanascha Wall, which is part of the outer rim of the volcano cone. We meet up with the trio from AAI. They smile, noting our stashed skis.

An hour later, I am elated to climb over the lip and stand on the summit of Cotopaxi. The rising sun sets on fire the ice-capped Andes peaks all around us. It is just touching the dark Pacific Ocean, well over 100 miles to our west. We can see Chimborazo, Cayambe, and other volcano cones.

The sulfur fumes escaping from rocks all around us are nauseating. The AAI guides, now our friends, offer us coca leaves to chew and it works.

Below us, the crater stretches over 2,000 feet wide and it is 800 feet deep. Half of the crater rim is permanent ice that glows in the sun. The ancient natives hereabouts named this peak Cotopaxi, meaning necklace of the moon. European climbers first reached this peak in 1877. But somebody must have beat them. Because there's a small cone in the middle of the crater called Cabeza de Inca and the Incas reached power here around 1500, before the Spaniards took them down.

It's time to ski. We climb back down the wall. At this altitude, it takes us fifteen minutes just to wrestle our skis on. We launch into our first two turns and quickly realize the wind has carved the terrain into frozen pipes we can't turn across. It feels like skiing across a series of street curbs.

We drop down another 100 feet and we are ready to go. I am an expert skier on the mountains around Utah but Mike and Steve are masters. Even with the advantage of my Alpine touring skis and bindings, Mike and Steve use their Nordic skis and techniques to show me how it's done. And then they come to a sudden stop.

A hundred yards to our left looks identical to where we are standing. And just below it are the unmistakable signs of a very recent avalanche. Very carefully, we glide off to our right.

The surface as we descend is very smooth and consistent corn snow, a little hard, and we've all skied tougher without a thought of falling. But here the cost of a fall is a long, unchecked glide into a crevasse or a long plunge onto the very sharp rocks below.

If you fall, the only way to stop your slide is the self-arresting grip at the end of your ski pole. It's actually a miniature ice pick you use to jab into the snow and hang on. Unfortunately, only Mike has a pair of poles with these grips. He shares one with me at Steve's gracious insistence.

We ski one at a time. One skier remains behind and one below. Just in case.

Down we glide. I am thinking only a few hundred feet to go when suddenly everything is wet and gray. I slide to a stop. I can't see anything but I can

191

hear Mike. We can't hear Steve. We are on the steepest part of the run and I ask Mike if we should just wait for it to clear. He reminds me it could take hours and we'd never be able to stand on this steep section that long. We have no choice.

After fifteen long minutes, we decide to go. I've figured out that Mike is somewhere below me and I don't want to run into him. It clears just enough that I can see his shape and he tells me to ski on down past him and wait four or five turns below. I handle it OK and then he skis down to join me. We fist bump with big grins. It's getting clearer. Now, our shouting gets us an answer from Steve. He says he's near the end about 200 feet below us. He wants to know what's taking us so long. Mike grins and says, "Oh yeah," and drops down the mountain.

I tell myself this is no different than thousands of turns I've made down dozens of icy runs and that I'm a damn good skier. I can handle this. And what the hell, the worst I'll do is slide on my ass the last hundred feet and stop. I launch into the gray soup.

Eight turns and I'm there. Steve and Mike greet me with backslaps and handshakes and I can't stop shaking and slapping them back. We are whooping and laughing, exhilarated, and maybe just a little relieved. Maybe a lot relieved.

An hour later, we are back at the hut. No one can recall people who have actually skied down Cotopaxi before. Our guide friends confirm it. They take our snapshots to put on the wall.

We toast our trip as a great success and the basis of some incredibly exaggerated stories when we get home. I decide I like this adventure travel stuff and vow to keep doing it the rest of my life.

Almost twenty years later, an avalanche wiped out the hut and killed a dozen skiers. I hear it's been rebuilt.

CHAPTER 57
December 19, 2015—Los Angeles, California

"Not exactly Santa . . . "

My early Christmas present in 2015 came during an LA visit with not-so-jolly Dr. Bob and it was nothing I had wished for. Two months ago, Dr. Bob ordered me off TRT because of my heart problem.

Now, he told me my days of TRT dancing were over indefinitely. I had to become virtually cancer-free before he would consider it again.

As Dr. Bob said, I had experienced too many setbacks and I had to acknowledge I already had my three strikes.

But you know, I am a stubborn and determined man.

I would continue searching for the path that would lead me to some yet undiscovered solution. That small but resilient cancer that refused to let go of my battered prostate was not going to win.

Technology was rolling out new breakthroughs all the time. Why not one for the boys ?

CHAPTER 58
March 30, 2016—Maui, Hawaii

"Fifty years ago I was a decent surfer."

The last of 2015 had ended with a thud. First, it was my bout with congestive heart failure, followed by another knockout when staunch supporter Dr. Bob delivered the unexpected bad news that I would have to end my TRT regimen for the foreseeable future.

As the days rolled into spring, I had one of my what-the-hell moments and decided what I needed was a big vacation in Hawaii with all the family. Between Michelle and me, that meant a family group of twelve headed to a week on Maui.

The sun was warm, the water was Hawaiian blue, and the white sand beach was under my feet as my grandson, Henry, and I ran toward the surf on our first day.

Back in my college days, I worked every summer at Ocean City, Maryland and spent many happy hours being a bodysurfer of first rank. This was the lesson I was going to give Henry that day.

As I splashed into the warm ocean to get out to where the waves were breaking, I turned back to see what was delaying my hopefully not-too-timid grandson.

Do you remember that movie, *Home Alone*? And the famous image of the boy with his huge eyes and wide open mouth about to scream?

That same expression was on my grandson's face as I heard him yell, "Papa, stop! Don't!"

The next thing I knew, I was suddenly being lifted high in the air as the ocean suddenly swelled up and then it smashed me face-down into the rough sandy bottom.

Stunned and choking, I got my feet under me and struggled to stand up. I was dazed, bewildered, and stumbling as Henry screamed and Michelle—who had seen the whole thing—came running into the water to hold me up. "My God! That wave came out of nowhere. One minute you were standing in waist-deep water and then a wall came up behind you!"

We figured out later it was like a rogue wave caused by conflicting currents. Little did I know at the time, but I was one of dozens of surfing disasters in the islands that day. The doctor who treated me at the hospital said I was his fifth bodysurfer of the morning . . . one of whom was now paraplegic.

I know I like to brag about unexpected adventure, but this one surprised me with cracked C1 and C2 vertebrae. I spent the next three days in Maui Memorial in traction, waking up often for a quick check to make sure my fingers and toes were still moving. It took two weeks of recovery before I could fly home.

I couldn't move my neck, of course, and for the next three months had to wear a head cage every day and night to stay immobilized. Years later, I still have the jerky moves of a chicken. And I gave up bodysurfing.

CHAPTER 59
October 7, 2016—Palm Springs, California

"The times, they are a-changin' . . . "

In the past twelve months, I've suffered and recovered from CHF . . . lost my TRT regimen on doctor's orders . . . cracked two vertebrae in the Hawaiian surf and worn a head cage . . . been humiliated on a simple west coast bike trip by a good buddy . . . and wondered if I would ever get back to the rugged lifestyle I loved.

So you can understand that when a chance came along to turn back the clock a bit, I jumped.

It was called Desert Trip, a rock festival to recall the legendary Woodstock of half a century ago, planned to coincide with the famous Coachella festivals in the desert outside Palm Springs.

The affectionate nickname was Oldchella because the music acts were all legends from the twentieth century and the target audience was aging yuppies and raging boomers. Michelle looked at me funny when I said we'd fit right in. She was a baby when I missed Woodstock.

Luckily, we scored some very scarce tickets and hooked up our Happy Camper mini-trailer to the car and set off for our camp spot in the desert. Well, actually it was next door to the green fields of a posh polo club where my old friend, Rick had played . He laughed when I called it a desert.

But we settled in for a weekend of nostalgia, kicked off on Friday night by a concert by none other than Bob Dylan. Dressed all in black, he took us back through all his great songs of the past decades. Listening to those anthems, it came as no real surprise when the word spread that he had just been awarded the Nobel Prize. Bob, however, never mentioned it.

Mellowing out in the glow of the Dylan magic, we were jolted to life by the familiar opening chords of Jumping Jack Flash as Mick Jagger and the Stones electrified the audience like no others can.

You know all the songs, even if Keith Richards can't remember the words. By the end of the night, we were dancing our asses off up by the stage beside Emma Stone and Woody Harrelson.

After a long day's recovery, we headed back for the Saturday night concerts, led off by the unique voice of Neil Young and his advice to us all to Keep On Rockin'. He was in great form that night and in equally good humor, especially when he looked out at the audience and dedicated his next song to, "You all know who you are," and brought us to our feet with Old Man. When he closed out with a full desert moon over his shoulder, singing Harvest Moon, it couldn't have worked better.

And then we were jolted out of our serenity by the clashing, all-too-familiar opening chords of Hard Day's Night as Paul McCartney bounded on stage. Two hours and many favorite songs later, Paul led 80,000 of us through the closing chorus of Hey Jude and said, "And now we finally get to someone under fifty!" as he brought a young singer named Rhianna onstage to join him. It might have been her first US appearance.

Sunday was another long, restful day strolling around watching all the other festival activities you always see at Coachella. It was highlighted by a monster foosball game with elastic banded people replacing those plastic players on normal game tables . . . like a miniature, enclosed, walled arena football game. You'd have to see it.

And then came the Sunday night finale.

First on stage, Roger Daltry, Peter Townsend, and The Who. As usual, Daltry brought the crowd to a frenzy, proving that Jagger is not the only one with all the moves. Townsend caught the desert mellow by not smashing any guitars and we all went wild with what seemed like a solid twenty minutes of Pinball Wizard.

And then, to close out the weekend, Pink Floyd's Roger Waters launched a spectacular sound, light, and video show of all their great hits, concluding with an equally long and never-ending version of The Wall.

We were exhausted. And I think Michelle now gets my music.

CHAPTER 60
December 8, 2016—Los Angeles, California

"Now that's more like Santa . . . "

By the end of 2016, I was again pissed and depressed about my low level of strength and stamina thanks to my continuing Estinyl program and pathetically low testosterone level. Even though my years of fighting this cancer had preserved all my precious D.U.P.E. functions, I was a long way from the virile, energetic man I wanted to be.

On top of that, I was still recovering from that bodysurfing head plant in Hawaii, regularly training to overcome the resulting concussion and balance problems.

So I was not feeling the holiday cheer when I went to visit Dr. Bob in LA this year. Even worse, it was my sixty-ninth birthday.

Dr. Bob amazed me with an unexpected gift—a proposal that he would support a relatively new technology for targeted focal prostate cancer treatment called HIFU. If it worked, he would put me back on TRT!

Dr. Bob smiled as I immediately started to google HIFU on my phone. He told me to relax.

HIFU is high-intensity focused ultrasound. It has been around for over twenty years and has treated over 65,000 men, mostly in Europe. Canadian doctors have been using it for ten years. Bob explained that our FDA had recently approved it for US use.

Basically, HIFU was the long-awaited rifle shot that could target just the bad guys and leave the good guys still functioning. It seemed to me that a focal cancer treatment, much like women's lumpectomies in lieu of mastectomies, might work. It used pinpoint focusing of sound waves to thermally destruct prostate bound cancer cells revealed by radiology and biopsies. It could also ablate other types of tumors.

But, of course, there was a catch. Dr. Bob insisted that I would need one of the newly-available C-11 isotope body scans before my HIFU procedure to show that my cancer was, indeed, confined to my prostate. And after HIFU, I would need another of those invasive and excruciating biopsies. Dr. Bob and Shahrooz felt my years of cancer management protocol had likely wiped out any cancer outside my prostate. The C-11 scan could verify this.

I'm in. Whatever. I go into full-bore mode.

CHAPTER 61
March 5, 2017—Culver City, California

"By the time I got to Phoenix . . . "

Catch-22 had nothing on prostate treatments. Dr. Bob says no TRT without HIFU. Dr. Bob says no HIFU without a C-11 scan. The only place in America doing C-11 scans now is the Mayo Clinic.

The Mayo Clinic is only doing C-11 scans for patients with prior surgery or radiation and a PSA at 2.0 and rising. They disqualify me on both counts. Which is too bad because they did the scan for free.

Before I go berserk, my 24/7 research mode uncovers an announcement that a new company called Phoenix Molecular Imaging (PMI) has launched their own C-11 program. Theirs is too new a program to be covered by insurance companies that, like the FDA and God, move in mysterious ways. But if I want to pay $3,000, they will fit me in at the end of the month.

C-11 isotopes can detect prostate cancer cells outside the prostate because PCa cells attract fat. The C-11 isotope clusters around fatty acids.

The scan goes well. I fly home on April Fool's Day. While still on the runway, I receive PMI's message that I have no cancer outside my prostate!

For the first time in over eighteen years, I can show uncontestable proof that my prostate cancer has not spread beyond my precious but beleaguered gland. In other words, I do not need any treatment that goes beyond my prostate. I'm eligible to receive HIFU

The armies of Jim are ready for the final battle!

CHAPTER 62
May 1, 2017—Los Angeles, California

"High five for the HIFU man."

I am on my way to meet Dr. Xavier Sainte, one of a handful of urologist surgeons in America with expertise in the as-yet-not-widely-practiced art called HIFU. I was referred to Dr. Sainte by Dr. Bob's long-time associate and my trusted advisor, Dr. Shahrooz Eshaghian.

A urologist! The very cancer specialist type I'd studiously avoided for more than eighteen years. But HIFU requires a urologist surgeon and Bob and Shahrooz are internal medicine guys who do not operate.

Dr. Shahrooz clued me in that Dr. Sainte and his bedside manner are not always an immediate charmer but there was no doubt about his skills.

Did you ever see the movie, *Doc Hollywood*? During the story, the lead character played by Michael J. Fox is lured to Hollywood with an offer too good to resist by an arrogant and immensely successful plastic surgeon played by George Hamilton. The Hamilton doctor is astounded that Fox's doctor character ultimately declines . . . but the audience is not surprised.

Now, you can imagine how my first meeting with Dr. Sainte goes. He looks like he assumes I know I am lucky to be sitting in front of him. I assume he will be impressed by my years of hard-won expertise in prostate cancer treatments . . . including the relatively unknown HIFU.

Those were all wrong assumptions.

Within five minutes of hearing my long story, the much-younger Dr. Sainte tells me, "If you were my father, I would advise you to remove your entire prostate as soon as possible."

Having just described my eighteen-year struggle to keep my prostate, I barely avoid telling Dr. Sainte where he can shove his advice. Instead, I politely but firmly tell him I am here to see him so I can keep as much of my prostate as I can and that I thought he was the man who could do it.

201

After a few seconds of silent staring, he gives me a tight smile and says, "Let's get you started."

I let out my breath and say, "Thank you. I appreciate that."

His smile widens as he says, "But first, let's get you set up for your biopsy."

I groan and nod my head. His staff schedules me for a July 6 biopsy.

CHAPTER 63
July 10, 2017—Glasgow, Scotland

"A lovely summer stroll across Scotland."

There's not a word of truth in the quote above. I spent six days hiking around Scotland and I never saw a ray of sun or an easy path. I've probably been wetter, for sure I've been colder, but seldom so much of both at the same time.

I'd like to blame it all on my friend, Colin. He's a little shorter, a little younger, and a travel buddy of mine with a thatch of white hair and the acerbic wit of the ex-film critic he is. But hiking across Scotland in July was my whim, so, at best, he's an unindicted co-conspirator.

We landed in Glasgow with not much more than our favorite trail running shoes and the daypacks we'd challenged each other to pack under ten pounds. Compare that to the suitcase you took on your last week's vacation.

Our timing sucked. We had a seventeen-hour Glasgow overnight because we just missed our connection to our launch point at Fort William, which is further north.

So what can we do with all that free time? I could tell you that what happens in Glasgow stays in Glasgow . . . but then you'd miss the story about lawn bowling.

Turns out our B&B near the University of Glasgow was across the street from the public lawn bowling pitches, enthusiastically supported by the local LGBT community. I won't bore you with the inside lore of lawn bowling but one fact you should know is that the ball is purposely lop-sided, so, it never goes where you point it. Which led to all kinds of inappropriate jokes from bystanders about my inability to go straight. You had to be there.

My loose goal with Colin is to walk coast to coast across Scotland. But before we can take the first step, a lively young Scottish lass we meet in a Glasgow pub persuades us we can't leave without seeing the town's famous orrery.

What is an orrery? Turns out I actually know. Because in the Newpark Town Center neighborhood I built in Park City I designed and constructed a million-dollar sun calendar for its central plaza and amphitheater. An orrery is a three-dimensional model of our solar system. The one in Glasgow is huge, it fills a room. It shows all the planets suspended in motion around the sun like a giant mobile. Why they have one in the middle of the Highlands, I never learned. Blew me away. Travel. Learn. Be surprised.

We're up early the next morning to catch our bus for the 100 mile ride to Fort William. The scenery is astounding, rolling past Loch Lomond and up the valley known as the Land of Giants. Misty mountains, sparkling lakes, glacier cliffs, dark forests, and waterfalls. We wind along the shore of Lake Katrine, the setting for Sir Walter Scott's, *The Lady of the Lake*. We spot Dumbarton Castle and stop in the picturesque village of Glencoe.

There are tourists with cameras every place you can stop a car. A reminder to me that I might have guessed mid-July is high tourist season.

In Fort William, most people visit the famous Ben Nevis distillery. Colin says we should not miss the Harry Potter train . . . a real-life nineteenth century Jacobite steam train, one of the few remaining in the world, that's featured in the movies. We decide to pass on both.

We are now in the Highlands. Looming above us is the original Ben Nevis, the tallest mountain in the British Isles. It marks the crossroads for two famous hiking routes, the West Highland Way and the Great Glen Way (GGW). It's the Great Glen Way that we will follow some seventy miles to Inverness and beyond.

Rain, mist, and fog pretty much limit our view to the path ahead. It's said that summer in Scotland is usually a couple days in July. We missed them. You wonder why the peak of the rainy, cold season would also be the peak tourist season. I suspect it may be because Scotland never has a warm, sunny season.

My other surprise was the GGW itself. It runs directly northeast from Fort William along a chain of Lochs and the famed Caledonian Canal. So, I expected your basic largely flat hiking path along the banks.

What we got was an up and down mix of forest paths, old drovers trails, former commando training tracks, and towpaths . . . plus an undulating up and down climb totaling 6,000 vertical feet. For most of the first seventeen miles or so, we saw no one else on the path. But we finally came to a highlight.

The Moy Swing Bridge, the last canal bridge of its kind in the whole UK.

When this Caledonian Canal was built over two hundred years ago, land owners whose property would be split by the canal demanded and won a crossing bridge in perpetuity.

What they got was a forty-foot long iron bridge which has two halves that swing together to form a single span across the canal. The bridge-keeper cranks the halves into position by hand. And, yes, the bridge-keeper has to row across the canal to operate one span at a time.

We learned most of this talking to Andrew, the bridge-keeper, who also lives in the 200-year-old cottage by the bridge. He said he didn't get much demand to open the bridge these days and it could get a bit lonely after tourist season. Not surprisingly, there didn't seem to be a Mrs. Andrew.

Our visit was a bright spot in Andrew's day, so, he graciously allowed both Colin and me to try cranking the bridge into place while he took some photos for his collection. We didn't ask.

After that excitement, a couple of phone calls revealed that every accommodation for miles around was taken . . . those pesky tourists again plus my reservations about reservations. So our friend Andrew, called Jock, the local taxi man, to run us eight miles east to grab the last room in the surprisingly-excellent Roybridge B&B.

Next morning, we cheat. Instead of going back to where we stopped south of Gairlochy, we have Jock take us five miles north of the town. Our rationale is driven by hard fact. Our now precious reservation for the next night's lodging is in Fort Augustus. This detour cheat will put us within twenty miles, about our maximum day's travel in this weather.

We step out of our warm taxi into monsoon rain and a dark forest path. Luckily, the weather breaks and sun peaks through soon after, as we start to cross a broad meadow. I'm puzzled to hear a low, throbbing buzzing just as the sun highlights thousands of bright yellow bumblebees busy pollinating acres of purple wildflowers.

It's an amazing, unexpected sight. And the bees turn out to be the only living creatures we see until we reach Fort Augustus. Where have all the tourists gone? Of course, I'd discovered long ago that a short hike away from anywhere that driving ends eliminates 90 percent of tourists on foot.

By the time we reach Caledonia Cottage, it is dark and late and we are wet and tired. Answering our knock, landlady Sheila—ancient and on a crutch—scolds us for being three hours past check-in. Colin decides he is offended and keeps muttering as we grab a late meal at the only open pub.

I go off to dry my clothes and collapse while Colin stays for the lively banter. The next morning, Sheila again has to wait for us, this time for breakfast, but she is all smiles, and cheers us on to a gorgeous day. Colin and his hangover are still offended.

Two days of flatland hiking has added to our confidence, so we decide that even our late start shouldn't keep us from detouring up the High Route. It's an alternate path through the mountains that overlooks Loch Ness and we can't resist.

Eight miles and a lot of vertical later, we agree it's beautiful, wet, and more than enough. We climb back down to loch level and I find a phone in the village of Invermoriston. Miraculously, the Lochside Hostel is only five miles away and they will hold their last room for us. All we have to do is trek up and down a last 1,000 vertical feet.

We are soon sitting in the best seats for a view of Loch Ness that we can imagine.

Our hostel is a gem. The lounge features two roaring fireplaces, an Italian biker playing the piano, and two dozen guests from everywhere but America. But we are the only hikers.

Like hostels all over the world, Lochside featured a big community kitchen where everyone brought their own food and cooked their own meals. Our room was small and clean and we shared the single bathroom with a half-dozen others. I'm a big fan of hostels. They are simple on purpose and they do the job without the bullshit.

Later that night in front of the fire, Colin and I agree that nearby Drumnadrochit will make a good end to our forty-five mile, three-day journey. Once you've seen half of the long and endless Loch Ness, you've seen all you need to see.

The next day we leisurely savore our last leg and happily climb into a taxi for the short drive to Inverness airport and a quick flight to our next destination—the mysterious Orkney Islands.

Ten miles beyond the northern tip of Scotland, there is an archipelago of some seventy islands where people have been living for over 6,000 years. I have no idea why. Most are tiny, most are bare of trees, and the surrounding waters offer some of the fiercest winds and currents in the North Sea.

Neolithic people lived there and left stone archeological puzzles that are a main industry today. Tribes of ancient Picts—the blue-tattooed people who fought everyone from Arthur to Caesar—ruled until AD 800. That's when hundreds of Vikings, land-starved across the sea in Norway, decided the week-long sail to the Orkneys made the flat, fertile fields a candidate for a good homestead.

Today, the Viking influence is everywhere and Orcadians speak a dialect that sounds vaguely familiar to both Scots and Norwegians.

We landed in Kirkwall, the largest and only town on the main island. About 17,000 live here. The next biggest island is home to less than 500. Our goal across island is the picturesque village of Stromness and Brinkies Guest House. The weather is near freezing and typically windy. But lodge owner Jevonne makes our stay warm and cozy.

We recall that fondly the next day as Jevonne's assistant, Laura ,drives us out to the famous ruins of Skara Brae with a bracing nine-mile hike back to town. Or so we thought.

Skara Brae is known as Scotland's Pompeii. It's a remarkably preserved Stone Age village which was apparently suddenly overrun by storm waves and sand as people hurriedly fled, dropping everything to run—just like

Pompeii—and leaving a fascinating record of life in 3000 BC. Think of Egyptian pyramids and Sumerian temples at about the same time.

We were properly awed and ready to hike back home for dinner. That's when a bemused Orcadian bystander mentioned that Laura's estimated nine-mile hike is really more like fifteen. We have no choice.

There is no path. So we strike south across farmers' plowed fields and rolling meadows, observed by hundreds of nonplussed sheep. Eventually, we come to cliffs overlooking the sea and follow the coastline south, hoping for a bend to the east and a way home to Stromness.

At times, barbwire fencing runs to the cliff edge and we have no choice but to climb over or crawl under. Neither works very well and you've all seen the comedic results in movies. Colin is not amused. Until the rabbit hole.

The tall grass that borders the cliff edge conceals where rabbits have dug four-foot deep holes just waiting for an aging American hiker. My right leg disappears down one. I think it's only because I am so tired that I collapse at once. Any energetic forward momentum would have probably snapped my leg.

Colin's laughs startle the sheep as I try over and over to climb out. But with one leg trapped so high above the other, I have no leverage. He relents and pulls me out.

Even with the unexpected adventures, it's a spectacular hike along the cliffs ---all wind and waves crashing and gulls shrieking. Eventually, the coast does turn to the east and we are thinking we are doing OK. No need to worry about darkness because summer in the Orkneys is when night barely comes.

We think we've come at least ten miles when we spot a road coming close to the cliffs and there's a car at the vantage point. Now, we start to hint to each other at asking for a ride but neither wants to be the one to surrender. We approach a young couple who are obviously tourists. Hearing about our unexpectedly long walk, they offer to give us a ride. We are quickly persuaded.

Two minutes down the road, Colin notes that the meadows to our right look remarkably manicured and he jokes about sheep mowing. The couple look around and laugh, "Oh, you mean the golf course?" Turns out we have hiked nearly the whole fifteen miles and had nearly reached Stromness's country club. A few minutes later, they drop us off in town with a wave and a smile.

After an evening of regaling Jevonne and an embarrassed Laura with our misadventures, we are up early the next morning to accept another ride with Laura to another ancient island wonder.

This is called the Ring of Brodgar and is a familiar-looking henge or ring of standing stones, similar to the one far to the south in England. This ring dates to 2500 BC, as old as the pyramids, and is buzzing with dozens of archeologists and hundreds of students, all busily sweeping away centuries.

Nearby is the oldest henge in the British Isles called the Standing Stones of Stenness. Like the much younger Stonehenge, the Standing Stones are huge dolmens weighing tons, placed in a careful circular pattern that is tied to rituals that would have occurred here as early as 3100 BC.

This time we catch a ride home. Comfortably riding along, we wonder at the oddity of such incredible monuments to human endeavor, stuck here on these tiny nondescript islands at the edge of the world. But we agree they are damn well worth the walk.

CHAPTER 64
July 29, 2017—Los Angeles, California

"I'm getting tired of the good news, bad news."

The bad news: Last night Shahrooz called me and told me my tumor is now a Gleason 9. They don't get much worse. He didn't want me to see Sainte without that warning. When I sit down with Dr. Sainte today, he starts:

Bad news: "Before we go over everything, I want to do an in-office, transrectal ultrasound scan."

The good news: "We can view the results while you're here."

The good news: My prostate right lobe is cancer-free, which is lucky because my right lobe is too full of calcium deposits that will block the HIFU focus.

The bad news: My cancerous left lobe has a few calcium deposits that must be removed in a routine pre-HIFU procedure.

A Gleason 9 tumor is like walking around with a time bomb up your butt.

All I want to know now is how soon I can get the HIFU and kill it. I now understand all those guys who said "Just get the damned cancer out."

Dr. Sainte says he'll have the needed approvals in a few weeks. It's complicated. But first, he needs me in for that pre-HIFU procedure to decalcify my targeted left lobe. We set it up for early August.

CHAPTER 65
August 15, 2017—Los Angeles, California

"No such thing as quick . . . "

D r. Sainte's routine procedure to decalcify my left prostate lobe is not pleasant but I get through it and am ready to talk about surgery dates.

Not so fast.

The after-effect of the decalcifying is that I must have a penal catheter inserted. And keep it there for the next two weeks. If you think that sounds painful and inconvenient, multiply by ten. I will never do this again.

I come back after the longest two weeks of my life, and the damn thing is removed.

The good news: Dr. Sainte confirms he can use the much less painful and obtrusive suprapubic catheter when I get HIFU. High five!

The bad news: What I have just experienced will take thirty days to heal. Dr. Sainte schedules a tentative surgery date for late September.

CHAPTER 66
October 15, 2017—Park City, Utah

"FDA red tape is killing me."

A lthough HIFU was finally approved by the our nation's FDA in 2015 only nine years after the rest of the world, that's only two years ago in FDA time . . . "Don't rush me."

They are having a hard time clearing me because I am a senior on Medicare.

That's right. The very age group most in need of effective prostate cancer treatments is the last group they are moving to qualify. And only one hospital has achieved Medicare HIFU clearance.

The agonizing wait is killing me, I decide. So throwing patriotism and financial prudence aside, I bolt for Canada where HIFU has been routine for years.

On October 10, 2017 my selected Canadian surgeon and I speak at length and he promptly schedules me for surgery on October 24. I immediately wire his Maple Leaf HIFU my $25,000 deposit.

Humming O Canada, I call Dr. Sainte's office and leave word I cannot wait any longer and I will be heading north in nine days.

Five days later, I get a late-night phone call. It's Dr. Sainte. He tells me I am making a big mistake by going to Canada. He lobbies hard for me to use him, claiming his equipment is much more precise and that he is, after all, the surgeon my own team suggested.

Dr. Sainte reminds me we have agreed on my preferred suprapubic catheter and that we have projected a less than 20 percent loss of tissue, which should mean I can escape the D.U.P.E. effect and walk out a happy man.

Then Dr. Sainte guarantees me a November 1 date with full approval from the FDA and Medicare.

I bite. And when I call Maple Leaf to cancel, they are a pleasant surprise when they offer me almost a full refund. I am counting the days until November 1.

CHAPTER 67
November 1, 2017—Los Angeles, California

"Another day that will live in infamy."

I wake up from surgery and it feels like I have lived through a sneak attack. That sharp pain I feel in my groin area is a penal catheter! The very thing I vowed to never endure again and the exact thing Dr. Sainte swore not to use.

The surgery authorization papers I signed specified a suprapubic catheter.

But that is not the worst. I just don't know it yet. Not for ten more days.

CHAPTER 68
November 10, 2017—Los Angeles, California

"We got it all . . . ?"

I am back in Dr. Sainte's office to have the damned penal catheter removed. The post-op pain meds have had me in a daze for the last ten days.

I barely protest when his nurse tells me the after-effects of the procedure will likely mean weeks of diapers and pads until I regain some control.

Dr. Sainte pops in for a quick look and seems surprised when I ask how my HIFU went. "You were still groggy when I talked to your wife. There was more cancer than we thought . . . both lobes. I showed her the image. But, congratulations. I am pretty sure we got it all. "

Michelle had related this surprising new turn but I wanted a lot more detail. This was not what I had expected. I had a lot of questions and I needed answers.

Dr. Sainte says my scans look good but it's too early, I need time to heal, and that we should wait until we have the next biopsy. We will go over everything in our next visit . . . and he rushes out to another surgery.

So the Gleason 9 tumor is gone and, except for the catheter problems, I am assuming some kind of success. I just wish I felt good enough to celebrate. I also prepared myself for months of urine leaking due to the extra prostate tissue he HIFUed or the penal catheter error.

The next day, I typed out a lengthy list of questions and demands for answers. But I ultimately decided not to send it to Dr. Sainte. I can't change anything anyway. I decided to embrace what gains I had and wait.

CHAPTER 69
February 10, 2018—Los Angeles, California

"Why aren't we celebrating"

I am back in LA again for my official follow-up with Dr. Sainte which got delayed by his tight surgery schedules and holiday travel plans. I also wanted to coordinate this with a same-day visit to Dr. Bob's office to discuss my hoped-for next steps toward resuming TRT.

The meeting with Dr. Sainte starts out tense as I bitterly complain about his decision to use the forbidden penal catheter. I had made myself very clear and our notes, as well as our pre-surgery sign-off, confirmed his suggestion and agreement to use the suprapubic alternative.

Dr. Sainte's answer is that it was a decision made in surgery for reasons he dealt with at the time and it had to be his call. He understands my being upset at the weeks of pain and diaper pads but assures me it will eventually heal.

Dr. Sainte says what's really important is what the next biopsy shows. He feels confident he removed the Gleason 9 tumor as well as the other cancer he didn't expect . . . but suggests the wise course is to get the biopsy done and deal with what the facts show.

I can't argue with that. Our visit time is up and we are due at Dr. Bob's office but I leave feeling like there are questions hanging in the air.

As we drove to my meeting with Dr. Shahrooz Eshaghian, Dr. Bob's associate, Michelle turned to me at one point and said, "It feels like Sainte doesn't really listen . . . "

After a brief review meeting with Shahrooz with me expressing my white-hot anger and he suggesting I focus on results . . . "Jim, you've got to feel good knowing that tumor is gone," we agreed he would handle any further conversations with Dr. Sainte. And I should not see him again other than for the planned May 1 biopsy to verify there's no cancer left in my prostate or what's left of it.

A three-month delay was required to allow healing and time for any residual cancer to emerge.

The good news: If my biopsy and MRI show me to be cancer-free, we can consider resuming my TRT as Shahrooz promised.

Michelle and I left for home, knowing there was nothing I could do to undo the past, and we resolved to be patient as we awaited the biopsy in three and the facts, all in three months.

That lasted for all of two days. Michelle and I reviewed the precise notes she had taken through all of my conversations with Dr. Sainte. And I got mad all over again . . . especially every time I had to change my diaper pad.

I felt I had been betrayed by some kind of an arrogant dismissal of my needs. I knew there had been no misunderstanding.

CHAPTER 70
May 1, 2018—Los Angeles, California

"So, am I cancer-free?"

In early April, I went in for an MRI scan which Dr. Eshaghian required in addition to the forthcoming biopsy. I was told it showed no trace of cancer.

On May 1, after sufficient healing time, I went back to Dr. Sainte's surgery center for the official post-op biopsy. I was again told it showed me to be cancer-free!

But I wanted more than just a one-line statement. I wanted to know what went on in my surgery, what decisions were made and why, and what was his comment about " . . . more cancer than we thought."

I wanted a discussion and closure with Dr. Sainte. Finally, a few weeks after my repeated calls, he surprised me with a callback.

Dr. Sainte quickly went right into a justification. He said the ultrasound radiology he used during surgery was much better than what he had used in his office, and that it showed much more cancer than he showed me on his office ultrasound radiology back on July 29, 2017.

In surgery, Dr. Sainte said he saw cancer in my right prostate lobe---the one that had repeatedly been shown to be cancer-free through biopsy and regular imaging for eighteen years, and which his own July 6, 2017 biopsy said was cancer-free and too full of calcium to be treated with HIFU.

He added that it was his midst-of-surgery decision to HIFU almost my entire prostate. I thought this was absurd.

No doctor would ever say a radiology image is more meaningful than an actual biopsy of tissue. This was not a crisis moment. Sainte could have stopped and given me a chance to decide.

Dr. Sainte also said that even my prostate left lobe had a larger diseased area than the 15 percent he'd agreed to HIFU.

How could this be and how could he be so certain?

Biopsy determines the actual presence of cancer. Biopsy always takes precedence over images. And how could his equipment show images so dramatically different?

A year later, I recall how stunned I was to hear a University of Chicago cancer expert who was helping me on this book exclaim, "That doctor really screwed you. Prostate cancer is slow-growing cancer and could not have spread from a small spot on one lobe to take over your entire prostate during the 117 days between your biopsy and surgery dates."

I will also never forget the slight surprise I heard in Sainte's voice during that last phone call when he said, " . . . um, you only have about 6 cc's of your prostate left."

An average older male's prostate is around 45 cc's. We had agreed and I expected him to remove about 15 percent, at most 20 percent of mine.

Instead, based on his in-surgery decisions, Dr. Sainte had taken almost 85 percent of my prostate.

The pinpoint, precisely-focused sound waves (HIFU) that had promised to be the answer to my decades of search became in that moment weapons of mass destruction --- equal in damage to any of the standard radical solutions I had spent nineteen years avoiding.

As I sat dazed and speechless, I guess Dr. Sainte took my silence as wordless assent. Because he continued that yes, he was sorry this meant I was now possibly going to be one of those living with the after-effects—the pads and diapers, unable to ever again enjoy sexual penetration without needling my penis, or even ejaculation. He said I should wait and see and meanwhile focus on the good news of finally being cancer-free. And with that, he wished me well and hung up.

Just as my shocked brain began to recover, in full-throated response I shouted into the phone, "Well, at least I got really fucked one last time!" But I think the line was already dead.

CHAPTER 71
May 24, 2018—Los Angeles, California

"Just get over it."

I am in LA at Dr. Bob's office once again. Today is a big day. Almost six months ago, Dr. Bob had told me I could not go back on TRT until I was shown to be cancer-free. And he suggested I look into HIFU.

You know what happened. Everyone who knows me knows what happened. To paraphrase an old biblical saying, "Man proposes and his doctor disposes."

I thought I could beat the system. I thought I could find the alternate path. And for nineteen years I did. Can't take that away. But in the end, the system that makes a surgeon all-powerful on the operating table in life-threatening circumstances was mistakenly mis-used as an excuse to maim me.

Think about that for a moment. I'll be coming back to it.

Today, I at least have some joy as Dr. Eshaghian hands me the long-awaited prescription for my testosterone. I turn around and head down the elevator to call on my old friends, John and Jessica, at Century City Pharmacy. Ten minutes later, I am once again slathering on the AndroGel. TRT #4 has begun.

CHAPTER 72
September 12, 2018—Havana, Cuba

"That's not how you get to Cuba."

In 2018, if you mentioned to someone you'd like to go to Cuba, almost anything they told you would be wrong. Ever since Obama opened up American travel to Cuba in 2014, and Trump partially blocked it in 2017, there's been nothing but confusion. In reality, though, visiting Cuba is as easy as visiting Canada . . . as long as you're willing to fudge just a little.

My friend Colin is a retired Minneapolis Star Tribune film critic and I am a retired builder. But since we've both published a few articles in our local newspapers, we figure that makes us journalists. And that's all it takes for the Cuban visa folks to officially welcome you, and it's one of the twelve State Department -approved visitor categories.

With our visas and tickets in hand, and nothing but a couple of panniers stuffed with T-shirts and shorts, we grabbed our maps and hustled on down to Havana, where we picked up our rental bikes and hit the road for a week-long, 250-mile ride back into time.

My TRT#4 was starting to turn back my years and, unlike our Scotland trek and Oregon biking, it was Colin who was struggling to keep up. The same Colin who suggested I use black biking shorts to help mask the persistent urine leakage due to Sainte's maiming.

For us, the route was a series of back roads and highways along the sparsely-populated south coast, from the seaside town of Trinidad through a big national forest and across the island to the north coast and back to Havana.

Yes, you see lots of beautiful crumbling architecture and restored 1950s cars, as long as you don't leave Havana. Our Cuba instead was beautifully uncrowded beaches, lush forests, hardscrabble farms, and sleepy small towns and villages.

Best of all was the network of Casa Particulars which are government-approved private homes offering clean rooms, good beds, blessed AC, and a lovely breakfast for the two of us . . . all for around $35 a night! And the cold cervezas were often two for $1.

And here's the other funny thing about prices. Everything has two. If you're a foreign tourista, you use CUCs, which is a special state currency that lets you buy things Cuban citizens don't and can't afford anyway. If you're a citizen, you use CUPs at your local store where you usually wait in line and hope things don't run out. It takes about twenty-five CUPs to equal one CUC.

Strangely enough, the currency works and nobody seems to mind the two classes.

Meanwhile, Canadian, European, and Latin travelers have been laughing and enjoying one of the world's least-crowded, visitor-friendly islands ever since the Russians left years ago. Now, it was our turn.

We stopped at a hole-in-the-wall jungle zoo where a guy draped small crocodiles around our necks. We drank $1 Cuba libres on the beach at the Bay of Pigs where Kennedy's ill-advised Cuban freedom fighters were routed. We climbed around a 400-year-old castle built to deter the real pirates of the Caribbean with tall walls, cannons, and a drawbridge. We were the only Yanquis in the stadium when we watched the Cienfuegos Elephants beat the Havana Yankees in a thrilling baseball game.

One night in Palpite, we sat on a rooftop drinking beer as our laundry dried on the lines overhead and we spent hours watching the village life unfold on the street below. Men laughed and smoked cigars outside a sports bar, lovers met, women gossiped, grandmothers called to children to come in, horse-cart taxis hawked rides, and the local policeman leaned against a wall and napped.

One afternoon we pedaled for miles through orchards where every 500 meters an identical abandoned four-story building stood empty with windows broken and cupolas on top. At the last one, we spotted a lone occupant, an old woman who told us these were the dormitories built by the Russians for the agricultural workers. Our guess is you'd find the same buildings still standing back home in Volgograd.

For our last-night dinner, we have to thank our host, Emilio, the resident beach bum at Playa Jibacoa, who roasted us fresh-caught sardines he in exchange for our last CUC-purchased cervezas.

Between us, we probably didn't spend $800 the entire week we were in Cuba. Sure, you can do Cuba the luxury way, using a guided day trip from a nice big cruise ship. But if you can ride a bike and wash your own underwear, take our advice and go see the world like it used to be. Because that's how you really go to Cuba.

CHAPTER 73
November 1, 2018—Park City, Utah

"I am not over it. And I promise you this . . . "

The day I was finally able to get back onto my TRT was like coming back from purgatory. And my life is so much better in so many ways. Except one.

It's been a year since an arrogant surgeon made a unilateral decision to overturn nineteen years and twenty-six days of my life and cancer management mission.

If you've read this far, you know what I went through to get to that surgeon's table and put all my hopes in his hands. You know what he did and why he says he did it.

I don't buy it. Based on the careful notes Michelle and I took during and after every meeting, we think Dr. Sainte was, to put it kindly, at best deceitful. Not due to maliciousness but certainly carelessness. He was obviously over-scheduled. He forgot important details. He scrambled to justify after the fact.

How else can you explain removing 85 percent of my prostate when our plan and his promise was no more than 20 percent?

I could go on, ranting for hours about the arrogance of some surgeons . . . the clubby protectionism of the old boys medical establishment . . . their slavish loyalty to theories they haven't updated since med school . . . the undeniable fact that much of medical practice lags twenty years behind medical science, especially for prostate cancer.

But I've heard the advice, "Don't get mad, get even."

So that's why I came down to one of two choices: sue Dr. Sainte's ass off— which would have taken years and cost me a fortune while his insurance paid his defense and, if I was close to winning, would have likely ended in a settlement so you would never have heard all this.

Or write this book. Not to persecute some asshole surgeon. But to protect and advise all the guys like me who were not going to get --- or even know about ---any choices but the same worthless ones we've been hearing for years. The ones that create legions of D.U.P.E.s who simply followed their doctor's orders.

I spent the next eighteen months collecting all my journals, photos, maps, and notes. Then I sat down to write the story of these two journeys.

One is the off-path journey all over the world which I have hiked ,biked and climbed for the last thirty-five years. It stops and starts and I hope it's still not over.

The other is this off-path trek I've pursued through the medical world. It doesn't have reliable guideposts, either. And you're just as much on your own with only your own resources to rely on.

In early 2020, just as the COVID 19 pandemic was sweeping the world, I holed up in my Park City home to write this book. I had lots of good help and support along the way. And I've got a few more things to share. Stay with me for a few more pages.

CHAPTER 74
December 24, 2020—Park City, Utah

"... sont les mots qui vont tres bien ensemble ... "

Michelle, my wife who joined me on so many adventures and who carried me through sixteen years of cancer, is no longer my wife. For all the reasons you don't or won't see coming, we grew apart. Too far to come back together.

Michell was my rock, my partner, my caregiver, and my pathfinder. And she will always be my love and my friend. For all of that, I owe her these words of appreciation.

I met Michelle two days after she met me. It was the summer of 2004 and I was in the third day of biking down Highway 1 along the Big Sur coast.

I didn't know it but a young St. Paul woman was driving by on her way to an Esalen workshop, wondering what kind of misguided fool would risk his life riding a bike on a no-shoulder highway with waves crashing on the cliffs below and with most drivers diverting their attention to the beautiful views. She mentally bet she was not likely to see that yahoo again.

The woman's name was Michelle, age thirty-six, and she was taking a well-earned break from her Midwest corporate executive grind to attend a two-day workshop on Integral Transformative Practice. That's typical Esalen-speak for one of those human potential-building group programs. If you don't know much about Esalen, I suggest you Google it, but it's kind of like Woodstock without the music and with much heavier lyrics.

Coincidentally, the guy on the bike was me, heading to attend the same workshop. I noticed her the first day, regretting that she was clearly twenty years or so younger and I was an old, divorced guy.

The last morning of the workshop, we were together in the breakfast line and chatting. She invited me to join her group table. It turns out we are the only two who are staying an extra night. I take a chance and tell her I am going to a concert on the Henry Miller Library lawn that afternoon, then hiking along the ocean cliff to a sixty-foot waterfall . . . and would she like to join me.

I get an enthusiastic yes. Later, I take another chance and reserve a table at nearby Nepenthe, a legendary Big Sur restaurant.

The concert, the hike, the waterfall, and the dinner are a success. Michelle confesses she saw me biking on the highway before she got here and thought I was daft. I confessed I was a prostate cancer warrior and explained my obsession with finding my own way to a cure. I also told her about my world traveling . . . mostly on a bike. We end the evening with a skinny dip in the Esalen hot tubs overlooking the ocean.

Two months later, Michelle flew to Park City to visit me. Eventually, she stayed.

Less than a year after Michelle and I met on the Big Sur, we were packing to leave Park City for a tandem bike tour across Australia. Over 1,000 kilometers into the trip, I was convinced this young lady could and would go anywhere with me . . . exactly the companion of my dreams.

I had stashed away a beautiful gold locket with the inscription, Will You Marry Me? But I hid the inscription under a small photo of us— just in case I sensed a no-win.

Luckily, I decided to ditch the photo and go with the inscription. It was a winner. A month later, we were back home and we eloped to Big Sur for the official ceremony.

A life of up, down, and all around began. In between my successes and failures as a Park City builder, Michele traveled beside me as a more than equal partner on treks across New Zealand, Wales, Turkey, Iran, Iceland, Greenland . . . and, of course, the trips you've read about here to Hawaii and South Africa

The biggest journey Michelle and I took together was the one where she did most of the heavy hauling. That's the cancer journey, of course, and—

believe me—it was not one I could have done without her. She picked me up, pushed me, held me, and basically saved me—more than once.

If any of my advice in this book becomes part of your plan, here's the single most important rule: You can't do it alone. You need a Michelle. I hope you have one.

So, now, before we let Michelle off our stage, let's celebrate with one last sample . . . an unforgettable trek we did across Nepal.

This story really begins in Lhasa, Tibet in 2006 when Michelle let me join her and fifteen Feng Shui experts on a three-week bus tour of China. During the tour, Michelle and I took an unauthorized detour with a car and a driver to explore the Friendship Highway from Lhasa to Kathmandu, in Nepal.

A hundred miles from Lhasa, we spotted and stopped to chat up Raji, a Nepalese guide leading three bike tour clients. A series of email conversations over the next year or so resulted in our custom- planned bike-camping tour with Raji from Lhasa to Kat . . . about 800 kilometers over 17,000-foot-high mountain passes.

Luckily for me, the Tibetan protests that proceeded the 2008 Beijing Olympics led to China closing all borders and our trip was postponed indefinitely. I was not in shape for a trip that tough. But Raji had a good alternative. Mountain biking, hiking, rafting, and camping from Kathmandu to Pokhara and back again. About 500 miles as the crow flies but, with the huge up and down climbs on obscure mountain paths, we probably doubled that.

This was to be Nepal's version of glamping . . . with a support car meeting us every night interspersed with the occasional hostel or hotel.

This was unlike the harsh and primitive nature of my other trips . . . not out of concern for Michelle but for my cancer-treatment weakened state.

Michelle and I flew into India and spent a few days at an ashram with some of Michelle's fellow yoga enthusiasts. The highlight for me was morning runs along the banks of the Ganges. I'd pass dozens of hovels occupied by Babas—sort of holy man beggars who lived from food donations even the poorest locals never failed to come up with. Babas tend to sport nothing but orange togas or loin cloths and a ghostly make-up from pale wood ash. Yet, I found a few very convivial. One morning I was floating down the Ganges to cool off from a run when a Baba I knew called and waved from the bank. Seems I was about to float through a flotilla of shrouded corpses . . . the poor man's burial ground.

That night Michelle and I stood on the river bank with thousands of people as they placed offerings in tiny paper boats they would then set alight and send downstream—a deeply religious light show not to be missed. We headed off the next day to Kathmandu for a few days of touristing. Then, it was on to the first leg of Raji's custom tour.

The first day we biked to Bakhorapur . . . perilous downhill coasting, tortuous uphill pedaling, burning legs, and little appreciation for the wild forests we're passing through. Really glad to find the support car that is called a sag wagon by bike trekkers everywhere. The acronym SAG stands for "support and gear" and our car team has already set up tents and dinner.

The next morning we're up early on our way to Somari Bonjang on a remote, barely passable route with lots of boulders and potholes to navigate. Rolling downhill just before noon, Michelle's front wheel disappears into a leaf-filled rut and the jolt sends her flying over her handlebars into an imperfect somersault.

Raji does his best medic thing to patch up Michelle's cuts and bruises . . . and thankfully there were no sprains or breaks. There is no alternative. No doctors. No ER. No medivac. Out here you are on your own. Michelle does not complain, thanks Raji with a hug, gets her bike back together, and pushes on.

We do not see anyone else on these remote paths but we do pass through several small, picturesque villages. Everyone comes out to wave.

At the end of another very long day, the sag wagon has again surpassed itself —this time with a tablecloth setting in our dining tent right down to the filled wine glasses.

Day three is the road to Gurkha, an area made famous by the legendary British Army platoons made up of Gurkha mountain troops. This so-called road is a rocky, twisting up and down climb that is the most challenging yet.

Again, it's Michelle who leads the way, even giving me the raised eyebrow the fourth time I called for a rest stop. Hey, I'm a sick man!

The mountain sides are rocky and the valleys are lined with pine forests, pocketed with small villages where often the only water supply is a communal spring. We're stopped in one for a lunch break when a mother and daughter sit down in the dirt near us. They don't say anything but empathetic Michelle offers the little girl a Snickers. That earns her a custom forehead paint job from the girl . . . one of those red, third eye Hindu thingamabobs.

When Michelle and I stand up to go, the mother points to our legs. We're sporting a half dozen blood-sucking leeches each. We have to light matches and hold them against each leech until it lets go. You can't just pluck them because the tiny teeth will stay in your skin. We're soon back on our bikes with a vow we will eat standing up from now on.

Another day, another trail-end meeting with the sag wagon. This time, we actually get a hotel, The Gurkha Inn. We put our bikes away, knowing tomorrow begins our hiking segment. As we set off on foot from Nayapul, it's the first of our tortuous days of mountain staircases, swinging cable bridges, and freezing waterfall spray.

This was part of a Middle Ages trade route that was in continuous use for centuries. I think some of the stone tea houses we stopped in may have served Marco Polo. In some places, we were the first white visitors in a generation. And the entire village would turn out to see us and listen to the strange voices. After passing through Tikhedhunga, Poon Hill, Ghorepani, and Ghandruk . . . there were no picture postcards . . . we stumbled back into Nayapul. Ready to sit down for a bit.

Raji obliged. With a rafting trip down the Kali Gandaki River. A tropical jungle tour through the Chitwan. And a lovely farewell night in Kathmandu at the Dwarika Hotel . . . in the same room previously let to Prince Charles.

And if you think Michelle sounds like a trooper here, you should've seen her in the Australian bush.

All those memories.

EPILOGUE

"Are enough doctors telling the truth? Is anyone listening?"

It's the Summer of 2021 as I write this and the year-long nightmare of the pandemic is finally lifting. Vaccines have given us hope. It's time to look ahead again. But before I do, a little important history . . .

Back in 2013, you may recall, I was bouncing back and forth with my testosterone treatments under the watchful eye of Dr. Bob and his team.

It was also the year a brilliant theoretical biologist from the University of Chicago, Dr. Edward Friedman, published an astonishing book, *How You and Your Doctor Can Fight Breast Cancer, Prostate Cancer and Alzheimer's.* It questioned accepted knowledge about the relationship between testosterone and prostate cancer. In his groundbreaking book, Friedman suggested entirely new ways to treat and defeat prostate cancer, maybe even breast cancer, based on theories about the hormones our own bodies produce. The author of the book's foreword, Dr. Paul Savage, suggested Friedman may deserve a Nobel Prize.

Friedman noted, " . . . fighting prostate cancer with testosterone is being used with terrific success by forward-thinking physicians worldwide, including a well-known California doctor . . . "

That was Dr. Bob.

Bob and his patients like me were alone back 1999. But by 2013, other doctors and scientists like Ed were realizing Bob was onto something.

By 2015, when I was again struggling with the ups and downs of on-and-off TRT, it still seemed no healing treatment was in sight. All standard PCa treatments vaporized, removed, or poisoned your entire prostate. They simply D.U.P.E.'d guys into living these greatly diminished, often depressing lives.

And yet, a 1995 Swedish study and a 2012 NEJM article about another study reported essentially the same thing: men who chose the standard destructive treatments typically didn't live any longer than guys who rejected entire prostate procedures. Sadly, it's unlikely many of their doctors told them about those studies.

Outlier doctors like Bob Leibowitz, Shahrooz Eshaghian, several Bob proteges, and a handful of others were successfully and systemically managing patients' prostate cancer and, according to their published follow-up data, getting better mortality results.

Their patients only suffered D.U.P.E. issues temporarily and then regained those functions unimpaired. Their PCa was managed using a variety of medications . . . anti-angiogenesis, 5-alpha reductase inhibitors finasteride and dutasteride, edgy newer drugs and, most controversially, estinyl and TRT. They also used a few mainstream drugs usually prescribed for other purposes such as metformin, citing evidence that those were anticarcinogens.

By 2015, HIFU prostate tumor treatment became available, promising millimeter precision tumor removal without risking adjacent prostate tissue. HIFU side effects remain largely un-studied but I've already offered one case history—my own. Some day we may regard HIFU as an advance similar to what happened for women when they demanded lumpectomies for partial tissue taking instead of devastating mastectomies.

In late 2016, Bob proposed that I explore HIFU to get the concentrated 15 percent of my prostate with probable cancer ablated. He postulated that preserving most of my prostate tissue through a focal HIFU would allow me to minimize D.U.P.E. risks and that retaining most of my prostate would preserve my cancer warning system, PSA* readings. Making me cancer free was his condition for me to resume my TRT. You all know how that worked out.

But think about what I gambled. For nineteen years, I battled prostate cancer and fought off any natural or interventional effects. I enjoyed normal plumbing functions, a healthy and unencumbered sex life, and a pretty adventurous travel regimen.

But then a man named Sainte offered me the golden apple. And a few month's after falling into his hands, I was as D.U.P.E.'d and maimed as every poor guy I warned. Yep, I have to sometimes wear the pads, I have embarrassing accidents, and old-fashioned intercourse has every problem you can think of—including the end of happy endings.

Imagine how I felt a few years later when Dr. Freidman said to me, "You know, that urologist who operated on you really screwed you. It's scientifically unfathomable that an indolent, slow-growing cancer could have spread like he said or that your Gleason 9 tumor could have grown 500 percent in the four months between his biopsy and the operation."

Unfathomable. Just how I could describe nineteen years of successful efforts wiped out in an afternoon.

It was about this time that I met two forward-thinking California doctors who had published a myth-busting book, *The Stem Cell Revolution* by Mark Berman, MD and Elliot Lander, MD. Lander was a urologist . . . would he offer stem cells as a solution for lost prostate cells?

Like Dr. Bob, Dr. Lander theorized that the tools to fight cancer and rebuild our bodies are already there within us . . . endostatins, angiostatins and, yes, testosterone and maybe estinyl.

And Dr. Lander's vision was evident after our first meeting. He'd started using MRI guided, millimeter precision, focal laser treatments for partial prostate ablation years before HIFU became available. And he was successful!

Lander's focal treatment side effects for penetration and urination only occurred in 2 percent or slightly more of his patients versus the conventional gold standard of care treatments of 30 percent to 70 percent. They experienced very few defecation and ejaculation problems. But Landers' focal MRI-guided prostate tumor ablation never got attention. Why? Because Lander was known as a stem cell guy. And big time urologists don't take notes from edgy stem cell guys.

Like Leibowitz, Eshaghian, Lander, Berman, and scientist Friedman, leading edge medical thinkers in America are generally either disparaged or dismissed until their edge has become mainstream. That's how medicine is practiced in our country. Mainstream standard of care doctors are encouraged by the system to dismiss edgy approaches their med school curricula didn't support. For fear of insurance loss and malpractice suits, they prudently practice defensive medicine . . . following standard of care treatments promulgated by their professional medical associations. As long as they talk the party line, they are fulfilling their pledge to do no harm.

But think about this. All those TV commercials that offer weird-sounding medicines for conditions you've never heard of? Half the commercial is a warning about bad side effects. They have to disclose them because the law says so. An everyday highly-promoted operation like laser eye surgery has to post page after page of possible harmful consequences. Even cigarettes and alcohol finally had to tell you the whole story. But guess who doesn't?

I would bet that most men whose doctors recommended the destructive standard PCa treatments were never told—by their doctor or hospital or even their insurance provider—about that 2012 article in the prestigious New England Journal of Medicine that showed the mortality rate was virtually the same between a group of prostate patients who were treated (and D.U.P.E'd) and a group of patients who did nothing.

And I'll bet even fewer men whose doctors recommended one of the standard treatments ever heard of a 1995 similar Swedish study with pretty much the same conclusion—whether you got D.U.P.E'd or not, you lived on about as long. But which group would you rather spend your last years in ?

I believe we deserve the truth. I cannot find any evidence that mainstream PCa surgery, radiation, and chemo standard of care procedures extend mortality as compared to doing nothing.

The American Medical Association (AMA), American Urological Association (AUA), and similar physician associations—as well as their their directors—should be held accountable for not revising their members' advisories . . . for not requiring member doctors to advise patients when there are zero mortality differences between debilitating treatments and doing nothing.

Imagine the enormous difference that would have made and could make in the quality of life for hundreds of thousands of men who suffered, perhaps needlessly.

Certainly, I think about it. And these days, I am doggedly pursuing off-path ways to get back to where I was pre-Sainte. There's a slim chance my poor battered prostate may be coming back . . . time will tell . . . as I follow Elliot's and Mark's stem cell protocols using a patient's own fat (adipose) derived stem cells, kind of like a patient using his own stored blood.

I believe the real science of stem cells—not the pop fiction in media reports—may be a game changer for me. These have no relationship with the umbilical cord or fetal tissue derived cells most people and doctors still associate with stem cell treatments.

Building on the protocols Dr. Bob laid down decades ago, we are slowly moving this super-tanker-sized medical establishment away from their comfortable dock, cautiously venturing into new waters.

I wish I could tell you we have seen the answers and they're on the way. I honestly don't know. The handful of brilliant doctors I found are showing us the possibilities. But are enough people listening?

Until then, here's my advice for you: Learn.

Browse through the appended WebMD Glossary and learn the lingo.

Study the appended "What I've Observed" sections which answer a lot of the questions I get asked.

Get copies of Elliot's and Ed's books. They are valuable learning and reference tools.

Get on the internet and learn some more.

There's no way around it. If you're not well informed and aware, you'll get D.U.P.E.'d.

One more thing:

Remember when I decided the best revenge I could have against my surgeon was to write this book and take all you guys out of his sights? I've gone one better.

I have set up a non-profit foundation with my co-writer, Rick Barrow, to support dissemination of the prostate cancer knowledge every man over forty needs, to support any of us who needs help and answers along the way, and to encourage tort attorneys to compel doctors' professional associations to advise members they must tell patients all the truth about the treatments they sell.

You can find more about the foundation at www.riding.com and thescalpel.com.

With it all, I have to say life is good. Even with the pandemic, I skied 100 days this winter, stayed in shape, and I'll be off on another of my trips by the time you read this.

So, if you're coming down a mountain trail one day and you spot a skinny white-haired guy with a bandana on his head and a bike up his ass, give me a wink.

Jim Doilney
Park City , Utah
July 30, 2021

ACKNOWLEDGMENTS

This book would never have occurred without Robert L. Leibowitz, MD (Dr. Bob), a brilliant oncologist who I believe has the world's most successful prostate cancer treatment and patient cohort. I owe my life to Dr. Bob, my doctor number eighteen out of the nineteen I met to find my path to cancer freedom. Bob should get a Nobel Prize for his work.

I thank Michelle Skally Doilney for sharing sixteen years of her life and for helping me through countless cancer treatments and endless discussions about how to write about them so others could benefit.

Rick Barrow, my co-writer, was somehow able to take my rambling storytelling and journals and reshape them into what we hope is a compelling narrative. He saw that my lifelong adventure journeys could be engagingly intertwined with my efforts to deny prostate cancer when others didn't. Without Rick's writing genius, this book would have been destined to collect dust with no chance of making a difference. If we have helped to guide you to your own path, it's largely because Rick is a great writer.

Shahrooz Eshaghian, MD and, until recently, Mary Duong, NP, managed my medical treatments when Dr. Bob was unavailable. I thank them for helping me through many emotionally and medically stressful years.

Edward Friedman, PhD, helped me understand the science underlying Dr. Bob's treatments. He should share in Bob's Nobel Prize for his pioneering testosterone replacement therapy explanations of Bob's approach.

Elliot Lander, MD and Mark Berman, MD, authors of *The Stem Cell Revolution*, have collaboratively helped me deal with a urologist's mistake.

I thank brilliant internist, Kim Scott. Kim has acted as my medical gatekeeper and collaborator as I navigated my way through medical decision-making.

Many other medical professionals helped me including Lydia Sar, RN; Maria Regalado; Lisa Huber, RN; Whitney Bailey, RN; and Sean Berman.

Writers' writers Natalie Goldberg and Rob Wilder taught me how to overcome writer's block through writing practice.

In various ways, Mary Carroll Moore and Gwen Hernandez helped in the early work on this book.

My most serious reader-reviewer has been Tammy Schlesinger, PhD. And I must especially thank the endless friends who read book excerpts: Barbara Courtney, Faye Slettom, Wendy Petersen, Steve Dering, Max Doilney, Molly Crosswhite, Tom Ligare, Jake Doilney, Jim Klopman, and Janet Miller.

Thanks to Lynn Ware Peek and David Windsor for giving me a prepublication book interview.

Thanks also to Simaima Lutu for assembling nineteen years of medical records that will be accessible on my forthcoming website, jamesallendoilney.com.

WebMD Prostate Cancer Glossary
© 2021 WebMD, LLC. All rights reserved.

Reviewed by Kumar Shital, DO on April 26, 2021

Abscess: a collection of pus caused by a bacterial or viral infection, fungus, or parasite.

Acid phosphatase: an older blood test for an enzyme produced primarily in the prostate. High levels may indicate infection, injury, or the presence or spread of cancer in the prostate.

Active surveillance: a treatment approach for prostate cancer that involves close monitoring with exams and tests.

Acute: abrupt onset of a medical condition that is usually severe; happens for a limited period of time.

Acute bacterial prostatitis: also called infectious prostatitis, a bacterial infection of the prostate gland that causes inflammation and swelling of the prostate. Acute bacterial prostatitis requires prompt treatment as the condition can lead to cystitis, abscesses in the prostate, or blocked urine flow in extreme cases. In some cases, acute prostatitis requires hospitalization.

Adjuvant therapy: treatment provided in addition to the primary treatment for cancer.

Adrenal glands: two glands that sit on top of the kidneys that make and release hormones such as epinephrine (adrenaline), which raises heart rate and blood pressure; norepinephrine, which causes constriction of blood vessels; and steroid hormones, including cortisone, which help reduce inflammation and control how the body utilizes fat, protein, carbohydrates, and minerals. Other steroid hormones produced in the adrenal gland are called androgens, or male sex hormones.

Adverse effect: negative or harmful effect.

Alpha-adrenergic blocker: class of drugs used to treat benign (noncancerous) prostate enlargement. These medications tend to relax the prostate muscles and improve urine flow. They are also used to treat hypertension.

Analgesic: medicine used to relieve pain.

Androgen: a hormone, such as testosterone and androsterone, responsible for the development of male sex characteristics.

Anemia: a condition when blood is deficient in one of three ways: 1) not enough red blood cells, 2) not enough hemoglobin, or 3) not enough total volume of blood. Hemoglobin is a substance in the red blood cells that enables the blood to transport oxygen through the body.

Anterograde ejaculation: normal forward ejaculation.

Antiandrogen drug: any medication that reduces or blocks the normal activity of an androgen hormone.

Antibiotic: medication used to inhibit the growth of or kill microorganisms. It is used for treating bacterial infections.

Anti-inflammatory: medication used to reduce pain, swelling, or other irritation, often caused by prostatitis.

Antimicrobial: a drug that kills microorganisms or prevents them from multiplying; antibiotics are naturally occurring antimicrobials. Antimicrobial medications are used to treat acute infectious prostatitis and chronic prostatitis.

Antibodies: proteins produced by the body to protect itself from foreign substances (such as bacteria or viruses).

Antigens: Foreign substances that cause an immune response in the body. The body produces antibodies to fight antigens, or harmful substances.

Antispasmodics: drugs that help decrease involuntary muscle spasms that may occur in the bladder.

Asymptomatic: no symptoms that disease is present.

Atrophy: wasting of tissue or organ due to disease or lack of use (as in muscle atrophy). The testicles can become atrophic due to disease, cancer, or abnormal development.

Axumin: a radiotracer which is used in conjunction with a PET scan to help pinpoint the location of any recurrent prostate cancer.

Azoospermia: the absence of sperm in the ejaculate.

Benign tumor: a noncancerous growth that does not spread to nearby tissues or other parts of the body.

Biofeedback: a method of learning to modify a particular bodily function, by monitoring it with the aid of an electronic device that may produce sight or sound signals. Pelvic floor biofeedback may help some patients who have an underlying pelvic floor neuromuscular dysfunction.

Biological therapy: treatment to stimulate or restore the ability of the immune system to fight infection and disease. This is also called immunotherapy, in some cases.

Biopsy: removal of a sample of tissue for study, usually under a microscope. A physician uses ultrasound to guide a small needle into areas of the prostate where abnormalities are detected. The needle is used to collect cells or tissue samples of the prostate. Usually six to fourteen biopsies are taken to sample various areas of the prostate. The tissue samples are then analyzed in a laboratory to help physicians diagnose a variety of disorders and diseases in the prostate.

Benign prostatic hyperplasia (BPH): also known as benign (noncancerous) enlargement of the prostate. Almost all men with normal hormonal function (those who produce the male hormone testosterone) will develop some enlargement of the prostate as they age.

Brachytherapy: Also called image-directed irradiation (and internal radiation therapy), a form of radiation therapy for prostate cancer. There are two types of brachytherapy for prostate cancer: low-dose rate (LDR) and high-dose rate (HDR). The most commonly used one is LDR. During this procedure, radioactive seeds are implanted into the prostate gland under ultrasound guidance. The number of seeds and their locations are determined by a computer-generated treatment plan for each patient. The seeds remain in place permanently and become inactive after a period of months. HDR brachytherapy is a newer treatment and involves the temporary placement of hollow needles in the prostate. These are filled with a radioactive substance for a period of minutes and then removed. This is repeated two to three more times over several days.

Cancer: a general term for more than 100 diseases marked by an uncontrolled, abnormal growth of cells. Cancer cells can spread through the bloodstream and lymphatic system to other parts of the body.

Cannulas: tubes that are used to help deliver something into the body or allow access into the body. Examples include a tube to hold an instrument called a laparoscope (see below) and other instruments that allow access to the abdominal cavity for laparoscopic surgery.

Carcinoma: malignant (cancerous) growth that begins in the lining or covering of an organ and tends to invade surrounding tissue and metastasize (spread) to other regions of the body.

Carcinoma in situ: cancer that involves only the tissue in which it began; it has not spread to other tissues.

Catheter (urinary): a thin, flexible, plastic tube that is inserted into the bladder through the penis/urethra to drain urine.

CAT scan: an X-ray technique using computer technology to produce a film showing a detailed cross-section of tissue. A CAT scan may be recommended so your doctor can check for swollen or enlarged lymph nodes, which might mean the cancer has spread. Generally, a CAT scan is only used if the cancer is large, of a high grade, or associated with a very high PSA level.

Chemotherapy: in cancer treatment, refers to the use of drugs whose main effect is either to kill or slow the growth of rapidly multiplying cells. Chemotherapy usually includes a combination of drugs, since this is more effective than a single drug given alone. There are several drug combinations used to treat prostate cancer.

Chronic: persisting over a long period of time.

Chronic prostatitis: a form of prostatitis that is usually caused by bacteria. Chronic prostatitis is the main reason men under the age of 50 visit a urologist. In some cases, chronic prostatitis follows an attack of acute prostatitis. The condition causes recurrent bouts of bladder and urinary infection.

Clear margins: areas of normal tissue that surround cancerous tissue, as seen during a microscopic examination.

Clinical trial: a research program conducted with patients to evaluate a new medical treatment, drug, or device. The purpose of clinical trials is to find new and improved methods of treating different diseases and special conditions.

Combined hormonal therapy or maximal androgen deprivation: a treatment method that combines suppression of testosterone production and androgen production by the adrenal glands. (See also: hormone therapy.)

Contraindication: a factor that makes use of a drug or other treatment inadvisable.

Cryobank: a place where cells, sperm, or embryos are frozen and then stored.

Cryopreservation: the process of freezing and storing sperm or embryos for later use.

Cystectomy: removal of the bladder.

Cystitis: an inflammation or infection of the bladder. When it is due to bacteria it is referred to as a urinary tract infection. When caused by inflammation it is called interstitial cystitis.

Cystoscopy: also called cystourethroscopy, a procedure where a tube is inserted into the urethra through the opening at the end of the penis. It allows the doctor to visually examine the complete length of the urethra and the bladder for polyps, strictures, abnormal growths, and other problems.

Cystoscope: tube-like device containing a light and viewing lens. A cystoscope is inserted into the urethra to examine the urethra, bladder, and prostate.

Digital rectal exam (DRE): a manual exam of the prostate. Because the prostate is an internal organ, the physician cannot look at it directly. Since the prostate lies in front of the rectum, the doctor can feel it by inserting a gloved, lubricated finger into the rectum. They will feel the prostate for hard, lumpy, or abnormal areas and to estimate whether the prostate is enlarged.

Dysuria: painful urination.

Ejaculate: fluid and sperm (semen) ejected from the penis during male orgasm.

Ejaculation: discharging semen from the penis during orgasm.

Ejaculatory duct: tube in the body where semen is deposited into the urethra.

Electrovaporization: a surgical procedure that uses electrical current to destroy excess prostate tissue.

Enuresis: involuntary urination.

Epididymis: a long tube-like coiled structure where sperm collect, mature, and pass. The epididymis is located above and behind the testicles. Matured sperm leave the epididymis through the vas deferens when they are ejaculated or reabsorbed by the body.

Epididymitis: inflammation of the epididymis.

Epidural catheter: a small tube passed into the space between the spinal cord and spinal column. Pain medication can be delivered through the tube.

Erectile dysfunction: See impotence.

Flow study: a test that measures the flow of urine.

Gene: the basic unit of heredity found in all cells.

Gleason score: a rating system that indicates how aggressive a cancer is. The higher the Gleason score, the more likely it is that the cancer will grow and spread rapidly. Pathologists often identify the two most common patterns of cells in the tissue, assign a Gleason grade to each, and add the two grades. The result is a number between 2 and 10. A Gleason score of less than 6 indicates a less aggressive cancer. A grade 7 and up is considered more aggressive.

Grade: a labeling system indicating how quickly a cancer is growing.

Hormones: chemicals produced by glands in the body. Hormones control the actions of certain cells or organs.

Hormone therapy: also called hormonal therapy. The use of hormone medications to treat cancer patients by removing, blocking, or adding to the effects of a hormone on an organ or part of the body. Hormone therapy may also include surgical removal of the testicles to prevent male hormones from further stimulating the growth of prostate cancer.

Hyperthermia: treatment which uses heat as a treatment to kill cells. See transurethral microwave thermotherapy (TUMT).

Immune system: the body's natural defense system against infection or disease.

Impotence: also called erectile dysfunction, a man's inability to develop or sustain an erection satisfactory for sexual intercourse. Though prostate cancer is not a cause of impotence, some treatments for the disease can cause erectile dysfunction

Infectious prostatitis: See acute bacterial prostatitis.

Inflammation: one of the body's defense mechanisms, results in increased blood flow in response to infection and certain chronic conditions. Symptoms of inflammation include redness, swelling, pain, and heat.

Intensity Modulated Radiotherapy: See radiation.

Interstitial Laser Coagulation (ILC): a technique used to treat an enlarged prostate. This technique uses two lasers to deliver heat to the interior of the prostate. A specially designed laser fiber is inserted into the prostate using instruments placed in the urethra. The procedure is usually done in the operating room, under local anesthesia to numb the area.

Intracavernous injection therapy: injection of medication into the penis to treat impotence. This type of therapy can be effective and successful for patients who have undergone radical prostatectomy (removal of the prostate) or who have received radiation therapy to treat prostate cancer. The overall success rate with injection therapy is up to 80 percent.

Intraurethral Therapy (such as medicated urethral system for erection or Muse): medication taken as a suppository placed in the urinary tube (urethra) to treat impotence. The medicine relaxes the muscle in the erection chamber, allowing improved blood flow into the penis and resulting in an erection.

Incontinence, **urinary**: loss of urinary control. Incontinence may be complete or partial and can result from prostate surgery or radiation therapy for prostate cancer.

Laparoscopic surgery (laparoscopy): a method of surgery that is less invasive than traditional surgery. Tiny incisions are made to create a passageway for a special instrument called a laparoscope. This thin telescope-like instrument with a miniature video camera and light source is used to transmit images to a video monitor. The surgeon watches the video screen while performing the procedure with small instruments that pass through small tubes placed in the incisions.

Laser surgery: destruction of tissue using a small, powerful, highly focused beam of light.

Local therapy: treatment that affects cells in the tumor and the area close to it.

Localized cancer: cancer that hasn't spread to other parts of the body. Localized prostate cancer is confined to the prostate.

Luteinizing hormone releasing hormone (LHRH) analog: a drug that blocks the production of testosterone by the testes to help stop tumor growth. These drugs carry a small risk of triggering diabetes, heart disease, and/or stroke. Before starting one of these drugs, patients should tell their doctor if they have a history of diabetes, heart disease, stroke, heart attack, high blood pressure, high cholesterol, or cigarette smoking.

Lymph: clear fluid that travels through the lymphatic system and carries cells that help fight infection and disease.

Lymph nodes: small glands located in many areas of the body that help defend the body against harmful foreign substances.

Lymphatic system: a circulatory system that includes an extensive network of lymph vessels and lymph nodes throughout the body. The lymphatic system helps coordinate the immune system's function to protect the body from foreign substances.

MRI: a test that produces images of the body without the use of X-rays. MRI uses a large magnet, radio waves, and a computer to produce these images. MRI may be used to examine the prostate and nearby lymph nodes to distinguish between benign (noncancerous) and malignant lesions.

Male infertility: diminished or absent ability to produce offspring.

Malignant: cancerous; can spread to other parts of the body.

Metastasize: to spread from one part of the body to another.

Nonbacterial prostatitis: the type of prostatitis that occurs when no definite infectious cause can be identified. Men with nonbacterial prostatitis often have a number of white blood cells (associated with infection) in their urine, but no bacteria are found.

Nonsteroidal anti-inflammatory drugs (NSAIDs): a class of drugs effective for reducing inflammation and pain without steroids. Examples of these drugs include aspirin, naproxen, and ibuprofen.

Obstruction: a clog or blockage that prevents fluid from flowing easily.

Occult blood: Blood in the stool that is not always visible to the naked eye. This type of bleeding is detected by performing a laboratory test on a stool sample.

Oncologist: a doctor who specializes in the medical treatment of cancer. Medical oncologists have a thorough knowledge of how cancers behave and grow. This knowledge is used to calculate your risk of recurrence as well as the possible need for and benefits of additional or adjuvant therapy (such as chemotherapy or hormonal therapy).Your medical oncologist generally manages your overall medical care and monitors your general health during your course of treatment. They check your progress frequently, reviews your lab and X-ray results, and coordinate your medical care before and after your course of treatment.

Oncologist, radiation: a doctor trained in cancer treatment using radiation therapy.

Oncologist, surgical: a doctor who performs biopsies and other surgical procedures specifically related to cancer.

Orchiectomy: surgical removal of the testes.

Palpation: a simple technique, when a doctor presses on the surface of the body to feel the organs or tissues underneath.

Patient Controlled Analgesia: a method of giving pain medication that is activated by the patient.

Pathologist: a doctor who specializes in analyzing tissue samples. In the case of prostate cancer, the doctor can examine prostate tissue samples under a microscope to detect the cellular makeup of the tumor, whether the cancer is localized or has the potential to spread, and how quickly it is growing. Pathologists can detect subtle differences in cancer cells that help your surgeon and oncologist confirm the diagnosis.

Penile prosthesis: See prosthesis.

Perineum: the area between the scrotum and anus.

Permanent radioactive seed implants: a form of radiation therapy for prostate cancer. During the procedure, radioactive implants are implanted into the prostate gland using ultrasound guidance. The number of implants and where they are placed is determined by a computer-generated treatment plan individualized for each patient. The implants remain in place permanently, and become inactive after a period of months. This technique is also referred to as low-dose rate (LDR) and allows for delivery of radiation to the prostate with limited effect to surrounding tissues.

Peyronie's disease: a condition that causes buildup of plaques and scarring along the walls of the erectile tissue of the penis. This condition causes curvature of the penis, especially when erect.

Platelets: substance in blood that helps prevent bleeding by causing blood clots to form at the site of an injury.

Post-void residual test: a test often performed with ultrasound imaging to detect how much urine is left in the bladder after the patient completes urination.

Priapism: persistent, painful, and unwanted erection. This condition requires immediate medical attention or it may result in permanent injury to the penis.

Prognosis: the probable outcome or course of a disease; the chance of recovery.

Prostate: a muscular, walnut-sized gland that surrounds part of the urethra, the tube that transports urine and sperm out of the body. The prostate is part of the male reproductive system. It secretes seminal fluid, a milky substance that combines with sperm produced in the testicles to form semen. The muscles in the prostate push semen through the urethra and out of the penis during sexual climax.

Prostate cancer: the most common form of cancer in American men and the second leading cause of cancer death in men. Cells in the body normally divide (reproduce) only when new cells are needed. Sometimes, cells will divide for no reason, creating a mass of tissue called a tumor. Tumors can be benign (not cancer) or malignant (cancer). Prostate cancer is a malignant tumor.

Prostate enlargement: See benign prostatic hyperplasia (BPH).

Prostate-specific antigen (PSA): a blood test used to detect elevated levels of this protein, produced by the prostate, which can indicate prostate cancer or other prostate diseases.

Prostate stripping: during a digital rectal examination, the doctor may massage, or strip the prostate to force prostatic fluid out of the gland and into the urethra. This fluid sample is then examined under a microscope for signs of inflammation and infection and helps to diagnose prostatitis.

Prostatic ducts: group of 20 to 30 tubes inside the prostate that collect and transport prostatic fluid to the ejaculatory ducts.

Prostatic fluid: fluid produced by the prostate that makes up a portion of the semen. Doctors believe the prostatic fluid contains a chemical substance that contributes to the viability of sperm for reproduction.

Prostatodynia: pain in the prostate.

Prostatectomy: See radical prostatectomy.

Prosthesis: an artificial replacement of a part of the body. A penile prosthesis may be considered if the patient has had erectile dysfunction for about one year following cancer treatment and nonsurgical therapy has either failed or is unacceptable. Prosthesis is an effective form of therapy in many patients, but it requires an operation to implant a device in the penis. Surgery can cause complications, such as mechanical failure or infection, which may require removal of the prosthesis and re-operation.

Prostatitis: an infection of the prostate. Prostatitis may also appear as an inflammation of the prostate with no documentation of infection. When no definite infectious cause can be identified, the condition is called nonbacterial prostatitis. A sudden bacterial infection of the prostate gland characterized by inflammation of the prostate is called acute bacterial or infectious prostatitis. Acute bacterial prostatitis requires prompt treatment to prevent other health problems. Chronic (long-lasting) prostatitis is the most common form of this disease, usually caused by bacteria.

Pulse oximetry: photoelectric device that measures the percent of oxygenation in the blood using a clip on the finger. It also measures the heart rate.

Radiation therapy: a form of cancer treatment that uses high levels of radiation to kill cancer cells or keep them from growing and dividing while minimizing damage to healthy cells.

Radical prostatectomy: surgery that removes the entire prostate gland plus some tissue around it. Radical prostatectomy is used most often if the cancer is thought not to have spread outside of the gland.

Radioactive Seed Implants: See brachytherapy.

Radiology: a branch of medicine that uses radioactive substances and visual devices to diagnose and treat a wide variety of diseases.

Radiologist: a doctor who reads and interprets X-rays and other radiographic images.

Recurrence: the return of a disease after a period of remission.

Remission: disappearance of any evidence of cancer. A remission can be temporary or permanent.

Renal: relating to the kidneys.

Renal threshold: the point at which the blood is holding so much of a substance, such as glucose, that the kidneys allow the excess to spill into the urine. This is also called kidney threshold, kidney spilling point, or leak point.

Renovascular disorders: diseases of the blood vessels of the kidney.

Retrograde ejaculation: ejaculation of semen backward into the bladder instead of through the urethra and out of the penis.

Risk factor: a factor that increases a person's chance of developing a disease or predisposes a person to a certain condition.

Scrotum: the sac of skin that contains the testes.

Semen: the fluid, containing sperm, which comes out of the penis during sexual arousal.

Semen analysis: test that provides information about the number and quality of the sperm.

Seminal vesicles: small glands near the prostate that produce some of the fluid for semen.

Sentinel lymph node: the first lymph node to which a tumor drains, making it the first place where cancer is likely to spread.

Sexually transmitted disease (STD): a disease that is spread by having sex with someone who has an STD. You can get an STD from sexual activity that involves the mouth, anus, or vagina. STDs are serious illnesses that require treatment. Some STDs, such as AIDS and genital herpes, cannot be cured.

Sildenafil: See Viagra.

Sperm: the microscopic cells produced in the testicles and transported by semen to aid in reproduction.

Stage: a labeling system indicating how far the cancer has spread, or the extent of the cancer. The stage of prostate cancer depends on the size of the cancer and whether it has spread from its original site to other parts of the body.

Systemic therapy: treatment that reaches and affects cells all over the body.

Temporary brachytherapy: a form of radiation therapy for prostate cancer during which hollow needles are placed into the prostate gland. These needles are filled with a substance that gives off radioactivity for a period of minutes. This is repeated for two to three additional treatments over a couple of days. This technique is also referred to as high-dose rate (HDR) and allows for delivery of radiation to the prostate while sparing its effect on the surrounding tissues.

Testes (testicles): a pair of rounded glands that lie in the scrotum that produce sperm for reproduction and the hormone testosterone.

Testosterone: the male sex hormone produced by the testes.

Thermotherapy: See transurethral microwave thermotherapy (TUMT).

Transurethral incision of the prostate (TUIP): surgical treatment for benign prostate enlargement. An instrument passed through the urethra makes cuts in the prostate to clear any blockages, but does not remove tissue.

Transurethral microwave thermotherapy (TUMT): also called transurethral hyperthermia. Used to treat benign enlargement of the prostate. During this procedure, microwave energy delivers temperatures above 45 degrees C (113 degrees Fahrenheit) to the prostate by way of an antenna positioned in the prostate using a special catheter.

Transrectal ultrasonography: See ultrasound, prostate.

Transurethral resection of the prostate (TURP): surgical removal of the tissue blocking the urethra, with no external skin incision. This is the most common treatment for symptomatic benign enlargement of the prostate.

Trocar: sharp, pointed instrument used to make a puncture incision in the abdominal wall. Used for placement of cannulas.

Tumor: an abnormal mass of tissue.

Ultrasound: a test used to diagnose a wide range of diseases and conditions. High-frequency sound waves, inaudible to the human ear, are transmitted through body tissues. The echoes vary according to the tissue density. The echoes are recorded and translated into video or photographic images that are displayed on a monitor.

Ultrasound, prostate: also called transrectal ultrasound. A probe about the size of a finger is inserted a short distance into the rectum. This probe produces harmless high-frequency sound waves, inaudible to the human ear, that bounce off the surface of the prostate. The sound waves are recorded and transformed into video or photographic images of the prostate gland. The probe can provide images at different angles to help the doctor estimate the size of the prostate and detect any abnormal growths or lesions.

Urethra: the tube that carries urine (from the bladder) and semen (from the prostate and other sex glands) out through the tip of the penis.

Urethral stricture: a narrowing or blockage of the canal leading to the bladder, discharging the urine externally.

Urethritis: inflammation of the urethra, which may be due to infection.

Urinalysis: a test that evaluates a urine sample to detect abnormalities. Urinalysis is important for diagnosing prostatitis, urinary infections, bladder and kidney cancer, diabetes and other conditions.

Urinary catheter: See catheter.

Urinary tract: the path that urine takes as it leaves the body. It includes the kidneys, ureters, bladder, and urethra.

Urinary tract infection: an infection of the urinary tract, usually caused by bacteria. The infection most often occurs in the urethra and bladder. It can also travel from the bladder into the ureter and kidneys.

Urination: discharge of liquid waste from the body.

Urologist: a doctor who specializes in treatment of the urinary tract for men and women, and the genital organs for males.

Vacuum constriction device: a cylinder that is placed over the penis to treat impotence. The air is pumped out of the cylinder, which draws blood into the penis and causes an erection. The erection is maintained by slipping a band off the base of the cylinder and onto the base of the penis.

Viagra: a drug used to treat erectile dysfunction.

Void: to urinate.

Voiding dysfunction: difficulty urinating.

Watchful waiting: an approach used for localized, slow-growing prostate cancer involving regular checkups instead of immediate treatment. See Active surveillance above.

X-ray: high-energy radiation used in low doses to diagnose diseases and used in high doses to treat cancer.

*

"What I have observed"

Jim's supplemental notes and Prostate Cancer Glossary

TAB – Triple Androgen Blockade, Dr. Robert Leibowitz's PCa baseline treatment.

** Per the American Cancer Society there will be about 248,530 new cases of prostate cancer and about 34,130 deaths from PCa in 2021.

** Anywhere you read cure or cancer-free, refer to WebMD's glossary term remission. Oncologists rarely intend to say cancer will not come back.

** My oncologist, Shahrooz Eshaghian, guessed that 75 percent of PCa-diagnosed patients submit to D.U.P.E.ing, temporarily or permanently affecting their ability to penetrate for sex and permanently giving up ejaculating. Unfortunately, many of Shahrooz's patients only find him after they've been maimed.

** 5 Alpha Reductase is an enzyme, sort of a saw that breaks testosterone into suspected cancerogenic metabolites, estradiol and dihydrotestosterone (DHT).

** Hematocrit (HCT) readings reflect the density of red blood cells in a person's blood. High readings indicate risk of stroke and other heart problems. Testosterone supplements can cause high HCT; hence, HCT should be closely monitored. An at home HCT and hemogloben test is available in Europe at swisspointofcare.com.

Jim's Prostate Cancer 101

These brief statements about Prostate Cancer (PCa) statements are necessarily incomplete. But I think they will be helpful for PCa patients.

Is it true that traditional PCa operations have not been shown to improve life expectancy?

Why does the American Academy of Family Physicians advise member doctors to not even run patients' PSA tests unless they commit to serve as PCa patients treatment gatekeepers so they can safeguard patients against unwarranted treatments that prostate specialists commonly use?

Many doctors say many men with PCa may need to do little or nothing. PCa patients do not have to have surgery or radiation on their prostates.

Do PCa patients demanding to get their cancer out understand they can focally destroy/ablate PCa tumors while sparing other prostate tissue, a partial prostate removal? This is somewhat like what women who have lumpectomies instead of mastectomies do to keep most breast tissue.

Focal treatment options include HIFU (high intensity focused ultrasound) or MRI guided laser.

It seems to me that PCa can be managed with drugs, allowing PCa patients to avoid or, if management didn't work or they change their minds, later radiate or remove their prostates.

Some leading doctors use finasteride and dutasteride, among other drugs for other purposes, to reduce testosterone conversion into dihydrotestosterone (DHT) and estradiol, a couple of postulated PCa promoters. Tracking PSA's rate of change, or doubling time, may be the best way to use PSAs. Sequential testing is needed. Continually rising PSAs warrant PCa management action.

A stable PSA indicates any PCa is not growing, negating the need for treatment and perhaps limiting action to watchful waiting.

Notwithstanding a Nobel Prize assertion to the contrary, research indicates testosterone does not cause PCa and may actually help control it if drugs preventing its breakdown into other hormones are taken.

It is possible to know if PCa has spread outside the prostate by using C-11 acetate, choline, or other isotope scans. These isotopes light up fatty acids which cluster around any fatty acid producing PCa tissue which has spread beyond the prostate. If PCa has spread beyond the prostate, PCa patients are not usually Focal PCa treatment candidates.

MRI guiding of biopsies can improve biopsy efficacy, offering better information than non-MRI guided biopsies.

Although testosterone may help patients control PCa, careful blood monitoring is needed because testosterone can cause red blood cell density changes and life-threatening risks.

Studies have shown that PCa patients given testosterone replacement therapy (TRT) after surgery or radiation were 50 percent less likely to have a PCa recurrence. One study has shown that men in their forties who had below normal testosterone readings and use TRT are two-thirds less likely to contract PCa as such men who do not use TRT.

Any man with any prostate tissue will have positive PSA readings.
It is my experience that medical community tribal practices may prevent doctors from referring patients to outside doctors who might do a better job or have better technology.